Perilous Journey

Debates on Security and Development in Assam

EDITED BY

RAKHEE BHATTACHARYA

SANJAY PULIPAKA

Maulana Abul Kalam Azad Institute of Asian Studies, Kolkata

MANOHAR

2011

Disclaimer
The views expressed in the various essays of this publication are those of the respective contributors and are not necessarily that of the editors.

First published 2011

ISBN 978-81-7304-904-0

Published by
Ajay Kumar Jain *for*
Manohar Publishers & Distributors
4753/23 Ansari Road, Daryaganj
New Delhi 110 002

Typeset by
Ajay Arts
New Delhi 110 002

Printed by
Salasar Imaging Systems
Delhi 110 035

Contents

Acknowledgements

This volume is the outcome of the Fourth National Seminar on North-East India titled 'Addressing Security and Development Issues in Assam', which was organized in Guwahati on 28 March 2009. This event was organized under the seminar series of the Maulana Abul Kalam Azad Institute's Long-Term Research Programme on North-East India. The Institute has initiated this programme in the year 2006 for a better understanding of the region by facilitating various academic activities in the form of seminars, symposia, workshops, and collaborations with scholars, academicians and policy makers from all the eight North-Eastern states.

This book would not have seen the light of day without the constant encouragement and guidance of Prof. H.S. Vasudevan, Director of Maulana Abul Kalam Azad Institute of Asian Studies (MAKAIAS). It is our privilege to thank Prof. Vasudevan for his cooperation in this endeavour. We express our deepest thanks to Prof. Jayanta Kumar Ray, Chairman of Maulana Abul Kalam Azad Institute of Asian Studies, who is the guiding force behind this project. His immense understanding and knowledge about the region has been helping us to work on this region. We also take the opportunity to thank Jaideep Saikia, the Security Analyst and author, based in Assam for his untiring support in making the Fourth National Seminar in Guwahati a success. We are grateful to Prof. Udayon Misra and Prof. Tilottoma Misra for steering and enriching the discussions at the seminar. We would also like to thank Sri G.M. Srivastava, former Director General of Police, Assam, for actively participating in the seminar. We must also thank all the administrative and finance staff of the MAKAIAS for providing all the logistical support to the seminar.

We are indebted to all the distinguished authors, whose contributions have given a shape to this book.

RAKHEE BHATTACHARYA
SANJAY PULIPAKA

CHAPTER 1

Introduction

Rakhee Bhattacharya

DEVELOPMENT-SECURITY FUSION: A REVISIT

Development and security are the two most basic concerns of the modern world. A fast-changing development strategy of recent times has extensively reconfigured the economy, polity, society and culture in a globalized flat world. This reconfiguration has also widened the gap in material gains between the privileged and the disadvantaged. Development in the modern world has not been able to address the challenges of poverty, inequality, and miseries of the underprivileged. The misery and sufferings of the poor have been further compounded by the emerging security issues in various parts of the world, leading to migration, displacement and further sufferings of the people who live on the fringes of development. All these have made conventional development and security dynamics across the world highly complex issues. Security now is closely interwoven with development in the perspective of faster transnational connectivity and greater human mobility. Frances Stewart[2] has hypothesized three connections between human security and development. By surveying developing nations, he argues that human security forms an important part of people's well-being and is therefore an objective of development. Lack of human security has adverse consequences on economic growth and poverty and thereby on development; and such lack of development or imbalanced development leads to horizontal inequalities, which is an important cause of conflict. To prevent such conflict, a region needs to be more secure, which can improve human development and economic productivity by attracting global investment. Once the country is more developed, it becomes more capable to support a security arrangement.[2] Thus the scope of security *vis-à-vis* development studies is increasingly widening. Earlier, the referent object of development was income growth and that of security was military power. Now there is a paradigm shift in our understanding of these issues, where both have become people-centric. The human race plays a pivotal role in the evolution of both development and security studies. Thus development which speaks widely about distributive mechanism and capability approach, and security which is a comprehensive concept of political, economic, sociocultural and diplomacy, are all directed towards betterment of human kinds. How and in what degree the condition of man can be improved and protected constitute the significant issues of both development thinkers as well as security experts.

Globalization, one of the contemporary development experiments, has changed the world order by 'accepting a whole range of new realities'.[3] Duffield, Beck et al.[4] have argued that during the 1990s globalization has impacted both development and security, and the closely interdependent world of today has more risks and uncertainties. Inequalities of wealth tend to widen the old disparities and encourage new forms of exclusion, all of which can lead to illicit, criminal and destabilizing forms of global flows and movements. Thus, on the one hand, it has increased global economic productivity and connectivity through increased trade volumes, transnational exchange, labour mobility, reduction of poverty and financial liberalization; while on the other hand, it has posed a grave threat to the world with a network of terrorism and other forms of non-traditional issues, such as illegal financial flows and other security related crimes. Networking of terrorists' groups in the name of religion, identity, regionalism, secessionism, ethnicity, etc., has created a convoluted parallel world, steeped in persistent threats, conflicts, avoidable bloodshed and public insecurity. Thus, apart from conventional threats of military action, non-traditional threats from non-state actors has emerged in today's world as an after effect of globalization. This has made state along with its institutions and citizens extremely vulnerable to unprecedented risks. Manwaring[5] argues that, 'security can no longer be considered only in terms of protecting national territory and interests against external military aggressions. Rather, security is being redefined more broadly to encompass stability; stability is dependent on the legitimate political, economic and social development, well-being of the global community'. Threat to security has multiplied due to cross-border and inter-group linkages. Ramana[6] argues that the nature of assistance that the terrorist groups secure as a result of the various linkages that they establish include financial and organizational support, weapons, training and operational synergy. This is a concern that is also becoming 'globalized' and has been polarizing the world to an alarming extent. The seamless world of today has more aggregate prosperity and wealth than at any other time in the past, and at the same time it has more cross-country terrorism than at any other time in the past. This problem of terrorism is becoming more aggravated with every passing day and is increasingly affecting the lives of common people. Therefore, one can no longer discuss economic prosperity and security perception in mutually exclusive paradigms; rather they need to be coined together to counter the threats that the modern world faces.

In the South Asian scenario, regionalism and separatism are still very strong obsessions, having their roots in economic, political, social, ethnic, religious and many other ramifications. Johnson argues,

> in a region of such diversity strong centrifugal forces are understandable, and, as economic problems or central government direction become unbearable, there are calls for separate states to be created. The legacy of partition, ethnic divisions, fears for the survival of a particular identity and threats to the homogeneity of the nation-state have generated conflicts in pockets across the region.[7]

Surrounded by unfriendly neighbours like Pakistan, Bangladesh, Nepal, China and Myanmar, India is persistently facing security threats emerging from these countries with which it could have forged successful regional partnerships for cooperation and development. These countries, which share porous borders with India, are constantly exporting terrorism to India to seriously destabilize the country's internal security. Such umbilical link across the borders has turned Jammu & Kashmir and the north-eastern region of India into perpetual trouble spots. The year 2008 was a year of bomb blasts and terrorism for India, extensive underground militancy support and cooperation of terrorist network transcending national borders took a heavy toll to innocent lives, and this has made it imperative for India to modernize and strengthen her internal security system. 'Team Manmohan' of the presently elected UPA government of 2009 has taken a vow to prioritize the issues of development and security. It is now being recognized that unless security is made foolproof, development so far achieved would be meaningless; besides the neglected and peripheral regions that is bracing security threats from across international borders would be even more marginalized and isolated from the mainstream, and all our rhetoric about inclusive development would turn out to be farcical.

NORTH-EAST IN FOCUS: EXPLORING ASSAM

'India's North-East illustrates the complexity of factors that led to conflicts and the difficulties that face any government in trying to resolve it. Ethnic, religious, economic, political and sub-national identities were all involved to a greater or lesser degree.'[8] Very recently the comments of Mizoram Chief Minister Pu Lalthanhawla[9] in Singapore reflected the mindset of the people of the region, when he said that 'Indians consist of three races—Dravidians, Aryans and we in North-East'. To resolve such sensitive issue like this in North-East India, one needs a deeper understanding of peoples' sentiments. A forum where both security and development are discussed together with people's participation is increasingly becoming important for this region. The region's geographical isolation and economic vulnerability have kept it in the backyard of India's development and prosperity and made it a fertile breeding ground for insurgency and terrorism. The governments both within the region and at the centre have adopted a security-first approach rather to address the problem of the region and adopting a development-centric approach. Innumerable government policies and development schemes have failed here due to such security risks. It is time therefore to combine and address the dual issues of development and security together—both their internal nuances and its international neighbourhood factors, with which North-East's destiny is closely tied up.

To understand the region, one necessarily needs to understand Assam first, which is the nodal state of North-East India, and anchors other smaller states in terms of connectivity, geography, economy, history and society. This is because Assam has been deconstructed and fragmented and all the other states of the region, except Tripura and Manipur were carved out of Assam on the basis of ethnicity and identity of their people. People of Assam still claim Shillong as the emotional capital of Assam. The state has the largest resource base in the region, human as well as natural resources. Assam's economic performance has gradually worsened from a very sound position due to its internal conflicts, to almost the bottom of the development ladder in the country. The insurgent movement and outfits like United Liberation Front of Assam (ULFA) that aimed for a sovereign Assam to be achieved through armed struggle has crippled the state during the last 30 years, drastically changed the socio-political and economic landscape of the state and bringing it on the verge of complete bankruptcy. As observed by Duffield and Newburg,[10] for achieving security, the pivotal condition is that a state needs to be identified as failed and fragile. Their findings show that the states, which were treated with relative negligence are now subject to renewed policy interest. The crisis states are vulnerable to subversion by regional extremism that is able to propagate separatism and alienation among the non-secured population. The failed states have multidimensional conflicts, as can be seen in Assam, ranging from ethnic issues to lack of development, internal conflicts and border disputes followed by large-scale infiltration. Johnson[11] argues that 'In Assam, the fear that an influx of "foreigners" into the state would dilute the local population and subordinate them economically to outsiders set off one of India's most serious insurgencies.' Wolpert[12] further argues that 'against the background of rising oil prices, which made the local oil reserves more attractive to the outsiders, and a contrasting feeling amongst locals that infrastructure and welfare had been neglected, the Assamese began to strike, riot and murder the Bangladeshi migrants. In 1983 the world's media was alerted to the problem of this remote region by the image of corpses floating down the tributaries of the Ganges and Brahmaputra.' Apart from this, Assam also has become a ground for ethnic conflicts. Several small ethnic communities have been fighting for their independent land in Assam, which creates the possibility of further fragmentation of the state.

Assam's political economy and its internal security began to deteriorate sharply since the early 1980s primarily due to underground militancy. Over the years, assistance and support of various kinds from various external agencies have found their way into the various militant outfits in Assam, making it even more volatile. Apart from Bangladesh, Pakistan, China, Myanmar, Bhutan, Nepal, there are also other countries like the US, Australia, Singapore and Thailand, Malaysia, Sri Lanka which act as conduits for such assistance flowing to the militant groups operating in the region in one way or the other.[13] This 'durable disorder'[14] that has hit Assam needs to be addressed effectively and the contradictory and often conflicting approaches taken today by various governments and security agencies should be reconciled to uniform principles and strategies to find a sustainable solution in the region. One possible approach could be meaningful engagement and better relations not only with the neighbouring nations but also with mainstream India. The mosaic of issues must find a uniform and inclusive approach for a solution that involves the people of the state and their economic betterment. Security cooperation and peace-building measures, both within the region and with the international neighbours can successfully lead to growth and development for all. Unless this is done, the geopolitics of Assam *vis-à-vis* the rest of the North-East soon manifest itself in some other form. 'A methodology that would ensure the presence of the law enforcing agencies in the foreign countries'[15] can also be an alternative for dealing with the global nexus of militancy in this region. Looking at the fragility of international borders and growing interconnectedness of terrorist network within and across the borders of Assam, it seems that the war on terrorism has further 'deepened the interconnection between development and security'.[16] The essays in this volume have addressed the vector of such complex issues that revolves around Assam and touches and affects all other North-Eastern states. This collection of experiences and opinions by some of the most prominent and veteran personalities and a group of young innovative scholars is intended to make this volume serve as useful inputs to our policy makers, scholars and thinkers and also members of the civil society.

The essay by Lt. Gen. S.K. Sinha that is the prelude to this volume, has made some extremely assertive and candid statements regarding Assam's security scenario. He refers to the continuous massive influx of illegal immigrants from Bangladesh in several districts and pockets of Assam. His long association with Assam since 1945 and deep understanding of the political nuances of the state has helped him to support and buttress his arguments with strong logic and facts. According to Sinha 'insurgency erupted primarily because the governments both at centre and the state were not checking the unabated influx of illegal migrants from Bangladesh. They too have legitimate grievances of neglect and discrimination by the centre.' This as he argued was the prime reason for the creation of ULFA. Sinha discusses the adverse history of political discourse in the region, which has eventually injected the feeling of insecurity in the Assamese mindset against Bangladesh. During the Congress regime in 1960s, he informs, such illegal flow of Bangladeshis was consciously encouraged due to 'vote bank politics'. He has finally crafted a three-pronged strategy for combating militancy in Assam, viz., unified command, economic development and psychological initiatives. Citing the bigger terrorism and security context in India in the recent days, Sinha concludes that the regional or local disputes and traditional antagonism between political parties should not suppress and exploit issues of vital concern to the nation like that of illegal infiltration; they should rise above petty considerations and address issues of national interest jointly; with the help of a strong government at the centre, such larger issues can be resolved.

In the next essay, Krishnan Srinivasan has looked at Assam and the rest of North-East in the context of Government of India's attempts and policies towards them, and expressed his concerns and scepticisms against those. He thinks the region is still not in the periphery of awareness and consciousness of the rest of India and argues that Assam does not exist in our news, but only in the 'breaking news'. Illegal migration is fast changing the demographic profile of Assam, and along with this, the 'unholy nexus' between politicians, civil authorities and insurgents of Assam is today a cancer, which can no longer be ignored. Issues of development and security in the state are mutually reinforcing each other and have to be addressed simultaneously. Any viable development model needs to consider the problems of endemic corruption, inefficiency, lack of investment and infrastructure, delivery of promises, improvement of the infrastructure of tourism, bringing in more democratization and transparency, along with meeting the challenges of militancy, illegal migration, HIV/AIDS and drug trafficking. But this author feels Assam has the biggest challenge among all the states in the region to address these developmental concerns due to the Bangladesh factor. Bangladesh is acting as a stumbling block for any initiatives in Assam and the rest of North-East. Therefore he thinks a state-by-state foreign policy approach with Bangladesh, especially with the present pro-India Sheikh Hasina government can change the scenario.

The concerns that were expressed by Sinha and Srinivasan on the level of influx of illegal migration in Assam are translated in terms of actual figures in Jayanta Madhab's essay. He makes an econometric analysis on the contour of such uneven population growth and distribution of population in Assam. Madhab also gives an empirical projection on the numbers of infiltrated population in Assam till the year 2020. In terms of figures, the Hindu population will decrease by 12.39 per cent, whereas the Muslim population will increase by 12.98 per cent, by 2020, with some districts poised to emerge with Muslims as majority among the population. This uneven growth of population will put enormous pressure on economic security in Assam in terms of the scarce land and means of livelihood. The author shares the hope of Srinivasan on the new political regime in Bangladesh under Sheikh Hasina and feels that a negotiation and settlement with her government on the infiltration issue in Assam needs to be chalked out. In the internal scenario, Madhab discusses the methodology of detection of immigrants after 1971 and thereafter and feels that a strong action needs to be taken against those immigrants who occupy government land. Besides, the government should simultaneously deliver on education, health, marriage act, family planning measures, which though much discussed is forgotten and ignored quietly due to vested political interests and vote banks in Assam.

B. Raman in his essay provides an excellent theoretical understanding of the dual paradigm of security and development in a strategic framework of counter-terrorism in India as a whole. He categorizes three kinds of terrorism, viz., indigenous, foreign-sponsored and foreign-aided. To deal with these, there are basically two approaches—counter-terrorist and counter-terrorism mechanisms. The former looks at terrorism as a threat to national security and therefore takes measures through security forces, while the latter addresses terrorism in a broader sense as a phenomenon, having multiple dimensions like political, economic, social and other aspects, and which needs a pragmatic political leadership and approach for handling. Raman has further tried to see the linkage between development and security in any counter-terrorism and counter-insurgency strategy. Development initiatives need to be taken simultaneously in any security sensitive-area like the North-East India, 'in order to demonstrate to people the dividends of observing law and order and keeping away from terrorist and insurgents'. Since there is no copybook for counter-terrorism, the author thinks a fine balance needs to be struck that is situation-specific.

In another essay, Sanjay Pulipaka also provides a theoretical approach, but at a different level than Raman's, to understand the functional relationship between security and development. He shows a relationship through certain specific parameters like horizontal inequality, ethnic conflicts and abundance of natural resources as a cause of conflict. He examines these issues by studying various nations across the world and establishes a strong paradigm to correlate such issues with the issues of conflicts and development. Economic growth according to him may generate 'overall inequality' across individuals irrespective of ethnic, religious and linguistic associations. Economic growth also leaves some regions behind, which results in horizontal inequality, with potential for generating conflicts due to the 'grievance factor'. The author further argues that abundance of natural resources also tends to intensify conflicts, which can be termed as the 'greed factor'. Thus oil-rich countries and precious stone-rich countries are found to be more prone to conflicts. Similarly, coexistence of multiple ethnic groups has a high propensity towards conflicts. Thus the author emphasizes that there cannot be one single reason for fuelling conflicts in a certain region, rather multiple factors are responsible for giving rise to conflicts, and North-East India's scenario needs to be understood properly by identifying such multiple factors which are causing such conflicts in the region.

Ali Ahmed in the subsequent essay also tries to see the issues of conflicts in theoretical framework by contrasting the tenets of the sub-conventional warfare doctrine of the Army with the counter-insurgency strategy implemented in Assam. This strategy he says has reduced conflicts to a manageable level within the state. However, conflicts have not been resolved due to the absence of a matching political prong to the military prong of counter-insurgency strategy. The author argues that in Assam the issues are complex, and a predominant military prong may not be sufficient to bring about conflict resolution and conflict termination. Assam rather needs a politically predominant approach. Such a resolution to conflicts can be achieved through concerted civil society efforts *in tandem* with governmental political initiatives where an ambience of conflict resolution would precede conflict termination. The author suggests a counter-insurgency strategy resulting in a secure environment through isolating the conflict zone, addressing the local aspirations, winning the hearts and minds and by creating public information system. This would help resolve the ongoing conflicts without over-dependence on violence as a policy tool. Army operations like 'Operation Bajrang' earlier and 'Operation Rhino' have by and large improved the law and order situation and have generated public confidence. But beyond military operations, along with the need to win the hearts and minds of people, the strategy needs to incorporate developmental initiatives, restoring liberty, initiating a political dialogue, energizing the diplomatic initiatives and encouraging civil society initiatives.

After these three essays, which are constructed on a theoretical frame, H.N. Das sets the issue of conflicts in Assam in a historical set up. He takes a very large canvas, going back to the historical immigration pattern in Assam and discusses how the assimilation and differences have evolved a rich society in the state and how it is now threatening this existing social order. Assam has historically remained the abode of immigrants like Hindu Aryans and Tai Ahoms for a long time, and this has manifested in a rich cultural diversity. Apart from this, a cross-section of population from several parts of India came here during the colonial time for economic reasons; and added to all these is the huge Muslim immigration in Assam which over time has changed the demography of today's Assam. Meanwhile the process of reorganization of states on the basis of language in India has caused grievances among the ethnic and tribal groups, and Assam has suffered the most from it, getting fragmented into all other states of North-East today, except Tripura and Manipur. This political reorganization in Assam has spawned various other ethnic and tribal communities develop divergent aspirations, giving rise to various sub-national demands. This has aggravated the multi-layered differences amongst various communities and became the source of conflict in Assam. It has also complicated the political scene of Assam on the one hand, and aggravated the financial responsibility of the state for development of such communities on the other. Thus Assam's five-year and annual plans have allocation for hills, tribes and schedule caste communities with separate pre-fix ratios for weightage to different sections of people. Due to the absence of absolute majority of any community, any political cohesion and economic development remains a distant dream; rather, a large Muslim community along with many small ethnic and tribal communities has reconfigured Assam terrorism in a different dimension, leaving many of the state's problems unresolved. Therefore, the author suggests administrative reforms and political diplomacy to resolve such issues.

Rangan Dutta also echoes the views of H.N. Das and mentions that ethnic divisions and their aspiration have already made Assam a fractured state, and any further fragmentation in any form will make it 'ungovernable'. It also will escalate mainfold the cost of the Union Government. The author thinks that the strategic position of Assam is extremely important for India, therefore its development will ensure India's stability, which can improve the relation with South-East Asia. Dutta proposes development in Assam through an education reforms measure, which would incorporate science and technology. Presently, the state's scientific research and higher education is of poor quality. A 'knowledge based' structure can transform the economy in Assam and in the whole of North-East India. The author urges for institutionalizing the involvement of scientific system in the state planning and development process and proposes certain measures for 'landlocked' Assam for its growth and development, citing the growth model example of 'landlocked' Delhi.

Another essay by Papori Chetia Phukan also establishes the link between insurgency in Assam and its manifestation of various ethnic aspiration and demands. She argues that inter-ethnic conflicts and insurgency are intertwined in the North-Eastern region of India and Assam projects several layers of ethnic, linguistic, religious and cultural heterogeneity, leading to the complexity of identity issue. She also subscribes the views of H.N. Das that Assam was the land of Aryans and Ahoms with a rich culture, but she thinks that the advent of British had to a large extent changed the landscape of Assam, which had sown the seed of separatism amongst ethnic communities which led to insurgency. The author also feels that factors like geographical distance, inaccessibility and backward economy are significant for insurgency in the region. Phukan makes a case study for two hill districts of Assam, viz., Karbi Anglong and North Cachar Hills to show the intensity of inter-ethnic conflicts. Unlike Rangan Dutta, who feels Assam cannot be fragmented any longer to meet ethnic demands, Phukan on the contrary feels that if such ethnic aspiration are ignored, it would certainly add to security vulnerability in Assam and therefore recommends a robust plan of action to settle the issue of inter-ethnic conflicts in Assam both from New Delhi and from Dispur, the administrative capital of Assam.

Amarjeet Singh presents a well-researched essay to show how insurgency in Assam has affected its development process over the years. He makes a very interesting comparison by categorizing the peaceful and disturbed states in North-East India through development indicators, and shows empirically how peaceful states are surging ahead and how the disturbed states are falling behind. In the disturbed state like Assam, insurgency is encouraging illegal taxation, delayed and non-implementation of development projects, ethnic displacement, loss of public property, affected tourism, all these directly are impeding the overall development scenario of Assam. Like Dutta, Singh also proposes some policy measures to deal with such a situation. There is clearly a need for a political dialogue involving civil society and strengthening the internal police force to handle the insurgency, which can also replace the central military and paramilitary forces in the region.

M.P. Bezbaruah makes a very interesting point by highlighting the nexus between underdevelopment and insecurity in Assam, which are reinforcing each other in a vicious circle. Before establishing such a nexus, Bezbaruah outlines a clear scenario of Assam during the post-Independence period and shows how cultural identity and ethic aspiration and later the threat of infiltration were the roots of many conflicts and led to the ultimate fragmentation of Assam. He therefore argues that development issue is not the sole cause of conflicts in Assam, rather 'failure to accommodate identity aspiration of the group has been as much, if not more, responsible for the prolonged adverse security situation in the state as the failure to expedite the pace of development'. While looking at the development performance of the state, Bezbaruah shows that intra-district disparity in development is largely responsible for feelings of anger and deprivation, which ultimately resulted in conflicts. To deal with such a situation, Bezbaruah suggests development programmes which incorporate peoples' participation, rather than creation of enclaves of industries, which fails to establish linkages with the rest of the economy. Simultaneously, security measures also need to be intensified for a conducive economic environment. Bezbaruah then says that these two conditions are necessary but not essential when the identity issue is rooted to conflicts, which needs to be addressed through deepening democracy by facilitating creation of a space for dialogue and tolerance and developing trust amongst the conflicting groups.

Rakhee Bhattacharya's essay also dwells upon development-conflict interface in Assam through an examination of a brief historical perspective. Bhattacharya's prime argument is that despite Assam and the rest of North-East being special category states eligible to receive liberal financial benefits from the central government, development in a sustainable manner has not been achieved so far. Over and above, to deal with the protracted conflicts, draconian laws and measures like the imposition of Armed Forces Special Power Act have been initiated and these have not resolved the security issue either. Rather, government has been burdened with a huge financial responsibility both for Assam's development and for security issues, and the huge funds that has been pumped in were misutilized and siphoned off. Bhattacharya tries to analyse empirically the cost of development and mentions the impact of underdevelopment and insecurity in the region under two broad heads: (1) economic performance, where she has explored the economic status of the region comparing it with other states in India; and (2) economy of insurgency as a parallel economy that has evolved in the region over the years and is as potent as the legal economy dominated by the government. She feels that a different structural paradigm is essential for the region to rebuild it by an inclusive approach through people's participation.

Binoda Kumar Mishra reviews the entire concept of security, which has emerged now with new dimensions through a deeper, broader and extended understanding. He looks into the security scenario of North-East India, which so far has been projected primarily through insurgent issues—and explores the reasons behind such insurgency as well as the present international networking behind it, highlighted also by others. The author then goes beyond this and tries to look for a new paradigm in the region with an alternative approach to the security scenario to evolve towards a permanent solution. He emphasizes the need to explore the new security dimensions like comprehensive, cooperative and human security paradigms for North-East India, encompassing environmental, economic, political, community, health and food security. He takes the concept of 'human security audit' of Kanti Bajpai to identify each of these broad security issues, and calls for a need to address these issues through the creation of functional institutions. These functional institutions can involve both government and non-government stakeholders, which can improve the level of local participations and erase the sense of grievance amongst the people of North-East India for various reasons.

The last essay in this volume, which is interestingly a photo essay by Dilip Banerjee explores and portrays through his own amazing photographs, the facets of turmoil at various levels in North-East India. His images vividly capture and depict the myriad issues as discussed and brought out extensively by other authors, such as challenges of confronting infiltration, operation of Indian security forces, the tough lives of insurgents, political agreements and election campaigns in the region. His photo essay finally sums up the complex interplay of security, politics and development issues in North-East India.

BREAKING THE IMPASSE[17]

All these essays by and large dwell upon the burning issues of Assam *vis-à-vis* North-East India, ranging from illegal migration from Bangladesh, to the all-pervading corruption and existence of the unholy nexus between politicians and insurgents, issue of cultural identities, inter-ethnic rivalries and their demand for dues as the pivotal causes of prolonged conflicts in Assam, which has affected economic development of the state significantly with an outflow of investment, shrinkage in sources of livelihood and poor economic opportunities. The essays create a platform for debates on many new apprehensions, rivalries, tensions, uncertainties and inquiries that Assam is facing today. To move away from the existing situation, a societal progress is a prerequisite, which also can reduce insecurity. A more inclusive and egalitarian development as between cultural groups is likely to lead to greater security.[18] Thus it is not only economic impediments that lead to insecurity and vice versa, rather to understand the nexus between underdevelopment and insecurity, one needs to go beyond economic reasons and should simulteneously look at cultural, economic, political and social factors. Assam is a glaring example of such a complex scenario where all these issues are present, justifying the necessity of comprehensive security measures. Stewart[19] argues that virtuous cycles can be created with high levels of security leading to development and development further promoting security. But such a virtuous cycle can more readily be broken because it is easy to have relatively high levels of security without necessarily experiencing economic growth, or to have high levels of security and economic growth, but not inclusive growth so the potential for conflict remains. The security-cum-stagnation can be seen in a number of Latin American countries and non-inclusive growth, seems to be occurring in some Asian countries too, like India and China. This is clearly not sustainable and can pose potential threats to security. Assam with her complex issues of conflicts needs an inclusive pattern of development rather than a solution based only on the military approach. To lower the propensity of violence and insurgency, it needs to lay down a roadmap backed by an integrated effort at all levels with people's participation and through the creation of 'functional institutions'. A fusion of development and human security keeping 'life' as the common referent object needs to be made before persistent conflicts become a terminal threat to sustainable development in Assam. To achieve this, Assam needs to redefine the concept of state sovereignty to imbibe 'responsibility to protect'[20] and should have a consolidated people's forum under 'human security now'[21] to restore long-term peace and embark upon a path of true development in this beautiful part of India.

NOTES

1. Frances Stewart, 'Development and Security', Working Paper 3, Centre for Research on Inequality, Human Security and Ethnicity, CRISE, University of Oxford, p. 1, available at http://www.crise.ox.ac.uk/pubs/working(eds.)paper3.pdf)

2. S.K. Agnihotri and B. Datta Ray, eds., *Perspective of Security and Development in North East India*, New Delhi: Concept Publishing Company, 2005, p. 13.
3. Tom Conley, 'Globalization and Rising Inequality in Australia—Is Increasing Inequality Inevitable in Australia?' Griffith University, 2004, p. 1, available at http://www.adelaide.edu.au/apsa/docs_papers/Others/Conley.pdf
4. U. Beck, *Risk Society,* London: Sage, 1992; M. Castells, *End of Millennium,* Oxford: Blackwell Publishers, 1998; S. George, *The Debt Boomerang: How Third World Debt Harms Us All,* London: Pluto Press, 1992; Mark Duffield, *Human Security: Linking Development and Security in an Age of Terror*, Department of Politics and International Relations, Lancaster University, 2005, p. 12. available at http://eadi.org/gc2005/confweb/papersps/Mark_Duffield.pdf
5. Max. G. Manwaring, 'Security of the Western Hemisphere: International Terrorism and Organized Crime', April 1998, available at http://www.ndu.edu/inss/strforum/SF137/forum137.html
6. P.V. Ramana, 'Networking the North East Partners in Terror', Institute of Conflict Management, ND, 2001, available at http://www.satp.org/satporgtp/publication/faultlines/volume11/Article6.htm
7. Rob Johnson, *A Region in Turmoil: South Asian Conflicts Since 1947*, New Delhi: Viva Books, 2006, p. 35.
8. Ibid., p. 203.
9. Rashmee Roshan Lall, 'Man in the Mirror', *Times of India*, 30 June 2009, available at http://timesofindia.indiatimes.com/Opinion/Editorial/TOP-ARTICLE-Man-In-The-Mirror/articleshow/4716863.cms
10. P.R. Newburg, 'Politics at the Heart: The Architecture of Humanitarian Assistance to Afghanistan', Global Policy Programme, *Working Papers No. 2*, Washington: Carnegie Endowment for International Peace, 1999; Mark Duffield, 'Human Security: Linking Development and Security in an Age of Terror', Department of Politics and International Relations, Lancaster University, 2005, p. 12, available at http://eadi.org/gc2005/confweb/papersps/Mark_Duffield.pdf
11. Johnson, op. cit., pp. 35, 203.
12. Stanley Wolpert, *A New History of India,* New York: Oxford University Press, 2000, p. 411, cited in Johnson, op. cit., pp. 35, 203.

13. G.M. Srivastava, Director General of Police, Government of Assam has made this statement in the seminar organized by Maulana Abul Kalam Azad Institute of Asian Studies at Guwahati on 'Addressing Security and Development Issues in Assam' on 28 March 2009. This report has also come out in *The Assam Tribune*, 29 March 2009.
14. The term is taken from Sanjib Baruah's *Durable Disorder: Understanding the Politics of Northeast India*, New Delhi: Oxford University Press, 2005.
15. Srivastava, op. cit.
16. Mark Duffield, 'Human Security: Linking Development and Security in an Age of Terror', Department of Politics and International Relations, Lancaster University, 2005, p. 16, available at http://eadi.org/gc2005/confweb/papersps/Mark_Duffield.pdf
17. Taken from Sanjib Baruah (ed.), *Beyond Counter-Insurgency: Breaking the Impasse in Northeast India*, New Delhi: Oxford University Press, 2009.
18. Stewart, op. cit.
19. Ibid., p. 19.
20. A Report of International Commission on Intervention and State Sovereignty 'The Responsibility to Protect', 2001, cited by Stewart, op. cit., p. 9, available at http://www.crise.ox.ac.uk/pubs/workingpaper3.pdf
21. Report of Commission of Human Security 'Human Security Now', 2003, cited by Stewart op. cit., p. 9, available at http://www.crise.ox.ac.uk/pubs/workingpaper3.pdf

CHAPTER 2

Security and Development in the North-East: A Case of Assam

Lt. Gen. S.K. Sinha

After Independence, for well over a decade, a debate raged in our country on the conflicting pulls of defence and development. Having won our Independence as a result of a non-violent struggle and having chosen the *mantra* of non-alignment after Independence, we ignored defence till the debacle in the Himalayas of 1962. As far as the North-East was concerned, being a distant land, it was not in national focus. It was ignored both for defence and development. Although the Naga rebellion broke out in 1956 the strategic importance of the North-East dawned on us only after 1962.

Security is a more encompassing term than 'defence'. In the context of the North-East, apart from defence, secessionist movements pose a serious threat to our national security. The unabated influx of illegal migrants from Bangladesh is a grave threat not only to the demographic contours and the economy of the region but also to the national security. Till recently, there were seven states in the North-East. Sikkim has recently been included, making a total of eight states. Assam is the major state of the region. Its population is more than double the total population of the remaining seven states. Its economy has a similar edge over the other states. Assam is rich in oil, tea and forest wealth besides having abundance of water resources. Many states of the region are former districts of Assam.

I have had a long association with Assam going back to the Second World War. Soon after getting my commission in the

Army, I was posted to Guwahati in 1945 before proceeding to Burma, now Myanmar. When the Naga rebellion broke out in 1956, my battalion was the first Army unit to be inducted into the Naga Hills, then a part of Assam. I served as a company commander, a brigade commander and a divisional commander combating insurgency in the North-East at different points of time. As Chief of Military Intelligence of the Indian Army and as the Vice Chief, I was closely associated in dealing with the security problems of the North-East. In my post-army career, I served as Governor of Assam for six years from 1997 to 2003. During this period, I was also Chairman of the North-East Council, which is equivalent to Planning Commission for the region. It coordinates the economic development of all the states in the North-East. Based on my long association with the North-East, I will share my views on security and development in the North-East in the following paragraphs.

Our border dispute with China remains unresolved. China claims the whole of Arunachal Pradesh as her territory. China has been trying to encircle India by developing bases in the Indian Ocean region, which is often euphemistically referred to as the 'necklace of pearls' around India. In the event of another war with China, North-East will be the most important theatre of operations. We must at all times have a strong military posture in the North-East to deter any adventurist action. The several ongoing militancy movements with a secessionist agenda pose a grave danger to our national security.

Sikkim and Mizoram do not have any militancy problem. The insurgency in Mizoram got resolved through a political settlement in the 1980s. Meghalaya and Arunachal Pradesh are also largely free from insurgency except for a spill-over effect from neighbouring states. The over half-a-century long insurgency movement in Nagaland has been dormant for the last twelve years as a result of a peace accord. The territorial demands of the Nagas for a Greater Nagaland incorporating districts from Assam, Arunachal Pradesh and Manipur, however, persist. Militancy continues in Manipur and Tripura. The former is the most disturbed state of the North-East. The militancy in Tripura is a result of ethnic conflict between the indigenous tribal population and the Bengali population from East Pakistan, now Bangladesh, which moved into the state after 1947 reducing the original tribal inhabitants to a minority. Assam has tribal insurgency of the Bodos and other small tribal groups in the two hill districts of Karbianglong and North Cachar Hills. Assam also has the ULFA insurgency movement of the Assamese people living in the Brahmaputra Valley. This is the largest insurgency movement in the North-East. In view of the geostrategic location of Assam, the ULFA militancy is the most dangerous for our national security. The tribal insurgencies of the North-East are due to the fact that the tribes had not been fully assimilated in the Indian culture and civilization. They are mostly in peripheral areas near the border. The case of ULFA militancy is different. The Assamese people living in the Brahmaputra Valley have been a part and parcel of the Indian civilization from the dawn of history. Insurgency erupted amongst them primarily because the government both at the centre and in the state was not checking the unabated influx of illegal migrants from Bangladesh. They also had legitimate grievances of neglect and discrimination by the Centre. All these militant groups have bases in Bangladesh and enjoy the support of the intelligence agencies of Bangladesh and Pakistan. Over the years, India has been blackmailed by Pakistan's nuclear capability and has not carried out any cross-border strike against militants operating in Kashmir from Pakistan or Pakistan-held territory. There is no nuclear angle to any cross-border strike against militants taking shelter in Bangladesh. Yet we have chosen to be passive in this regard. No wonder we are viewed as a soft state!

As Governor of Assam for six years, I was very proactive in combating militancy in the state and I achieved a fair measure of success. I will take the liberty of dwelling on the problems of the state in some detail. The main cause for militancy in the state has been the unabated influx of illegal migrants from Bangladesh. This problem has a long history going back to early twentieth century. The indigenous people of the state have been very concerned about being made an ethnic and religious minority in their own state. It started with the formation of the Muslim League in Dacca in 1904 and their demand for a Banga-Islam, a

Muslim State comprising Bengal and Assam. This was much before the movement for Pakistan was started. In terms of population, Assam was less than one-tenth of the then Bengal. The partition of Bengal by Lord Curzon in 1905 led to Assam being merged with the newly-created Muslim majority of East Bengal and Assam losing its status as a separate state. In 1911 the partition of Bengal was annulled, but the people did not forget that during those six years they had been reduced to a small ethnic and religious minority in the newly formed state. The British government encouraged the migration of hardy Muslim peasants from North Bengal to Lower Assam to clear the forests and cultivate the land. Mullen, the Census Superintendent of Assam, in the Census Report of 1932 compared this large-scale migration of what he called Mymensinghias (North Bengalis) with the silent invasion of an army of ants. He felt that soon a stage will come when the people of Assam will find themselves at home only in Sibsagar district of Upper Assam. During the Second World War, Assam had a Muslim League Ministry of Sir Sadaulla. On the pretext of implementing the Grow More Food campaign, Sadaulla settled a large number of Muslims from North Bengal in lower Assam. The then Viceroy Lord Wavell in his book *Viceroy's Journal* wrote that the Muslim League Ministry was trying to 'Grow More Muslims' in Assam under the cover of Grow More Food. The Cabinet Mission Plan of 1946 catered for grouping of provinces. Hindu majority provinces were in Group A, Muslim majority provinces in Group B, and Bengal and Assam in Group C. In the latter group Assam would have lost its identity in view of the huge disparity in the population of the two states. Bordoloi, the then Congress Chief Minister of Assam, feared that this grouping would eventually lead to Assam becoming a part of East Pakistan. Thus, even though the Congress High Command had supported the Grouping Plan, Bordoloi raised the banner of revolt on this issue. Mahatma Gandhi supported Bordoloi, and the Grouping Plan ultimately got shelved and Assam was saved. At the time of Partition, Jinnah on a visit to Guwahati had boasted that he had Assam in his pocket. After Partition, Pakistani leaders and intellectuals continued to cast a covetous eye on Assam. Zulfikar

Ali Bhutto in his book *Myths of Independence* wrote, 'It would be wrong to think that Kashmir is the only dispute that divides India and Pakistan, though undoubtedly the most significant. One at least is nearly as important as the Kashmir dispute, that of Assam and some districts of India adjacent to East Pakistan. To these Pakistan has very good claims.' Sheikh Mujibur Rahman in his book on East Pakistan wrote that Assam has abundance of space and resources. East Pakistan must include Assam to be financially and economically strong. Several leading intellectuals in Bangladesh have been talking in terms of 'lebansraum' (living space). The continuing illegal migration into Assam has to be viewed against this historical background. In the late 1960s, B.K. Nehru was the Governor of Assam. He was a member of the ruling dynasty and his cousin Indira Gandhi was the prime minister at the time. He initiated measures to stop illegal migration from then East Pakistan. He was told to 'stop the nonsense'. In pursuit of its vote bank politics, the Congress had not only ignored but was encouraging migration from Bangladesh. In his autobiography, *Nice Guys Finish Second*, B.K. Nehru laments that for the old generation of Congressmen, national interests were paramount but for the new generation party interests mattered more. In the early 1990s, Lt. Gen. Jameel Mahmood, the then Eastern Army Commander took up this matter with Hiteshwar Saikia, the then Chief Minister of Assam and Jyoti Basu, former Chief Minister of West Bengal, advising them to take effective steps to stop this massive infiltration otherwise the borders of India in the east will have to be redrawn. He also wrote to Army Headquarters about his apprehension of a Kashmir-type situation developing in Assam. On 10 April 1992 Hiteshwar Saikia stated in the State Assembly that there were 3 million Bangladeshi illegal migrants in Assam. Two days later under pressure from some MLAs he stated at a Press Conference that there were no Bangladeshi illegal migrants in Assam. On 6 May 1997, Indrajit Gupta, the then Communist Home Minister of India had told the Parliament that there were 10 million Bangladeshi illegal migrants in India. It was estimated that of these, 4 million were in Assam. On 14 July 2004, Shri Prakash Jaiswal, the then Union Minister of State for Home told the

Parliament that there were 12 million illegal Bangladeshi migrants in India. The following day Dr Manmohan Singh on a visit to Guwahati, presumably under local pressure told the media that the figure quoted by his junior colleague in the Parliament was not authentic. A week later Jaiswal told the Parliament that the figure mentioned by him was based on hearsay!

The then Chief Election Commissioner, Shri Shakdher at a meeting of Chief Electoral Officers in 1978, expressed concern at the alarming increase of voters by 34.98 per cent in Assam in 10 years and if this continued at that rate, soon the indigenous people of Assam will be reduced to a minority in their state. He also referred to the demands of political parties to include the names of migrants who are not Indian citizens, in the voters' list. A few months later during the by-election of Mongoldoi, it was found that names of 70,000 illegal migrants had been included in the voters' list. This led to the start of a students' movement demanding detection, deletion and deportation of illegal migrants in Assam. ULFA was started as an armed wing of the movement with a secessionist agenda. That was the start of militancy in Assam. Since illegal migration had been the root cause of militancy in Assam, on taking over as Governor of the state in 1997, I carried out research of the problem. I also extensively toured the border and interacted with numerous people to get their views on the matter. Based on this, I made out a 42-page printed report which I submitted to the president with a copy to the prime minister and the chief minister of Assam. I brought out that successive governments in the state and at the centre had ignored the problem. This posed a grave threat not only to the demographic contour of the state but also to the national security. This report was serialized in full in all newspapers of Assam. This took the people of the state by storm. I was hailed as a true friend of Assam. This report became a landmark document and started being quoted both nationally and internationally while examining this problem. In my report, I made several recommendations like border fencing, photo identity card, repeal of IMDT Act and so on. The latter was highly discriminatory, designed to facilitate illegal migration. The Foreigners Act applied to the rest of India under which a foreign national had to establish his claim to be granted Indian citizenship. The IMDT Act applied to Assam only and under this Act, the onus of proof was with the state to establish that an individual was not an Indian citizen. There were provisions in this Act, which were favourable to an illegal migrant. The police could not act *suo motu* against any illegal migrant and it did not have the power to search or arrest an illegal migrant who had been convicted by a court. At least two citizens of the locality had to lodge a complaint at the police station and deposit a token amount before the police could take cognizance and start investigation. I am afraid, no action was taken by the government on my report to the president. A public interest litigation was filed in the Supreme Court. The apex court struck down the IMDT Act and in its judgement quoted extensively from my report. The UPA government brought back the IMDT Act through the backdoor by amending the Foreigner's Act.

We crafted a three-prong strategy for combating militancy in Assam—unified command, economic development, and psychological initiatives. It is amazing that we had been fighting insurgency in the North-East for over forty years, but had not established a unified command. Thus, different elements of security forces were functioning as competing rather than complementary forces. A unified command was set-up in Assam for the first time in 1997. It achieved spectacular results. 2,500 militants were killed in encounters, 3,000 surrendered with weapons and Rs. 1.25 crore was recovered in cash. This virtually broke the back of the militants but they still had their camps intact in Bhutan. Ultimately, the king of Bhutan acted and the Bhutan Army attacked these camps in 2003, and in a highly successful operation they destroyed all the camps. By the end of 2003 the ULFA was virtually wiped out.

The second prong of economic development was pursued vigorously. We hit a jackpot with our shallow tube well project. Before 1947, Assam was self-sufficient in rice, the staple food of the people of Assam. With the steep increase in population and stagnant levels of rice production, the situation had changed. Assam had become a rice deficit state and had to import rice from other states. Cultivation in Assam was dependent on the monsoon and the state used to have only one crop a year. During winter months, cultivable land used to lie fallow for want of water for irrigation. The Green Revolution that had come about in the rest of the country had not touched Assam. The water table in the Brahmaputra Valley is high. We decided to have 1 lakh shallow tube wells. Each tube well with pump costs Rs. 21,000. The state government was in no position to provide funds for this project. We obtained Rs. 14,000 per tube well from the Government of India and the farmers had to raise Rs. 7,000 from their cooperatives. We insisted on their contribution so that they had a stake in the project and they looked after it. It was almost a miracle that we were able to install one lakh shallow tube wells in one year. From a rice deficit state, Assam became a rice surplus state. Like other states that had benefited from the Green Revolution, Assam also now started having two to three crops a year. Production of paddy increased by 11.53 per cent and *rabi* crops by 6.93 per cent. The annual income of the average farmer had gone up by Rs. 51,000 to 1 lakh. The Planning Commission hailed this as a great success story and we were able to bring about a mini-economic revolution in the state.

The third prong of our strategy of psychological initiatives was equally successful. We stepped up the conventional measures like free medical camps, renovating schools, vocational training and so on. For the first time a pronounced emotional content was introduced in these initiatives, which touched the heart of the people. My report on illegal migration prepared the ground for it. I declared that my mission was to make the people of Assam proud of their past and the rest of India proud of Assam. I tried to project the three icons of Assam about whom little was known outside the state as our national heroes. These are, Shrimant Shankardev, the patron saint of Assam, Veer Lachit Borphukan, the legendary military leader, and Lokpriya Gopinath Bordoloi, the great statesman. Documentary films were prepared on each of them and showed on the television. Lachit's statue was installed at the National Defence Academy and a gold medal was introduced there for the best performer in the academy. A posthumous Bharat Ratna was obtained for Bordoloi, nearly fifty years after his death. The Guwahati airfield was named after him and his 11 ft tall bronze statue was installed inside the

Parliament building at Delhi. These measures had a tremendous impact on the people. Their feeling of alienation disappeared and they were brought back into the national mainstream. I started being referred to as more Assamese than any Assamese and a true son of the soil of Assam. The ULFA which at one time were hailed as heroes and had wide support among the people were now totally isolated from people. The measure of success obtained in bringing about a mind change among the people can be gauged from two facts. First, 81 militants over a period of a couple of years were apprehended in different incidents in rural areas by unarmed villagers. Half of them were lynched and the other half handed over to the police. Second, on the ULFA Raising Day of 7 April at Sibsagar Grounds where ULFA had been raised, I took the surrender of over 300 ULFA militants with the function witnessed by an appreciative audience of some 10,000 people. The gains achieved in tackling militants by 2003 got squandered away in subsequent years. I will touch upon this later.

I have discussed at length how we tried to meet security challenges from 1997 to 2003 when I was the Governor of the State. I feel that the strategy evolved there with suitable modifications to suit local conditions can also work elsewhere. I will now turn to development issues.

Partition wrought havoc to the economy of the North-East. With the loss of the entry-port of Chittagong, North-East virtually became a landlocked region with no outlet to the sea except through a circuitous route to Kolkata port. Goods from Tripura to the sea or vice versa had to travel an extra 1,400 km adding to their cost. The Brahmaputra was no longer available for river transport as in the old days. Surface routes by road and railway used to be from Kolkata through present Bangladesh to the North-East. These had now to be developed through the Siliguri corridor. There had been a population explosion in Assam along with the large influx of illegal migrants. Before Partition, Assam had been a food surplus state and the per capita income of its people was over 4 per cent higher than the national average. Today Assam is a food deficit state notwithstanding the fact that the shallow tube wells made it self-sufficient and even surplus in rice. The per capita income of the people of Assam is 31 per cent lower than the national average. Hydel projects, the new temples of India, came up in other parts of the country and initially none in the North-East. Thus the region was left out of the benefits of the Green Revolution. No doubt the Government of India has undertaken various measures for the economic development of the region but a lot more needs to be done. The North-Eastern states have been given special category status, which means that central aid going to them is 90 per cent grant and 10 per cent loan. States that are not in this category get central aid under different terms, 70 per cent loan and 30 per cent grant. Surface transport, both rail and road, has been developed through the Siliguri corridor. North-Eastern Council with governors and chief ministers of all the states of the region as members of the Council, was set-up in 1971. I was the chairman of this Council when I was Governor of Assam. It functions like a Planning Commission for the North-East. We concentrated on infrastructure development for the region. Some of the major projects undertaken by the Council were, Rangamati Hydel Project completed with an outlay of 1415 crore, North-East Power Corporation, Regional Institute of Medical Science, Shankar Netralaya, regional roads and so on. Despite all these, we have a long way to go to bring the North-East at par with the rest of the country.

After 2003, ill-conceived efforts were made to win over the ULFA by suspending operations when they were on the verge of extinction. The remaining ULFAs who had escaped from Bhutan were surrounded in the jungle in upper Assam. Suspension of operations was ordered and they were allowed to escape. Indirect talks through a Peace Consultative Group were opened. These talks dragged on for more than a year and at the end, true to their style, the ULFAs backed off. They were playing for time to regroup and reorganize, and managed to achieve their objective. This was not the first time that the ULFA had led us up the garden path. The ULFA again started their acts of violence but now there was no popular support for them among the people. When a militant outfit is defeated and has lost popular support, there should be no need for talks with them, chasing the chimera of a political settlement. The ULFA movement had been launched to stop illegal migration from Bangladesh. It now reneged against its ideology by facilitating this influx. It began acting in support of Pakistani and Bangladeshi intelligence agencies and functioning along with Islamist outfits. Jihadi terrorism, which had started in Kashmir had spread to the hinterland of India. City after city in the country have been suffering jihadi terrorism. The biggest serial bombing in Assam that took place on 30 October 2008 and the Mumbai terror attack on 26 November 2008 sent shock waves throughout the country. Besides, numerous acts of Naxal violence have been taking place in the country. A virtual red corridor has been established in seven states with 57 districts affected by this menace. Never before, the security scenario in the country has been so grim. To deal with this grave challenge we need a strong government at the centre. Parliamentary elections are to be held shortly.[1] In 1977, the Indian electorate had given a clear mandate against Emergency and in 1980 against a strife ridden and non-performing government. Forecast for the coming election is that neither of the two national parties will get a clear majority. They will then be at the mercy of the blackmailing tactics of regional parties. The security situation in the country including the North-East is so grave that in the event of a fractured mandate the two national parties should bury their deep-rooted antagonism and form a coalition in national interest, providing a strong government at the centre. Despite their sharp differences, the Conservative and the Labour parties in the UK had formed a coalition government during the Second World War. We need to learn from that example.

NOTE

1. This talk was delivered on 28 March 2009, at Guwahati, before the election results were declared on 16 May 2009. The election results took everyone by surprise with the Indian electorate giving a clear mandate for a stable government.

   Lt. Gen S.K. Sinha's Report: 'Report on Illegal Migration into Assam', submitted to the President of India by the Governor of Assam, 8 November 1998, can be accessed at http://www.satp.org/satporgtp/countries/india/states/assam/documents/papers/illegal_migration_in_assam.htm

CHAPTER 3

Security and Development Issues in Assam

Krishnan Srinivasan

CONNECTIVITY

The North-East region of India comprises eight states with only 2 per cent bordering India—the rest of the frontiers are with Myanmar, China, Nepal—and in Assam's case with Bhutan and Bangladesh. India's trade with the countries bordering the North-East may have gone up several times, but no impact is seen in the region because this commerce is through the seaports. Despite the many regional groupings like BIMSTEC, BCIM, Mekong-Ganga Initiative, and ASEAN, there is a lack of connectivity and an excess of security inhibitions in the North-East that preclude the seizing of opportunities leading to positive outcomes.

The Government of India gives the impression that it is ambiguous about closer integration between our North-East and the adjoining countries. Among these apprehensions are that trans-border ethnic solidarities may develop to the strategic advantage of other countries, illegal migration may increase, so might extremism and fundamentalism, and India may lose control over the economic situation. Considering India and China are among the fastest growing world economies, trade through the recently opened Nathu-la Pass should improve prospects for the whole North-East which has only about half of India's growth rate. But the optimistic prospects envisaged for commerce through Nathu-la do not look as if they will ever materialize. If the North-East opens up, would it be primarily for our exports or only for import of cheaper Chinese goods that benefit from an advantageous exchange rate? Such questions obsess the officials in New Delhi who always err on the side of caution.

SECURITY

Our North-East region is one of the most complex in Asia, with about 200 ethnic groups, languages and dialects. These societies have lived in a degree of isolation not only from the rest of the country but from each other, and both legal and illegal migrations have created new fault lines in traditional societies. The whole area, where parochialism transcends nationalism or even regionalism, is in uneasy transition, and needs extremely deft and skilful management. At the same time, a major constraint in people's minds involves the security situation in Assam. With headlines stressing some terrorist incidents, it is always a surprise to outsiders when people speak approvingly of what a fine place Assam is to live in. Assam does not exist in our news, but only in the 'breaking news'. The ground reality is somewhat at variance with the perception. In general terms, the Barak Valley is without problems and so is most of the Brahmaputra Valley. In the Bodo area there is generally tranquillity. But it is true that the United Liberation Front of Assam (ULFA) seeks innocent targets, and there is a degree of insecurity felt by non-Assamese communities in parts of the state, such as the so-called 'Biharis' in upper Assam and the entrance to lower Assam.

From 2005 to 2007 the number of insurgency fatalities in the North-East, including military and civil, was between 700 and 1,000 each year. I do not have the figure for Assam separately, but terrorist incidents in Assam between 2008 and 2009 reveal the extent of sub-nationalism, ethnicity, communal politics and foreign involvement. These atrocities have been perpetrated apparently by a Muslim terrorist group [ISF-IM: HuJI-ULFA (Harkat-ul-Jihad-al-Islami)] with methods which strongly suggest affiliations with Bangladesh. The demographic patterns in Assam due to illegal migration and other factors are contributing to this tension. Assamese speakers have become a minority in the state, and twelve out of twenty-three districts have a minority community population of 35 per cent and over.

With these challenges is the stark fact, which we should never ignore, of the unholy nexus between the political life and civil authority of Assam and the insurgents. If we recognize that there are seepages of development funds to the terrorists, we need to ask why those responsible for such rampant abuses are never named and shamed, let alone brought to book. Unless we take a hard look at this accursed nexus which is like a cancer in the whole of the North-East, we shall never be able to come anywhere near to considering the reality or making a proper diagnosis.

The question can arise whether lack of security is an impediment to development in the sense that insecurity can very quickly undermine the positive aspects of development, and years of patient progress can be brought down by violence. On the other hand, development, asset and job creation are antidotes to violence, whereas the absence of development breeds alienation and discord. So which aspect should come first—the fight against terrorism or steps towards economic development? Both aspects are mutually reinforcing and have to be implemented at the same time.

DEVELOPMENT

There is a tendency to assert that the North-East is not 'integrated' with the rest of India because of ethnicity and insurgency, but this is only partly true. Although ULFA, Bodos in the form of the Bodo Security Force (BSF) and other militants have infested the state of Assam for 30 years, this state has a tradition of higher learning, educated and skilled people, including in English, and a very large number of Assamese are working successfully elsewhere in India and abroad.

Assam is a key state in terms of security and development. It abuts the rest of the states of the North-East and has the sole connecting corridor with the rest of India. Of the 39 million people in the North-East, Assam has 68 per cent with the highest density of 340 per sq km. Therefore, unless Assam is developed, the region as a whole will not progress.

The North-East Council was set-up as early as 1971 and has been revamped many times since. Health and education are identified as priorities, along with employment and food security. The public's interest in participating in development is high. But while multiple recommendations are drawn up, minimum identified needs have not been met despite the massive funds poured into the region. There has been great wastage and massive corruption. Effective means to prevent this have not been devised, let alone implemented, and pumping in money leads to distortions in the economy unless there are investments in real assets.

It is important to assess the level of people's participation and delivery of promises. The need to protect the socio-cultural practices of various ethnic groups and to give them an effective say in running their own institutions has often been underlined, but there is a problem of adequate devolution to the minority tribes. Most of the plains of Assam, barring the Bodo area, are covered by the panchayati raj and municipal committees, and in the hill areas there are provisions that give greater powers to local institutions to protect people from land alienation, and they can set-up autonomous councils. But there is still a demand for democratization and transparency because there are legitimate fears of loss of identity, and the demand by various ethnic groups for more autonomy has to be addressed. Various ethnic fractures meanwhile prevent cooperation in anti-militancy, illegal migration, HIV/AIDS and drug trafficking.

So 'Shining India' does not exist in the darkness of Assam's villages and islands, where the only signs of prosperity are owned by political leaders, officials, contractors and those who collaborate with, or practice violence and corruption. To blame terrorism and illegal migration for the breakdown of political authority and responsibility is not the whole picture. Much of the problem is also caused by the abdication of responsibility and the peoples' trust by the decision makers; to use a currently fashionable term, the lack of 'good governance'. Individuals can make a difference, as is shown by the results achieved in a few spheres of development by some dedicated individuals, for example' in the health sector over the past three years. If there were more examples like this, the lack of development in the state would not be any concern.

EXPLOITATION OF ASSETS

Progress of North-East depends on the creation of assets in power, infrastructure and economic opportunities. Over 90 per cent of the natural resources in the North-East like fresh water, forest cover, hydroelectricity, biodiversity and minerals are not exploited. There is practically no private sector involvement. The entrepreneur does not need tax breaks and incentives—what he looks for are raw material sources, the potential market and good logistics. It is almost a cliché to say that the North-East has tremendous potential. If you ask the Confederation of Indian Industry (CII) 'why are you not there?' you will get the answer that it has a regional office at Guwahati. The potential is not taken seriously; it is not seen as real or achievable though the natural and human endowments are such that the state of Assam could be transformed. The shift from agriculture to industry and services is at a snail's pace even compared to the rest of India.

Why not make a start with the redevelopment of waterways? In the nineteenth century the British used the Brahmaputra and Barak rivers and brought us tea, jute and oil. We need to make investments that will transform the rivers into lines of contact and commerce again.

Tourism could change the North-East. The 'Incredible India' campaigns ignore the region, which is itself incredible! The infrastructure for tourism is poor, but infrastructure is equally poor in south-west China, Tibet, Nepal and Bhutan which are all also landlocked. Yet those countries and regions by far surpass the tourist numbers to the North-East, and so does Myanmar. Why have there been no specialized promotions, like adventure tours, tours for descendants of Second World War veterans, wildlife, temples, nostalgia (for tea planters and Baptists) or eco-tourism? Air connectivity to the neighbouring countries is non-existent, and the permit raj of inner line, restricted area, and protected area permits speaks for itself. The paranoia of the union government about the North-East has contributed to the lack of development.

BANGLADESH

One of the greatest setbacks to the development of Assam, and for that matter the whole of the North-East, has been the creation of East Bengal alias East Pakistan, and now the state of Bangladesh, which has been like a dagger or time-bomb in the heart of North-East's progress. There have been resulting problems created like support to insurgencies, impediments to transit trade, smuggling, border issues and illegal migration. These matters would require a seminar in themselves, but it is to be hoped that with a new government in Dhaka, elected by a large majority, and at least in fine words, displaying goodwill towards India, that some of these problems may finally get resolved.

I have been a strong advocate, while bearing in mind that only the union government has authority over foreign policy, of allowing state governments surrounding Bangladesh to play a much stronger role in setting the agenda for relations with that country—whether in respect of common rivers, trade and transit, illegal migration or issues like adverse possessions and enclaves. I understand that there was to be a delegation of one union minister and the chief ministers from the neighbouring states to Dhaka in the months of March-April 2009, but the Bangladesh Rifles mutiny and then Indian election schedule put a stop to that. I would humbly suggest that this is not at all the right approach—there needs to be not a collective mission to Dhaka, but an individual state-by-state one, since they all have distinct issues with Bangladesh, and the Bangladeshi politicians need to be invited also, for example to Guwahati, to be told, and taken to see, at first hand, about the state's concerns.

CALCOM CEMENT : A RAY OF HOPE

Let me end on a very positive note. The per capita national consumption of cement is 130 kg while in the North-East it is only 90 kg. While this reveals the lack of sufficient development in the region, there is some better news. The biggest foreign investment, and in fact the only one, in the whole of the North-East is in a green-field cement plant right here in Assam. The foundation stone ceremony took place on 7 March 2009 and there was one union minister along with the chief minister of Assam and five other ministers of the Assam government in attendance, which shows the importance of this project. The plant will be located in the districts of Nagaon and North Cachar

Hills on a 250 acre plot with an estimated production of 1.9 million tonnes a year. The promoters are the BK Group of Companies, and the total investment is about Rs. 500 crore. The state government is investing in 10 per cent of the equity with Rs. 11 crore, and several private and public sector banks have funded the debt of Rs. 267 crore. For the first time ever in the North-East, private equity has been received from two multilateral funding agencies in Germany and the Netherlands. This involvement will, among other things, ensure that the company will meet all the highest international standards of environment and pollution control. It should therefore become a model for the whole nation. The project will give jobs to 15,000 people. I hope it will be the forerunner of many more projects of similar scope and importance. Then we will see the state being transformed and flourish as never before. We all look forward to that day.

CHAPTER 4

The Contours of Uneven Population Growth in Assam

Jayanta Madhab

INTRODUCTION

The illegal immigration movement in Assam is now thirty years old and still unabated. As a consequence of this movement, the economy of Assam has been badly affected. During this period, the state domestic product increased by about 3 per cent per annum on average while India grew at an average of 6 per cent per annum, thus widening the disparity between Assam and India. In this context it was felt necessary to do a statistical exercise to estimate the post-1971 illegal immigrants and also to analyse the consequences of delayed action. Earlier, a study was done under the auspices of Omeo Kumar Das Institute of Social Change and Development, Guwahati, restricting its analysis up to 1991. This study, however, extends up to 2020 and in two parts. First, it endeavours to estimate the illegal immigrants and secondly, it projects the Hindu and Muslim population of Assam on district basis up to 2020. Limitations of the study are also spelled out.

It has been observed that the state of Assam is experiencing quite an uneven growth of population so far as different religious groups are concerned. The Muslim population in 1971 was 3,592,000 which stood at 8,240,000 in 2001 registering a 129 per cent increase over the above period. On the other hand, Hindu population rose to 17,296,000 in 2001 from 10,604,000 in 1971 showing an increase of 63.09 per cent during the period. The Christian, Sikh and other religious groups together registered a strength of 4,28,000 in 1971 and 1,118,000 in 2001 showing an increase of 161 per cent during the same period. This third group constitutes only 4.28 per cent of the total population of Assam in 2001 as such a percentage increase of population of this group will not affect largely in absolute term, whereas an increment of growth of Muslim population, sharing 30.92 per cent of total population, has a significant bearing in their total population. It is noteworthy that while percentage shares of Hindu population to total population of Assam had gone down to 64.8 per cent in 2001 from 72.51 per cent in 1971, that of Muslim population rose to 30.92 per cent in 2001 from 24.56 per cent in 1971.

Table 4.1 presents the growth rate of population in Assam according to religion since 1971.

The plausible reason of higher population growth of Muslims as compared to that of Hindus is the high birth rate of Muslims in addition to immigration from Bangladesh. It is quite interesting to note that the percentage share of Muslim population to total population is increasing in all states as well as at the national level. What is surprising is that while in some states, viz., Gujarat, Maharashtra, Karnataka, etc., the increase in percentage share of Muslim population is very nominal, in the case of Assam it is too high, registering 7.6 percentage points, increasing the share of Muslim population over the period, 1961 to 2001. Another state showing similar pattern is West Bengal recording 8 percentage points increase share of Muslim population over the same period. The figures in Table 4.2 present the percentage share of

TABLE 4.1: GROWTH RATE OF POPULATION IN ASSAM: BY RELIGION

Year	Hindu (%)	Muslim (%)	Others (%)
1971-91	41.90	77.42	132.42*
1991-2001	14.95	29.31	12.54

Note: * In 1971, growth rate for Christians and others declined due to separation of Meghalaya and Mizoram from Assam. After that normal increment shows high trend.

Source: Population Census, RGI.

Hindu and Muslim population of some major states with sizeable Muslim population for the year 1961 and 2001 as per population census data.

The figures in Table 4.2 present a national phenomenon of decreasing trend of percentage share of Hindu population except for the states of J&K and Gujarat. It is noteworthy that share of Hindu population in Assam has slightly reduced by 1.5 percentage points during 1961 to 2001. In the neighbouring state, West Bengal, the share of Hindu population has gone down by 6.3 percentage points during the same period. The other states have recorded lower reduction in percentage points of Hindu population.

Going through the data on percentage increase of Hindu and Muslim population during 1961 to 2001, Assam recorded the highest (198 per cent) increase of Muslim population among the states having a sizeable Muslim population. The figures in Table 4.3 present the percentage increase of Hindu and Muslim population during 1961-2001.

The statistics in Table 4.3 presented by population census data has generated a sense of curiosity among different circles on the future of Assam. The wild guess may promote fear psychosis among certain section of the population. But no methodical study hitherto has been made to estimate the projected population of Assam across different religions.

On the above issues, there is a need for estimates of projected population of different religious groups in Assam across various districts made on the basis of scientific methodology. To meet this demand, an exercise has been attempted for this purpose.[1]

MIGRANTS AND THEIR OFFSPRINGS DURING 1971-2001

In this section an attempt has been made to present the estimated number of international migrants for the period 1971-2001. The period earlier to 1971 is not taken into account since the cut-off date for identification of illegal migrants is March 1971 as per the Assam Accord. It is well known that the population census definition of 'migration' has undergone changes over time. In

TABLE 4.2: PERCENTAGE SHARE OF HINDU AND MUSLIM POPULATION OF SOME MAJOR STATES OF INDIA: 1961-2001

Year	India	Assam	Jammu & Kashmir (J&K)	Uttar Pradesh (UP)	Bihar	West Bengal (WB)	Gujarat	Maharashtra	Kerala	Karnataka
Hindu										
1961	83.4	66.4	28.5	84.7	84.7	78.8	89.0	82.2	60.8	87.4
2001	80.5	64.9	29.6	80.6	83.2	72.5	89.1	80.4	56.2	83.9
Muslim										
1961	10.7	23.3	68.3	14.6	12.5	17.2	8.5	7.7	17.9	9.9
2001	13.4	30.9	67.0	18.5	16.5	25.2	9.1	10.6	24.7	12.2

Source: Population Census, RGI.

TABLE 4.3: PERCENTAGE INCREASE OF HINDU AND MUSLIM POPULATION BETWEEN 1961-2001

	India	Assam	J&K	UP	Bihar	WB	Gujarat	Maharashtra	Kerala	Karnataka
Hindu	125.8	119.4	196.6	114.6	175.6	111.1	145.9	139.3	173.9	115.3
Muslim	194.3	198.0	179.3	185.0	137.2	189.8	163.2	238.5	159.7	177.6

Source: Population Census, RGI.

1971, census migration data were collected for the first time on the merit of place of last usual residence in addition to the place of birth. In the 1981 census, the coverage of enquiry on migration was further extended by collecting data on reasons for migration from place of last residence. The same exercise was continued in 1991 and 2001 census. The results in tabular forms provide distribution of migrant population by place of last residence, duration of residence and reason for migration. The data on inter-districts, intra-state and inter-state migration as well as immigration from abroad are also available in tabular forms. It is worth mentioning that these estimates were generated on the basis of 10 per cent samples.

Further, the reliability of the census migration data is dependent on the cooperation of the respondent. There is every likelihood that the illegal migrants would not divulge their actual place of birth and last residence. Mr Pakyntein, the Superintendent of Census Operation, Assam (1961) in *Census of India, Assam 1961 Report*, expressed his doubt about the reliability of census migrant data. He stated that 'it appears that the people who mostly concealed their birth place are those coming from East Pakistan. In 1951, people who returned their birth place as Pakistan number 8,31,872 but in 1961, the number of such people is only 7,74,869.' The Assistant Director of Census Operation Assam 1971 also remarked that 'this figure is also not reliable and cannot be used to make any valid estimate of growth of either immigrants themselves or the total population of the State excluding immigration'.

The study carried out by Omeo Kumar Das Institute of Social Change and Development (OKDISCD), Guwahati, under the guidance of Prof Atul Goswami in the publication *Population*

TABLE 4.4: INTER-STATE AND INTERNATIONAL MIGRANTS TO ASSAM

Period	Interstate migrant (A)	Total migrants (B)	International (B – A = C)
1971-91	2,90,625	9,76,969	6,86,344

Source: Anil Sakia (ed.), *Population Growth in Assam 1951-1991*, New Delhi: Akansha Publishing House, 2003.

Growth in Assam 1951-1991 has estimated the international migrants to Assam during 1971-91 as 6,86,344. The estimate has been arrived at by deducting the interstate migrants on the basis of 1991 migration table of population census.

The authors expressed their apprehension that 'the possibility of a section of inter-state migrants first entering other neighbouring states, viz., West Bengal, Bihar, Meghalaya, Tripura, etc., subsequently migrating to Assam and reporting the initial place of entry as the place of birth cannot be ruled out'. In such eventuality the above estimates of international migrants would be underrepresentative.

In spite of the above limitations and knowing that it may be an underestimation, an attempt here has been made to find out the probable number of international migrants and their offspring

TABLE 4.5: DECADAL MIGRATION, BIRTH RATE, DEATH RATE AND NATURAL GROWTH RATE IN ASSAM

Decade	Migrant	Birth rate	Death rate	Natural growth rate
1971-81*	3,43,172	33.05	14.89	18.60
1981-91*	3,43,172	33.15	13.47	19.68
1991-2001	1,30,966	28.89	19.93	18.96

Note: * The estimated number of migrants which was 6,86,344 during 1971-91 has been equally distributed in the period 1971-81 and 1981-91 as there was no census operation in 1981 in Assam.

Source: For birth rate and death rate: Sample Registration System (RGI). (The rates are overall, i.e. irrespective of religion.)

TABLE 4.6: MIGRANTS AND THEIR OFFSPRINGS: BIRTHS, DEATHS AND NUMBER OF OFFSPRINGS OF MIGRANTS IN ASSAM

Decade	Migrant and their offspring	Birth	Death	Offspring of migrants
1971-81	3,43,172	1,13,418	51,098	62,320
1981-91	7,48,664	2,48,182	1,00,845	1,47,337
1991-2001	10,26,967	2,96,691	1,01,978	1,94,713
1971-2001 (Total)	12,21,680	-	-	-

Source: Based on author's estimates.

during 1971-2001 taking into account the international migration during 1971-91 as 6,86,344 as estimated by Prof. Atul Goswami.

Taking 1971 as the cut-off year for estimating the migrants, the above estimates place the figure at 12,21,680 at the beginning of 2001. This figure is arrived at by cumulatively adding migrants, their offsprings and fresh migrants. Thus at the beginning of 1981, migrants and their offsprings numbered 4,05,492; to this figure, 3,43,172 (fresh migrants during 1981-91, Table 4.5) is added and the result is 7,48,664. Same way, migrant's offsprings and fresh migrants in 1991-2001 stands at 10,26,967. And finally, after its offsprings are added, the total number comes to 12,21,680. It needs to be reiterated that this is the minimum figure. In reality, it could be anything above this. As per estimates of Prof. Atul Goswami and others, the migrants with their offsprings stood at 4915058 during the period 1951-91. The census migrant data also reveals that bulk of migrants to Assam is from Bangladesh. Out of the total migrants of 1,30,966 during 1991-2001, 1,14,844 (88.7 per cent) were from Bangladesh and 11,209 (8.6 per cent) from Nepal.

The estimates of migrants and their offsprings presented here are underestimated as the overall natural growth rate, i.e. irrespective of religion is applied for arriving at the estimates. It may be mentioned that birth rate of Muslims is quite high in comparison to persons belonging to other religions, the reasons of which are described in the later part. Therefore it may be assumed that international migrants between 1971 and 2001 would be in excess of 12 lakh.

METHODOLOGY FOR PROJECTION OF POPULATION ACCORDING TO RELIGION UP TO 2020

Three different approaches have been attempted to project the population of Assam according to district and religion as follows:

Method 1: Applying General Fertility Rate (GFR) to state total population of Hindu, Muslim and others as per 2001 census and then moving forward estimates up to 2020 has been worked out. Thereafter, breaking them up as district-wise share of religious groups as per 2001 census.

Method 2: In this method GFR are applied directly to the district-wise population of Hindu, Muslim and others groups as per 2001 census and then moving forward.

Method 3: In this method, decadal variation of different religious groups for each districts as per 2001 population census are used.

Three different sets of estimates are generated through application of three different methods mentioned above. It may be mentioned that separate estimates for religious groups other than Muslim and Hindu would not be made as their population size is too small to arrive at a valid projection. As such they are clubbed as others.

ASSUMPTIONS AND LIMITATIONS

1. The GFR as available for the latest year data of Sample Registration System (SRS) conducted by Registrar General of India is used. It may be noted that SRS estimates provide different GFR for different level of education of women belonging to child bearing age, i.e. 15 to 49 years at state level. The state level GFR of SRS are used for different districts uniformly as GFR at district level is not available. It is observed that GFR is highest for illiterates and decreases with higher level of education of women in the reproductive age group. In the case of Muslims, GFR for the illiterate women as estimated through SRS which, is 135 is considered to be useful for the following reasons:
   - Immigrant Muslims consists of bulk of the Muslim population in Assam. Most of the female of these groups are known to be illiterate.
   - Polygamy is largely prevalent in this section of the population.
   - Practice of family planning among them is negligible.
   - Early marriage and re-marriage is common.

   In the case of Hindu and other groups, GFR for education of middle level is 88.4.

The above assumptions are made as the separate GFR according to religion is not available.

2. The RGI has provided sex-wise population in different age groups at state level. This information is used to estimate the percentage of women in child bearing age. This ratio is taken to be identical for all the religious groups at the state as well as at district level. The ratio is estimated at 24.67. Taking this ratio as constant number of female belonging to reproductive age groups are estimated for state as well as at district level for different religious groups and for different years by forward movement.
3. Estimate has been attempted for erstwhile 23 district of Assam as per 2001 census and estimates as per prevailing new 27 districts of Assam could not be made due to data constraints.

FINDINGS

Through application of methods I, II and III as mentioned earlier, the percentage share of population belonging to Hindu, Muslim and others to the total population of Assam in 2020 will be as follows:

TABLE 4.7: PERCENTAGE SHARE OF HINDU, MUSLIM AND OTHERS TO THE TOTAL POPULATION OF ASSAM

Method	Hindu	Muslim	Others
2020 (estimates)			
Method I	51.40	43.00	5.60
Method II	52.50	43.90	3.60
Method III	52.00	44.30	3.70
2001 census	64.89	30.92	4.19
1991 census	67.13	28.43	4.44

Source: Estimated from 2001 Census Data, Census of India, Assam.

The pattern of percentage share in regard to different religious groups will witness a phenomenal change across districts over the period under study. Table 4.8 depicts the changes in

TABLE 4.8: DISTRICT-WISE PROJECTION OF SHARE OF HINDU, MUSLIM AND OTHERS IN 2020 IN ASSAM (FIGURES IN %)

Districts	Hindu			Muslim			Christian and Others		
	2001	2020	Change %	2001	2020	Change %	2001	2020	Change %
Dhubri	24.74	17.75	-6.99	74.29	81.60	7.31	0.97	0.65	-0.32
Kokrajhar	65.60	65.89	0.29	20.36	24.00	3.64	14.04	10.11	-3.93
Bongaigaon	59.18	48.04	-11.14	38.52	50.10	11.58	2.30	1.86	-0.44
Goalpara	38.22	29.04	-9.18	53.71	65.02	11.31	8.07	5.94	-2.13
Barpeta	40.19	28.66	-11.53	59.37	71.00	11.63	0.44	0.34	-0.10
Nalbari	76.05	64.92	-11.13	22.10	33.39	11.29	1.85	1.69	-0.16
Kamrup	72.80	60.16	-12.64	24.78	37.61	12.83	2.42	2.23	-0.19
Darrang	57.74	45.15	-12.59	35.54	49.21	13.67	6.72	5.64	-1.08
Sonitpur	76.00	63.24	-12.76	14.89	28.96	14.07	9.11	7.80	-1.31
Lakhimpur	79.06	70.38	-8.68	16.15	25.11	8.96	4.79	4.51	-0.28
Dhemaji	95.95	94.62	-1.33	1.84	3.13	1.29	2.21	2.25	0.04
Morigaon	52.21	39.88	-12.33	47.59	59.97	12.38	0.20	0.15	-0.05
Nagaon	47.80	33.94	-13.86	50.99	65.13	14.14	1.21	0.93	-0.28
Golaghat	85.94	80.74	-5.20	7.91	13.09	5.18	6.15	6.17	0.02
Jorhat	92.86	89.38	-3.48	4.77	8.16	3.39	2.37	2.46	0.09
Sibsagar	88.21	82.73	-5.48	8.17	13.61	5.44	3.62	3.66	0.04
Dibrugarh	90.79	87.36	-3.43	4.49	7.71	3.22	4.72	4.93	0.21

Tinsukia	89.48	86.59	-2.89	3.48	6.03	2.55	7.04	7.38	0.34
Karbi Anglong	82.40	80.35	-2.05	2.20	3.85	1.65	15.40	15.80	0.40
N.C. Hills	69.91	73.58	3.67	2.49	3.42	0.93	27.60	23.00	-4.60
Karimganj	46.70	34.45	-12.25	52.30	64.80	12.50	1.00	0.75	-0.25
Hailakandi	41.11	32.03	-9.08	57.63	67.09	9.46	1.26	0.88	-0.38
Cachar	61.37	48.78	-12.59	36.13	49.10	12.97	2.50	2.12	-0.38
Assam	64.89	52.50	-12.39	30.92	43.90	12.98	4.20	3.61	-0.59

percentage shares as per estimates arrived at by following method II.

To summarize the Table 4.8, Table 4.9 depicts the projected changes between 2001 and 2020. It shows clearly that in 2001, 17 districts had a majority Hindu population, while in 2020 only 13 districts will still remain Hindu majority districts.

Similarly, Table 4.10 reveals the position of different districts as per their share of Muslim population. It is interesting to note that while in 2001, 6 districts had a Muslim majority, by 2020, 8 districts would have Muslim majority population. Most of the Muslim majority districts are curiously neighbouring Bangladesh.

Table 4.10 indicates that by 2020 some additional Hindu majority districts will be converted to Muslim majority districts.

So far as Christian and other religious groups are concerned these groups as a whole have a comparatively nominal share of total population of the state. The share of this group to total population of Assam was 4.20 per cent in 2001 and will register

TABLE 4.9: CHANGES OF SHARE OF HINDU POPULATION IN 2020 BY DISTRICTS

% share of Hindu population	As per 2001 census	As per 2020 estimates
Less than 30	Dhubri	Dhubri, Goalpara, Barpeta
30-40	Goalpara, Barpeta	Morigaon, Nagaon, Karimganj, Hailakandi
40-50	Nagaon, Karimganj, Hailakandi	Bongaigaon, Darrang, Cachar
50-60	Bongaigaon, Darang Morigaon	Kamrup
More than 60	Kokrajhar, Nalbari, Kamrup, Sonitpur, Lakhimpur, Dhemaji, Golaghat, Jorhat, Sibsagar, Dibrugarh, Tinsukia, Karbi-Anglong, N.C. Hills, Cachar	Kokrajhar, Sonitpur, Lakhimpur, Dhemaji, Golaghat, Jorhat, Sibsagar, Dibrugarh, Tinsukia, Karbi-Anglong, N.C. Hills, Nalbari

TABLE 4.10: CHANGES OF SHARE OF MUSLIM POPULATION IN 2020 BY DISTRICTS IN ASSAM

% share of Muslim population to total population	As per 2001 census	As per 2020 estimates
Less than 30	Kokrajhar, Nalbari, Kamrup, Sonitpur, Lakhimpur, Dhemaji, Golaghat, Jorhat, Sibsagar, Dibrugarh, Tinsukia, Karbi-Anglong, N.C. Hills (13 districts)	Kokrajhar, Lakhimpur, Dhemaji, Golaghat, Jorhat, Sibsagar, Dibrugarh, Tinsukia, Karbi-Anglong, N.C. Hills (10 districts)
30-40	Bongaigaon, Darrang, Cachar (3 districts)	Nalbari, Kamrup, Sonitpur (3 districts)
40-50	Morigaon (1 district)	Darrang, Cachar (2 districts)
50-60	Goalpara, Barpeta, Nagaon, Karimganj, Hailakandi (5 districts)	Bongaigaon, Morigaon (2 districts)
More than 60	Dhubri (1 district)	Dhubri, Goalpara, Barpeta, Nagaon, Hailakandi, Karimganj (6 districts)

3.61 per cent in 2020. In N.C. Hills district the percentage share of Christian and other minor religious groups together is the highest among the districts being 27.60 per cent and the 2020 estimates indicates that it will slide down to 23 per cent. The district with relatively higher share of population of this groups are Karbi-Anglong (15.40 per cent), Kokrajhar (14.04 per cent), Sonitpur (7.48 per cent), Goalpara (8.07 per cent), Tinsukia (7.04 per cent) and Golaghat (6.15 per cent). The 2020 estimates suggest very nominal change in percentage share of the group in all districts.

CONCLUSION

The closeness of the three sets of estimates arrived at through three different approaches suggests that the methodology adopted is in order. However, under representation of the estimates could not be ruled out as the estimates are based basically on census population figures which are usually widely criticized as under reporting. Moreover, some experts on this subject express their apprehension regarding presentation of ground realities through the SRS data.

The distribution of projected population according to religion is as per erstwhile 23 districts of Assam as on 2001. If the Bodoland Territorial Area Districts (BTAD) are taken into account, the percentage share of Muslim population will further increase in the following districts—Dhubri, Bongaigaon, Barpeta, Darrang, and Nalbari because of carving out of areas with less Muslim population to form the BTAD districts.

As the Total Fertility Rate among immigrant Muslim is too high as compared to other religious groups, the Muslim dominated districts will witness further increase in population. The situation will be aggravated further if illegal migration from Bangladesh continues. This phenomenon will be responsible for higher population density as well as reducing land-man ratio (effective land) in particular districts. The reduction in land-man ratio will have an adverse effect on the economy of the rural people, particularly the immigrant Muslim, majority of whom depend on an agribased livelihood. The situation will compel them to move to other districts in search of land and livelihood. Free movement of population irrespective of religion across districts will lead to movement of Muslim population from Muslim concentrated districts like Dhubri, Goalpara, Barpeta, Nagaon, Hailakandi, Karimganj, etc., to other districts and will thereby change the demographic pattern of all the districts. In such an eventuality fear psychosis will develop in the minds of the erstwhile residents of the districts thinking that they will be deprived of economic opportunity and the outsiders will grab the land and other assets they are presently enjoying. It will create social conflicts as has recently been witnessed in the districts of Tinsukia, Dibrugarh, Jorhat, Lakhimpur, etc. It needs no emphasis to explain that the constant social conflict looming large will be a major future deterrent of growth and development of the state.

The estimates of Hindu population cover Hindu migrants from Bangladesh. It may be observed that after 1971, the migration of Hindu population from Bangladesh to Assam is decreasing and is now negligible. As per 2001 census, the bulk of the migrants were from Bangladesh (88.7 per cent) and migrants from Nepal to Assam constituted only 8.6 per cent . As a result of this, Hindu population growth rate as well as their percentage share to total population are bound to decline further in future. The study clearly suggests that by 2020 the ethnic composition of the population of Assam will undergo rapid change where the difference of share of population between Hindu and Muslim will be very thin.

REFLECTIONS ON THE ISSUE

Large-scale immigration from Bangladesh started from the third decade of the last century, and continued unabated leading an anti-illegal immigration movement in the late 1970s and early 1980s, culminating into an agreement between the Government of India and the All Assam Students Union (AASU) and the Assam Gana Sangram Parishad (AGSP) in 1985. As a result, the people of Assam elected the movement leaders to form government twice in the 1980s and 1990s. Despite this, the immigration problem remains a major issue, which is yet to be solved. This resulted in instability which in turn manifested in low economic growth from 1970s to 1990s. Assam, which was at the time of Independence, one of the high per capita income states now can be counted only from the bottom.

The Assam Accord (1985) between the Government of India and AASU and AGSP stated quite clearly that (1) foreigners who came to Assam on or after 25 March 1971 shall continue to be detected, deleted from electoral rolls and expelled in accordance with the law; (2) the international border will be made secure against future infiltration by erection of barriers like walls, barbed wire fencing and other obstacles at appropriate places. These are two vital agreements to identify, deport and check further illegal infiltration. But, even after 24 years of the conclusion of the agreement, the Government of India has yet to honour the commitments.

The density of population in Bangladesh has always been high and is now a little over 1,100 per sq km, which is more than three times that of Assam. Rural poverty and earlier exploitation due to the zamindari system in Bangladesh compelled them to migrate to Assam. The Muslim League Ministry in Assam in the early 1940s provided incentives to come to Assam for the Grow More Food campaign. Economically, Bangladesh has done well in recent years. Its economic growth rate recorded a 5-6 per cent per year and the population growth rate has come down to 1.7 per cent which is lower than India's 2.3 per cent. Bangladesh needs to be congratulated for the success on these two fronts. As regards the population growth, however, it seems strange that the same stock of population in Assam has a growth rate double that of Bangladesh (3.2 per cent). One explanation could be a lot of people may have migrated from Bangladesh to various parts of the world including Assam and elsewhere in India. Another concern is that some environmentalists predicted that because of global warming, half of Bangladesh would be under water in about fifty years. Obviously this will have further implications for Assam. India, Bangladesh and other developed countries need to work on this issue.

The Bangladesh government now headed by Sheikh Hasina needs to be cultivated to appreciate the problems of Assam. Indeed, India should provide aid to Bangladesh to develop the border districts of Bangladesh so that some of the immigrants may find it worthwhile to go back to their country of origin. A prosperous Bangladesh is an asset for Assam. It can also solve Assam's problems to a certain extent.

Internally, the Government of India must in all earnestness detect the post-1971 immigrants, delete their names from the electoral rolls and try to deport them in a time-bound manner. However, the Government of India's record earlier in deporting illegal immigrants is hardly worth mentioning. It is easier to provide these illegal immigrants with one-year work permit to be renewed after a gap of six months on the basis of good conduct and without voting rights. They must be barred from buying and occupying land. No land can be transferred in their name. They may also be encouraged to settle down in other states of India.

A number of suggestions have been put forward in various forums to control the high rate of population growth irrespective of religion. Some of these are:

- To see that every child gets a minimum education up to high school, irrespective of sex and religion. This is because an educated person has better knowledge about health, hygiene and family planning besides some job skills.
- Family planning needs to be encouraged vigorously. The government should consider disincentives for having more than three children.
- Registration of marriage should be made compulsory and marriage below the age of 18 should be made illegal. More than one spouse at a time should be discouraged through education and incentives and disincentives. In fact, a unified civil code will be preferable.
- Strong action should be taken against those who occupy the government land.

These suggestions have been aired and discussed in various forums but without any result. The problem is that the main political party in Assam depends on these vote banks, and the opposition party, which was established to find a solution to this problem, now thrives on this issue. In the meantime, Assam suffers.

In addition, Assam's immigration issue is not well understood by the rest of India. After all immigration is a universal phenomenon; we all are immigrants at one point of time. Hardly any country is immune to it. There was Muslim migration to Assam for many centuries. Assimilation was not a problem. Then why is this movement? Amongst the various reasons one could cite the following: First, it may be remembered that there was an anti-Bengali movement when the erstwhile British rulers changed the official language from Assamese to Bengali for some time. Second, Jinnah demanded Assam as part of Pakistan but had to settle for a part of it. Third, when Bangladesh was formed, it was originally conceived as a secular state, but later on declared as an Islamic Republic. The Hindus at the time of Partition formed 22 per cent of the population in East Bengal, now it is less than 9 per cent. Fourth, many Bangladeshi political writers including top leaders have argued for inclusion of a part of Assam into Bangladesh. Further, Bangladesh has given shelter to about 10 radical Islamist organizations over and above Assam's and North-East's revolutionary organizations like ULFA, etc. These are old stories, but the apprehensions of the people of Assam remain with the continued illegal immigration from that country. On top of it, the sincerity of the Government of India in solving this vexed problem is being questioned. People often wonder that if the much longer border in the Punjab and Jammu & Kashmir could be sealed within a couple of years' time, why does it take a quarter of a century to complete the border fencing in Assam, Meghalaya and Tripura.

Time passes, the movement goes on. The communal harmony, of which Assam was proud of, suffers, and the economy of Assam moves at snail's pace, creating further problems for the communities there and the government.

NOTE

1. B.N. Das who retired as Joint Director of Economic and Statistics of Assam has provided statistical assistance for the study.

CHAPTER 5

Security and Development in Counter-Terrorism and Counter-Insurgency Strategies

B. Raman

India faces three kinds of terrorism—the indigenous one by some sections of our own people, the foreign sponsored and the foreign-aided. Indigenous terrorism itself has different motives—political and religious, as in the case of the terrorist groups in Jammu & Kashmir (J&K); purely religious as in the case of the jihadi terrorist groups operating outside J&K; ethnic as in the case of Assam; and ideological and economic as in the case of the Maoist or Naxalite groups operating in the tribal belt of central India.

Foreign-sponsored terrorism is mainly due to jihadi organizations such as the Lashkar-e-Toiba (LET), Harkat-ul-Mujahideen (HUM), Harkat-ul-Jihad-al-Islami (HuJI) and Jaish-e-Mohammad (JEM) operating from Pakistani territory and HUJI operating from Bangladesh. Their members are Pakistani or Bangladeshi nationals or other foreign Muslims and their activities in the Indian territory are sponsored by the intelligence agencies of these countries in order to serve their own purpose. The intelligence agencies of Pakistan and Bangladesh have a common purpose of creating a polarization between the Muslim and Hindu communities in India. Pakistan's Inter-Services Intelligence (ISI) has the additional purpose of forcing a change in the *status quo* in J&K through terrorism.

Foreign-aided terrorism refers to indigenous terrorist groups receiving assistance in the form of training, financial assistance and arms and ammunition from the terrorist organizations and the intelligence services of Pakistan and Bangladesh. Examples would be the Khalistani terrorists who used to be active in Punjab and Delhi till 1995, the Kashmiri terrorist groups, the Students' Islamic Movement of India (SIMI), and the so-called Indian Mujahideen (IM) and the United Liberation Front of Assam (ULFA). Assisting them helps the purpose of creating instability in India and keeping the Indian security forces preoccupied with internal security problems.

There are two approaches dealing with terrorism—the counter-terrorist and counter-terrorism. The counter-terrorist approach deals with terrorism as a threat to national security and seeks to put out of action the terrorists, their leaders and organizations through the use of the security forces. While incorporating the security dimension, the counter-terrorism approach treats terrorism as a phenomenon with many aspects such as political, economic, social, religious, etc. The counter-terrorism approach underlines that counter-terrorist methods will not be sufficient to deal with the threat effectively. In addition, the political, economic, social and other aspects have to be addressed simultaneously by the political leadership.

There is only one way of dealing with foreign-sponsored terrorist groups—through counter-terrorist methods. Foreign nationals indulging in acts of terrorism in our territory have to be neutralized by the security forces without any mercy. The use of such terrorists by Pakistan and Bangladesh amounts to indirect aggression in our territory. There are two methods of dealing with foreign-sponsored terrorists—passive defence and active defence. Passive defence refers to strengthening the internal security measures in our own territory in order to make it almost impossible for Pakistani and Bangladeshi terrorists to operate here. Active defence refers to our right to take our counter-terrorism operations to the territories of Pakistan and Bangladesh in order to pre-empt their plans for a terrorist strike in our territory.

Countries facing the menace of foreign-sponsored terrorism adopt a mix of passive defence and active defence methods. India follows a policy of only passive defence. The Indian political leadership is not prepared to consider active defence. Passive defence, however, requires effective preventive capability. Active defence requires an effective and deniable retaliatory capability. We have not built for ourselves such a retaliatory capability. After the Mumbai terrorist strike of 26-9 November 2008, many foreign terrorism experts have assessed that India may continue to face such strikes because it does not have either an effective preventive or retaliatory capability. This assessment needs to be taken seriously by our political leadership and policy makers and appropriate correctives in our strategy introduced.

In the case of purely indigenous terrorism, effective physical security alone will not produce enduring results unless accompanied by appropriate political action to address the anger and grievances of the community from which the terrorists have arisen. Unaddressed anger is a common root cause of all types of terrorism—whether ethnic, separatist, religious, jihadi or ideological. Even in the case of the indigenous terrorists, those who take to terrorism have to face the consequences of their action. At the same time, it is important to prevent the flow of new recruits to the terrorist organizations. This can be done only by identifying the causes of anger in the community and addressing them.

For many years, there has been an endless debate in the community of security analysts about the linkage between security and development in any counter-terrorism or counter-insurgency strategy. Without effective security, there cannot be satisfactory development. Without satisfactory development, there cannot be effective security. Hardline security analysts—who believe in the security first approach—even argue that if substantial funds are sanctioned for development in the terrorism or insurgency affected areas, much of that money might leak into the coffers of the terrorists or insurgents. This is an unwise approach, which would be counter-productive. Fortunately, our political leaders have rejected the arguments of such hardline security experts. They have been trying to give simultaneous attention to requirements of security and development even at the risk of some of the funds allotted for development leaking to the terrorists or insurgents.

At the same time, the priorities tend to be misplaced. For example, in the Naxalism affected areas we tend to focus more on development packages for the affected areas. It is important to pay equal, if not more, attention, to the development of the tribal areas not affected by Naxalism in order to demonstrate to people the dividends of observing law and order and keeping away from terrorists and insurgents.

In the North-East, there has been peace in Nagaland and Mizoram. Arunachal Pradesh has remained unaffected by insurgency. In Tripura, there has been a decrease in insurgency. We should have undertaken a crash programme for the economic development of these areas to provide a demonstration of peace dividend for areas which have given up insurgency or for areas which have remained away from insurgency. But the importance of this has not been realized by our policy makers so far.

The third type of terrorism in which Pakistani and Bangladeshi terrorist organizations and intelligence services use our nationals for acts of terrorism calls for a nuanced approach. Just because some of our nationals are acting at the behest of Pakistanis and Bangladeshis, we should not look upon the entire community with suspicion. Our aim should be to identify grievances—legitimate or otherwise, in the community, which are exploited by the Pakistanis and Bangladeshis and try to address them.

There is no copybook on counter-terrorism, which can apply to all situations and to all kinds of terrorism. Our strategies should be tailor-made to suit different situations and to deal with different kinds of terrorism. There should be a fair balance between the requirements of security and development in strategies dealing with indigenous terrorism.

CHAPTER 6

Security and Development: Exploring Interface between Inequality, Natural Resources, Co-Ethnics and Conflict

Sanjay Pulipaka

In the recent past, scholars and practitioners working in the realm of conflict resolution have been stressing on the need to understand and act on the inter-linkages between development and conflict. Quite often, many policy prescriptions state that conflicts cannot be resolved as long as underlying economic grievances remain unaddressed. However such statements are vague, as they do not highlight the exact interrelationship between various economic grievances and conflict. While it is indeed necessary to focus on development and conflict inter-linkages, there is also a need to disaggregate the concepts of development and conflict, and focus on the inter-linkages between the disaggregated units. This paper seeks to explore the role of economic factors that are responsible for the initiation of a conflict. In the process, the role of economic grievances, more specifically economic inequality and the role of natural resources in the initiation of a conflict and its duration are explored. While the resource dependence theories of conflict focus on the economic determinants, it must also be remembered that conflicts tend to get initiated in multi-ethnic states in a geo-political context. Hence, the political factors determining the duration of conflicts should also be examined.

INTRODUCTION

Conflicts are complex, multi-dimensional and often more than one cause propels a country to witness a civil strife or an insurgency. Significantly, since the Second World War, more than inter-state conflicts, intra-state conflict has been the most common form of conflict.[1] This trend picked up momentum after the end of the Cold War. As one can see in Fig. 6.1, while the number of civil wars has been increasing since the Second World War, the number of civil wars in 1990s registered a dramatic increase. Many countries that experienced political and economic transition in the post-Cold War era, were plunged into large-scale violence along ethnic lines. The collapse of the ideological conflict gave space for the explosion of ethno-political conflicts. These ethno-political conflicts went against the popular beliefs that greater economic integration and interactions will overtime erase primordial identities. However, the experience of the post-Cold War world has been to the contrary.

Intra-state conflict can be defined as contest between organized parties over government, territory and/or resources. One of the parties may or may not include government.[2] Intra-state

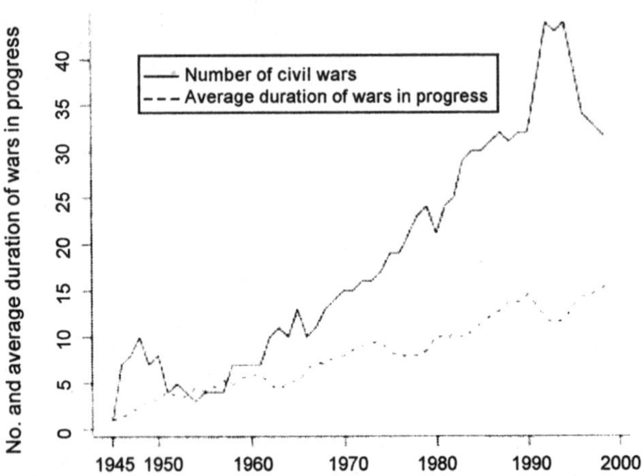

Source: James D. Fearon, 'Why Do Some Civil Wars Last so Much Longer than Others?', *Journal of Peace Research*, vol. 41, no. 3 (May, 2004), p. 276.

FIG. 6.1: NUMBER OF CIVIL WARS

conflicts may emerge due to prevalence of grievances among various groups of people that their legitimate interests are being undermined by existing political and economic order. Such grievances are not static as they keep changing over time depending on the evolving political dynamics. Perception among certain ethnic and religious groups that they are being denied their legitimate share of political power may fuel an inter-state conflict. Ethnic and religious groups may also demand separate political entities if they perceive that their identity is under threat. Intense competition among the elite and inability of state institutions to modulate such competition often results in failed states and civil war, which tend to continue for extended periods of time. External actors instigate and interfere in the affairs of others resulting in the emergence of civil war. However, for the emergence and sustenance of civil conflict, it needs to be legitimized by real or imaginary grievance(s). Often economic exploitation, economic neglect by existing authorities and prevalence of economic inequality are cited as supplemental or core causes for the emergence of an intra-state conflict.

POVERTY, ECONOMIC GROWTH AND CONFLICT

There seems to be a positive correlation between poverty and emergence of violent conflict. For instance, World Development Report 2003, points out that lower incomes and poor growth, largely explains high incidence of conflict in Africa.[3] High levels of poverty make recruitment of cadre by various violent groups easier, as the costs of participation in violent movements, in terms of loss of income and livelihoods, are very low for the recruits. Prevalence of extreme poverty also reduces capacity of the state to redistribute wealth between various ethnic groups. This incapacity of the state to redistribute resources exacerbates the ethnic cleavages in a society. As a consequence, severe poverty provides necessary conditions for the emergence and sustenance of civil conflicts. Further, Juha Auvinen and Wayne Nafziger based on econometric analysis of 124 developing countries, state that man-made Complex Humanitarian Emergencies (CHE) are a consequence of various economic factors such as high levels of inequality, higher share of military expenditure in GNP, stagnation and decline of income, along with other factors such as a tradition of violent conflict.[4] However, according to SIPRI, man-made CHEs tend to occur more in low and middle income countries, than in higher income countries.[5] A stagnant economy or negative growth, in low and middle income countries, reduces the capacity of the state to redistribute wealth among various groups, which tends to generate civil conflict. In non-democratic countries, a contracting or decelerating economy pushes elites to adopt more repressive measures to continue their rent-seeking exercises, which creates necessary conditions for the emergence of conflicts or complex humanitarian emergencies. The above evidence prompts us to believe that faster economic growth will help in mitigating the conditions that fuel conflict. However, the relationship between economic growth and conflict is non-linear.

'Economic growth' in itself is neither benign nor malignant. The social and political system in which the economic growth takes place determines the long-term consequences of economic growth. Faster economic growth may reduce the possibility of intra-state conflict and give opportunities to individuals to have a better lifestyle, and propel people to move away from conflict-generating ideas. Faster economic growth will also provide government with greater financial resources, which can be used for redistributive effect. However, Simon Kuznets argued that an increase in per capita income is accompanied by an increase in inequality and over time the inequality tends to subside.[6] This implies that economic growth in the short-term has a tendency to generate inequality. In this context, we must remember that economic inequality has both quantitative and qualitative dimensions. Per capita incomes, family incomes, Gross Domestic Product (GDP), literacy levels can be easily compared across time and space. Such comparisons help us determine the levels of inequality among different regions of a country or among different segments of a population. However, inequality can also manifest in terms of differences such as quality of school education and health care services. However, such qualitative differences are difficult to measure. Given this challenge, most of the studies on inequality tend to focus on the quantitative dimension of inequality rather than on the qualitative dimension of it.

While economic growth has many positive spin-offs, it may also generate 'overall inequality'. Overall inequity is defined as income inequality between individuals irrespective of ethnic, linguistic and religious grouping that they might belong. However, individual deprivation alone does not lead to large-scale socio-political conflict, as large-scale socio-political conflict requires perceptions of group deprivation. Notions of individual deprivation tend to have lower potential of propelling mobilization of people in large numbers and creation of organizational frameworks, which are prerequisites for large-scale socio-political conflict. However, it is distinctly possible that while a country as a whole is registering decent economic growth, some regions or provinces may not be registering similar levels of growth, resulting in 'horizontal inequity'. If different ethnic groups populate different parts of a country and one part of a country registers faster economic growth, then such horizontal inequality has greater potential to generate conflict. Ted Robert Gurr by studying 233 communal groups found that systematic discriminatory treatment of a group *vis-à-vis* other groups in a country prompted the discriminated group to act in defense or promotion of the group's self-defined interests.[7] Ted Gurr points out that the strategies of action, protest or rebellion, by the discriminated group will be contingent on complex interplay of group status and political context.[8] Horizontal inequity in the context of multi-ethnic, multi-lingual, multi-religious society tends to fuel demands for economic equality in the garb of identity politics, demands for autonomy and independence. Horizontal inequity makes it easy to indulge in antagonistic political communication against certain ethnic groups. The feelings of 'Us *versus* Them' can be easily generated in the context of horizontal inequity. All this creates sufficient conditions for the emergence of violent conflict in polities characterized by horizontal economic inequality. For instance, pointing out that horizontal inequalities have many dimensions such as economic, political and social, Frances Stewart states that overlap of geographic inequities and cultural differences prompt demands for independence or autonomy.[9] It should be noted that even the privileged adopt multiple strategies (such as contesting or co-opting) to protect their status. Privileged groups might avert a conflict by showing magnanimity towards the underprivileged if it enjoys very high status.[10] On the other hand, the privileged might also fight to protect their resources from being encroached on.[11] The possibility of conflict between the privileged and underprivileged tends to be higher in case of slight disparity as the chances of wining tend to be high.[12]

Does horizontal inequity automatically result in conflict? What is the role of regime types and electoral systems in modulating the discontent that emanates from economic deprivation? We might be tempted to argue that democracies tend to respond better to the needs of the people. Hence, democracies also respond better to the demands for equal distribution of wealth and therefore, are more adept at resolving conflicts that emanate due to horizontal inequalities. On the contrary, Gudrun Østby argues that being more responsive than autocracies, does not guarantee that democracies are better at avoiding/ preventing conflicts due to horizontal inequity.[13] Gudrun Østby, using demographic and health surveys from 55 developing countries during 1986-2003 argues that more than autocracies, semi-democracies and democracies with regional horizontal inequity have greater potential for civil conflict.[14] This may be because, in democratic countries, given the competitive nature of polity, politicians tend to play one ethnic group against the other for political gains often leading to violent outcomes. On the other hand, severe repressive measures in an authoritarian regime curtail free flow of information, airing of opinions and free interactions of people and groups. All this ensures that 'grievance sharing processes' and open expression of grievance are effectively curtailed.

Economies transiting from state-based economy to a more free market economy also generate horizontal inequities. Mismanaged transition from state-based economy to more free market economy tends to generate severe stress in the political system. Significant problems that transitioning economies face are the problems associated with raising expectations and anxieties. Transitioning economy generates anxiety as the certainties of the old order are increasingly questioned. On the other hand, faster economic growth in a transitioning economy induces rise in expectations. Often there tends to be a mismatch between rise in expectations and the capacity of a growing economy to meet those expectations. This mismatch or a gap between expectations and achievements fuels discontent among large masses of people. Further, economic transition tends to alter existing relationships between various groups in a society. Some segments of society, due to various historical reasons, tend to be better equipped to reap the benefits of an opening economy. As investors prefer to build on the existing infrastructure, opening up of the economy tends to benefit the regions that are already endowed with substantial infrastructure facilities, fuelling regional disparities. Such skewed economic transition may exacerbate the already existing religious and ethnic fault lines. For instance, Susan Woodward argues that structural adjustment programme in Yugoslavia resulted in 'socially polarizing and politically disintegrating consequences'.[15] According to Susan Woodward, austerity measures and economic measures aimed at Westernization to reduce tariffs resulted in severe hardships for be common people prompting them to court assertive nationalist ideologies and resulting in the break up of Yugoslavia.[16] Similarly, a few international organizations in 1991 reportedly advised the government in Sierra Leone to privatize state-run enterprises.[17] These privatization processes of state-run enterprises provide an opportunity for the rulers to 'cleanse them of politically threatening patrimonial hangers' and provided the ruling elite an opportunity to take control of the precious resources.[18] This is not to say that all transitions from state-based economy to a more free market economy tend to result in violent conflict or civil war. A mismanaged economic transition exacerbates the inequities between various groups of people, which provides for fertile conditions in which a large-scale violence or civil war may emerge.

NATURAL RESOURCES AND CONFLICT

It is evident from the above discussion that economic factors such as inequality, more specifically horizontal inequality, tend to fuel conflict. However, not every instance of horizontal inequity results in conflict. The grievance of inequality is present in many countries and yet not all of them experience civil conflict. This means that operation of various constraints ensures that prevalence of widespread inequality does not automatically push people to take up violent actions. Lichbach using the game theory demonstrated that rational actors, even in the face of domination and exploitation, will not rebel due to collective action problem.[19] However, this collective action problem can be circumvented if violent conflict provides incentives such as confiscation of resources belonging to richer sections of population.[20] Therefore, inequality may provide the necessary conditions but not sufficient conditions for the emergence of a conflict. Taking this argument forward, Collier and Hoeflller argue that more than 'grievance' it is 'greed' that plays an important role in conflict and point out that financial and military viability are important determinants for the emergence of civil conflict.[21] Using data from 78 large civil conflicts (1960-99), Collier and Hoeflller observe that countries with abundant natural resources and a large diaspora tend to have higher risk of conflicts.[22] Noting that predatory behaviour may not be the main objective of rebel organizations, Paul Collier in his recent work observes that the feasibility of predation—use of force to extort goods or money—to finance conflict determines the risk of conflict.[23]

It should be noted that the presence of natural resources in abundance does not always result in negative consequences. Natural resources can make significant contribution to the economic development of a country. Abundance of natural resources opens up substantial sources of revenue for the government and makes a country self-reliant. Easy availability of natural resources also ensures that production costs of various industrial products are reduced substantially thereby making them internationally competitive. All this will ensure that a country will have necessary resources at its disposal to manage numerous demands emanating from various ethnic groups. However, a country may also suffer from resources-curse. A country with abundant natural resources, such as oil, shows greater propensity to become undemocratic.[24] Further, a country with prevalence of abundant natural resources is prone to witness conflicts within.

Mining and trading of diamonds is often cited as a glaring example of natural resources fuelling conflict. Diamonds which are used for funding rebellions are often termed as 'conflict diamonds'. According to United Nations, 'conflict diamonds are diamonds that originate from areas controlled by forces or factions opposed to legitimate and internationally recognized governments, and are used to fund military action in opposition to those governments, or in contravention of the decisions of the Security Council'.[25] In countries such as Angola, Ivory Coast, Sierra Leone, Democratic Republic of Congo, and Liberia, conflict diamonds played a significant role in sustaining various kinds of conflicts. Since these diamonds ensure substantial financial resources, the armed groups were able to maintain fairly large number of personnel and equipment with lot of firepower over extended periods of time. For instance, Angola witnessed several civil wars between 1975 and 2002 resulting in the loss of 1.5 million lives and during these civil wars, the rebel groups financed their operations by trading diamonds.[26] Similarly, it is quite well known that in Sierra Leone the civil war got exacerbated due to the easy availability of diamonds. The civil war resulted in the death of thousands of people and many became amputees. In Sierra Leone alluvial diamond mining contributes half of the country's exports and for ten years (1991-2002), the Revolutionary United Front in Sierra Leone financed its rebellion by smuggling diamonds.[27]

In countries such as Myanmar, mining and trading of precious stones, such as jade, are enabling various ethnic groups to maintain armed/military forces and to prolong their struggle with the government there. Similarly, in Afghanistan cultivation of opium is fuelling the conflict in a big way. Afghanistan accounts for almost 90 per cent of the world's opium production and most of this opium (about 98 per cent) comes from seven provinces in the south-west Afghanistan, which are strongholds of the Taliban.[28] This clearly indicates a nexus between opium production and the intensity of conflict. The resurgence of the Taliban can also be attributed to their capacity to finance their activities from the drug money.

The role of oil in sustaining many non-democratic regimes has been documented well.[29] The conflict propensity of the societies that have oil abundance is now well known. It is indeed tragic that in spite of the presence of large amounts of oil, large segments of the Nigerian population continue to live in the midst of poverty. Further, the Nigerian delta region has been a focus of persistent political instability due to proliferation of armed groups belonging to local ethnic people, which survive on finances generated from stolen oil from pipelines and ransom collected from kidnapping of oil workers.[30] The Nigerian experience is not unique as many oil-producing countries have gone through similar experiences. Pointing out that oil-rich countries are twice as likely to experience civil war as a non-oil-producing one, Michael L. Ross observes that this is so because oil wealth makes it easier for rebels to propagate their grievances and finance their rebellions.[31]

The above examples give a general picture about the inter-relationship between the easy availability of natural resources and conflict. The exact role of natural resources in initiation of conflict and duration of conflict needs to be understood in greater detail. Drawing on the cross-national econometric studies, Michael L. Ross, identifies the following regularities pertaining to natural resources and conflict: First, the presence of abundant oil resources and increased dependence on these resources has a greater propensity for the initiation of the conflict; second, unlike oil resources, the presence of precious stones, opium and illicit drugs are not strongly related with initiation of conflict. Rather, they are strongly related in prolonging the duration of conflict once the conflict gets initiated.[32] In a similar study, Regan and Norton using data from Minority at Risk (MAR) project spanning years 1976-97, argue that the presence of natural resources such as diamond does not bear much relationship with the onset of civil conflict.[33] However, once anti-state violence or civil conflict begins, exploitable natural resources—localized, valuable, and easily recoverable—play a significant role in sustaining these conflicts.[34] The duration of a conflict is also contingent on the location and nature of conflict. Based on the analysis of 128 cases of civil war, James D. Fearon, observes that duration of civil wars in the peripheral regions of a state based on the 'sons of the soil' ideology, focusing on 'exploitation of fuel and mineral resources in their traditional areas', tend to last longer than the rest of civil wars.[35]

CENTRALITY OF 'PERIPHERAL' CONFLICTS

Peripheral regions of a state are logistically conducive for long-lasting civil wars. Peripheral regions with disenchanted and dispersed ethnic groups spilling into neighbouring countries also provide necessary conditions for the emergence of long-lasting civil wars. More specifically, concentrated ethnic groups spilling over national boundaries tend to fuel conflicts in the form of either irredentism or secessionism.

The state apparatus usually tends to have greater potential to generate material and financial resources to combat rebel groups. Rebel groups, on the other hand, are often constrained by the absence of easy access to financial and material resources. The biggest challenge for the rebel groups is to sustain their activities in the face of mounting losses of men and material. Peripheral regions provide easy access to financial and material resources. The writ of the state in the peripheral regions tends to be weak, which enables establishing and running of small-arms manufacturing units without hindrance. For instance, United Wa State Army (UWSA), located in the north-eastern border regions of Myanmar, reportedly established small-arms and ammunition manufacturing units.[36] Apart from enhancing its capabilities, UWSA is reportedly supplying equipment to various groups in North-East India and Myanmar.[37] Similarly, movement of arms across borders has emerged as a significant threat to national and regional security in Africa.[38] Once the possibility of constant supply of financial and material resource is assured for the rebel groups, then the pressures for a negotiated settlement tends to be lesser. As a consequence, the rebel groups tend to take hard-line positions prolonging the conflict. Further, as the peripheral regions facilitate easy movement across the borders, the rebel groups can withdraw into the neighbouring state to escape violent/repressive tactics of the government. The possibility of movements across borders makes it difficult for the government to isolate and contain the rebel groups.

The presence of ethnic kin/co-ethnics in neighbouring countries gives these ethnic groups a platform to voice their concerns in the international arena. Support to their ethnic kin/co-ethnics across the international borders in neighbouring countries increases the complexity of the conflict. Once the ethnic kin/co-ethnics in the neighbouring country get actively involved, the initial grievances such as demands for fairer political and economic processes tend to take a backseat, and demands for complete secession tend to be articulated with great fervour.

Theoretically, state has complete monopoly over coercive apparatus within a territory. Therefore, ceding territory to another political institution hits at one of the central principles of the existence of the state. It is precisely for this reason that states which have been bifurcated or have lost territory, tend to experience large-scale political convulsions. Given the demand to alter the state boundaries, which any state will find it difficult to comply, conflicts on the periphery tend to get prolonged. The support to the rebel groups need not be always from the formal state institutions of the neighbouring country. Quite often, due to strong presence of ethnic kin/co-ethnics, many organizations that fall within the realm of civil society end up supporting the rebel groups operating in another country. The formal involvement of a neighbouring country means that the actors for a negotiated settlement are relatively easy to identify. However, diffused support from various social groups located in the neighbouring country makes it very difficult to identify various actors for a negotiated settlement.

Quite often, the state apparatus of the neighbouring country and other regional powers support various actors in a country's civil war because of ideological considerations, shared religious identities and for strategic purposes. Such involvement increases the intensity of conflict and also prolongs it. For instance, a United Nations (UN) report in 2006 pointed out that about 10 countries (Ethiopia, Eritrea, Djibouti, Egypt, Iran, Libya, Saudi Arabia, Syria, Uganda, and Yemen) have either armed or trained various groups in Somalia.[39] Involvement of such large number of countries means that local people living in the midst of civil war have lost control of the rebellion. Their grievances and aspirations no longer determine the course of the conflict. The trajectory of the civil war, in such instances, is being increasingly determined by outside forces. Given the preponderant presence of various countries in a 'civil war', comprehensive regional solutions to address a civil war are often advanced. However, given the diversity and multiplicity of actors, consensus on regional solutions will be difficult to arrive at. Further, the category of 'intra-state conflict' or 'civil war' fails to capture various processes that mark such conflicts.

CONCLUSION

The above discussion demonstrates that the presence of economic inequality is not a sufficient condition for the initiation of conflict. Along with grievances such as economic inequality, there are other variables which act as inputs for the initiation of conflict. Easily extractable natural resources constitute a significant variable for the initiation of conflicts. As resource-dependence theorists point out, rebellion comes into play if the economic benefits of armed violence outweigh risks involved in it, which implies that rebels act as 'a rational-predators'.[40] Such metaphors help us understand the processes that enable rebel organizations to survive and propagate their cause. However, there is a need to go beyond economic determinants and also examine the politics of grievance construction and the strategies of neighbouring states. This discussion also throws up a few pointers for further research with reference to North-East India. There is a need to examine if North East India is a victim of 'overall inequality' or 'horizontal inequality'. There is a need to determine the exact nature of inequality, its components, its operation at sub-regional level and steps that should be taken to redress the situation. There is a need to bring into relief, organizational dynamics of various insurgent groups in North-East India. Along with the strategies of various neighbouring countries *vis-à-vis* conflicts in North-East India, there is a need to focus on the role of co-ethnics and natural resources in the conflicts of North-East India. Addressing some of these will give us better understanding of numerous conflicts in North-East India.

NOTES

1. Halvard Buhaug, Scott Gates, Håvard Hegre and Håvard Strand, 'Global Trends in Armed Conflict', Centre for the Study of Civil War, International Peace Research Institute, Oslo (PRIO), available at http://www.regjeringen.no/nb/dep/ud/kampanjer/refleks/innspill/engasjement/prio.html?id=492941
2. This definition is an expanded version of the definition given by PRIO. Definition given by PRIO makes it mandatory for government to be one of the contesting parties. For details see, Halvard Buhaug, Scott Gates, Håvard Hegre and Håvard Strand, 'Global Trends in Armed Conflict,' *Centre for the Study of Civil War Report*, International Peace Research Institute, Oslo (PRIO) available at http://www.regjeringen.no/nb/dep/ud/kampanjer/refleks/innspill/engasjement/prio.html?id=492941
3. World Bank, *World Development Report 2003: Sustainable Development in a Dynamic World*, Washington DC: World Bank and Oxford University Press, 2003, p. 156 available at http://www-wds.worldbank.org/external/default/WDSContentServer/IW3P/IB/2002/09/06/000094946_02082404015854/Rendered/PDF/multi0page.pdf
4. Juha Auvinen and E. Wayne Nafziger, 'The Sources of Humanitarian Emergencies', *The Journal of Conflict Resolution*, 43(3), June 1999, p. 267.
5. As cited in Juha Auvinen and E. Wayne Nafziger, ibid., p. 268.
6. See Simon Kuznets, 'Economic Growth and Income Inequality', *The American Economic Review*, 45(1), March 1955, p. 1-28.
7. Ted Robert Gurr, 'Peoples Against States: Ethnopolitical Conflict and the Changing World System: 1994 Presidential Address', *International Studies Quarterly*, 38(3), September 1994, p. 349.
8. Ibid.
9. Frances Stewart, 'Development and Security', Working Paper 3, Centre for Research on Inequality, Human Security and Ethnicity, CRISE, Queen Elizabeth House, University of Oxford, p. 12.
10. Frances Stewart, Graham Brown and Luca Mancini, 'Why Horizontal Inequalities Matter: Some Implications for Measurement', CRISE Working Paper, no. 19, June 2005, p. 5.
11. Stewart, op. cit.

12. Stewart, Brown and Mancini, op. cit.
13. Gudrun Østby, 'Horizontal Inequalities, Political Environment, and Civil Conflict Evidence from 55 Developing Countries, 1986–2003,' Post-Conflict Transitions Working Paper No. 7 Policy, *Research Working Paper; No. WPS 4193*, World Bank, available at http://econ.worldbank.org/external/default/main?pagePK=64165259&theSitePK=469372&piPK=64165421&menuPK=64166093&entityID=000016406_20070409112538
14. Ibid.
15. Susan L. Woodward, *Balkan Tragedy: Chaos and Dissolution after the Cold War*, Washington: Brookings Institution Press, 1995, p. 383.
16. Ibid., pp. 79-81.
17. E. Wayne Nafziger and Juha Auvinen, 'Economic Development, Inequality, and Humanitarian Emergencies', October 2001, available at http://www.k-state.edu/economics/nafwayne/ecdev10-1.pdf
18. Ibid.
19. Mark Irving Lichbach, 'Will Rational People Rebel against Inequality? Samson's Choice', *American Journal of Political Science*, 34(4), November 1990, p. 1073.
20. Ibid., p. 1074.
21. Paul Collier and Anke Hoeffler, *Greed and Grievance in Civil War*, Centre for the Study of African Economies, World Bank, 13 March 2002, p. 1.
22. Ibid.
23. Paul Collier, *Economic Causes of Civil Conflict and their Implication for Policy*, Oxford University, April 2006 available at http://users.ox.ac.uk/~econpco/research/pdfs/EconomicCauses of Civil Conflict-Implications for Policy. pdf, p. 3.
24. See Thomas L. Friedman, 'The First Law of Petropolitics', *Foreign Policy*, May/June 2006.
25. United Nations, 'Conflict Diamonds', 21 March 2001, available at http://www.un.org/peace/africa/Diamond.html
26. 'Background on Conflict Diamonds', Diamondfacts.org, available at http://diamondfacts.org/conflict/background.html
27. Ibid.
28. UNODC, 'Afghanistan Opium Survey 2008', August 2008, available at http://www.unodc.org/documents/publications/Afghanistan_Opium_Survey_2008.pdf
29. For details see, Friedman, op. cit.

30. 'Nigerian Oil Fuels Delta Conflict', *BBC*, 25 January 2006, available at http://news.bbc.co.uk/2/hi/africa/4617658.stm
31. Michael L. Ross, 'Blood Barrels Why Oil Wealth Fuels Conflict', *Foreign Affairs,* May/June 2008.
32. Michael L. Ross, 'What Do We Know about Natural Resources and Civil War?', *Journal of Peace Research*, 41(3), 2004; 337-56.
33. Patrick M. Regan and Daniel Norton, 'Greed, Grievance, and Mobilization in Civil Wars', *The Journal of Conflict Resolution*, 49(3), June 2005, p. 334.
34. Ibid.
35. James D. Fearon, 'Why Do Some Civil Wars Last so Much Longer than Others?', *Journal of Peace Research*, 41(3), May 2004, p. 283.
36. Brian McCartan, 'China Drawn into Myanmar's Border Strife', *Asia Times*, 28 May 2009 available at http://www.atimes.com/atimes/Southeast_Asia/KE28Ae01.html
37. Ibid.
38. For details see, Virginia Gamba, 'Small Arms Foster Social Turmoil', *Africa Recovery*, vol. 12, vo. 1, August 1998, p. 24.
39. Richard Beeston, 'These 10 Countries are Fanning Civil War Hate, says UN', 16 November 2006, *TimesOnline* available at http://www.timesonline.co.uk/tol/news/world/africa/article638363.ece also see 'Powers Stoking Somali Conflict', *BBC*, 15 November 2006, available at http://news.bbc.co.uk/2/hi/africa/6149276.stm
40. James Ron, 'Paradigm in Distress? Primary Commodities and Civil War', *Journal of Conflict Resolution*, 49(4), August 2005, pp. 443-50.

CHAPTER 7

Applicability of Sub-Conventional Operations Doctrine to Counter-Insurgency in Assam

Ali Ahmed

Following the presidential proclamation declaring Assam a disturbed area and ULFA as an unlawful organization, assistance of the Army was solicited and *Operation Bajrang* was launched in November 1990.[1] Ever since, the Army has been deployed—and restrained—alternatively in its counter-insurgency operations against different insurgent groups in Assam.[2] Its showing has been to its credit,[3] even if the Assam problem, counter-intuitively, continues to persist.

This paper argues that though the insurgency situation in Assam has been reduced to the levels manageable by the police, insurgency persists due to the political prong of national counter-insurgency strategy not having kept pace with the military prong. This paper contrasts the military prong of the operations in relation to the other prongs of national power, which according to the Army's sub-conventional doctrine requires to simultaneously address an insurgency situation. It recommends that civil society organizations require to continually pressurize both the government and the insurgents to come to a negotiated settlement so as to bring about conflict termination. This way a decisive turn of security would pave the way for further deepening of security through development. It makes its case so through the prism of the Indian Army's sub-conventional operations doctrine.

The Army's sub-conventional operations doctrine was released in end 2006.[4] The learning experience in Assam over almost a decade and a half has no doubt contributed to its evolution. Though this doctrine was released after over half-a-century of involvement in countering insurgency, it does not imply that the Army had no doctrine prior to then.[5] It has earlier had a pamphlet on counter-insurgency operations guiding its actions.[6] The pamphlet was updated in 1990 to incorporate the lessons learnt by the Army at some cost in Sri Lanka.[7]

However, the need to articulate a sub-conventional doctrine was felt primarily because of its continuing experience with proxy war in J&K and in countering insurgency in the North-East. This was part of the larger doctrinal efflorescence in the military in general over the turn of the century with all three services and the integrated headquarters periodically releasing their doctrines on various facets of warfare.[8] This is in keeping with India's democratic traditions of openness and debate.[9] It helps place the organization on the same page in its approach to insurgency. In being released as a public document it is also an attempt by the Army to draw the attention of policy makers and for the public debate to vexed questions that have troubled the Army in such situations such as 'command and control' and the need for a political resolution.[10] In particular, the doctrine covers the place of the military prong with respect to the other elements of national power that are to be co-extensively employed in counter-insurgency, such as political, economic and diplomatic power.[11]

The specific argument in this paper is that in respect of Assam the political prong—addressing *conflict resolution*—not having kept pace with the military prong—engaged in *conflict management*—the desired, and possible, political dividends have not been achieved. It would appear that the case of Assam is an unfair test case since the Assam problem is a very complex one consisting of the ethnic insurgencies, ethnic rivalries, tribal unrest and illegal immigrants.[12] Nevertheless, the applicability of the Army's sub-conventional warfare doctrine to countering insurgency in Assam is explored in this paper since the Army has succeeded in bringing levels of violence down to levels considered manageable by an upgraded police force assisted by the para-military forces.[13]

From a perusal of official statements of the Army it can be surmised that the deployment of security forces have met with considerable success. The Army's self-assessment is that insurgent 'support base is severely eroded and activities are on a low key due to own operations'.[14] Thus the Army appears to have met the requirements of the end—as envisaged in its doctrine—of a security environment in which the levels of 'law and order' that can be handled by the police.[15] The desired end state of creating conditions that are conducive to the attainment of political objectives can be said to potentially exist in the current status of the insurgency in Assam.[16]

The Ministry of Home Affairs' (MHA) Annual Reports corroborate the Army's perspective of an improved situation. A clear trend for the better can be discerned over time. The 1999-2000 and 2000-1 reports described the militancy as assuming 'serious dimensions' that has 'effected the very functioning of the democratic state'.[17] The 2003-4 Annual Report concludes that 'analysis of the data indicates that the law and order situation in Assam remains vitiated'. In 2007-8, 'the security situation in Assam continued to be a matter of concern'. The Ministry of Defence's (MOD) Annual Report states that

> [T]he multi dimensional approach adopted by the GOI to address insurgency problems in the North-East (NE) states has brought about a perceptible change in the overall security environment in the region. There has been a marked reduction in violence levels and the general situation in the NE region is *well under control* (italics added).[18]

The ground situation in Assam, as evidenced from media headlines, testifies to this to an extent. Upper Assam has been relatively peaceful after a split in ULFA's 28 Battalion.[19] The middle level leadership has dwindled, with a disconnect developing between the cadre and the senior leadership based in Bangladesh. Discontent amongst lower rung cadres is leading to surrenders. A split has occurred in the National Democratic Front of Bodoland (NDFB) with a larger faction preferring dialogue and expelling the Bangladesh based hardline leader.[20] Suspension of Operations agreements with NDFB (2005),[21] Dima Halim

Daogah (DHD) in 2003 and the United People's Democratic Solidarity (UPDS) (2002) continue in place, even if with some delicacy.

The MHA believes that this improvement has been brought about by a 'two pronged strategy to persist with counter-insurgency operations and concurrently win hearts and minds has paid good dividends'.[22]

> The strategy to 'improve the situation in the NE includes accelerated infrastructural development, stress on employment, good governance and decentralization, building friendly relations with neighbouring countries, willingness to meet and discuss legitimate grievances of the people and assist the state governments to combat militancy.[23]

Post-economic liberalization, the overall strategy—applicable also in the rest of India—appears to bring about a rising economic tide that lifts all boats. In case of the North-East this would translate into insurgents—self-styled defenders of the various ethnicities—abandoning insurgency to enable their communities to bandwagon with the rest of India on this upward economic trajectory. An increasing pie would proportionately increase the share of all the contending communities, thereby ending the perception of relative deprivation, resulting alienation and their apparent need consequently to take up arms.[24] The aspect of identity is being addressed through a move away from the earlier belief that with modernization the various ethnic groups would joint the Indian 'mainstream'.[25] This belief in the proverbial 'mainstream' and its beneficial effects has been substituted with the idea that the ethnic mosaic that comprises the North-East is an example of a multi-cultural and multi-ethnic India that instead requires to develop along its own unique trajectory. Towards this end, there are efforts to project India's Look East policy through the NE as the springboard,[26] the eventual happy circumstance likely to eventuate over a period of time.

There being a sobering reality to contend with, however, management of violence in the interim would continue to be of importance. Of the over 1,000 deaths in NE in 2008, 36 per cent were in Assam. The bomb blasts of October in Assam, Tripura and Manipur indicate the external-internal linkages between the ISI-DGFI-HuJI-ULFA-NDFB.[27] The latest ethnic clashes in the same month resulted in 55 dead and 2 lakh displaced, adding to the over 1 lakh already in camps from earlier clashes of last decade. The less visible consequence—of some import from human security point of view—is that 'every year, an average of 250 women and 200 girl children go missing in Assam. The actual number is higher being easy prey in camps of internally displaced persons.'[28]

Clearly, there is an equal potential for reversion to more disturbed conditions here that would do with a greater urgency in the approach to the political prong of strategy. Conflict resolution therefore needs to take centrestage as against the present focus on conflict management. On this issue, the doctrine has a controversial take. The Army, being subordinate to the political echelon in our democratic system, has wisely restricted its reflection on the nature of the resolution to stating that, 'When employing the Army in Low Intensity Conflict (LICO), management rather than conflict resolution will be the political objective.'[29] This is understandable. Nevertheless, conflict resolution should remain the political *aim*, with conflict management being only a *means* to a larger end.[30]

The doctrine goes on to say that 'the end state sought by the national counter-insurgency campaign is *conflict resolution*, which generally succeeds *conflict termination* (italics added)'.[31] Here it is apparent that the doctrine has mistakenly borrowed from a conventional warfare template in which conflict termination, in the form of a ceasefire, precedes conflict resolution through negotiations. In the counter-insurgency setting this should logically be the other way round, in that conflict resolution would precede or at least be coextensive with, the endgame leading up to conflict termination. The doctrine states that conflict resolution entails 'demilitarization of the conflict zone and shaping the environment wherein the remaining difference can be pursued without violence'.[32] Demilitarization can only succeed conflict resolution—conflict resolution being taken as an outcome of political engagement between the state and the insurgent group leading up to cooperatively arrived at mutually beneficial solutions. For instance, though there is a ceasefire on in Nagaland for about a decade now, conflict termination cannot be deemed to have taken place. There conflict resolution is underway, meaning that conflict resolution precedes conflict termination.

The paradox that usually develops is that once the security situation is manageable there is little incentive for the government to progress the political prong of strategy. Believing it has the cards, it prefers instead to exhaust the insurgent adversary. This is arguably a major lacuna in dealing with troubled regions, be it J&K, Nagaland and Assam. Persistence of violence, and threat of violence, even in an improved security situation testifies to an imbalance in the progress made by various prongs of national power. In such a circumstance, the insurgent attempts to use violence to announce presence and continued credibility, as a means of dialogue with the state. Insurgent actions in Assam and elsewhere in the NE, is seemingly a manifestation of an ethnic group's desire to be heard both in the provincial capital and in Delhi. This indicates that a meaningful dialogue with the group could bring about conflict transformation. Holding this up is the attempt on both sides, that of the security forces and the insurgent, to reach the elusive 'position of strength'.

A plausible reason for a situation in which both sides attempt to reach a position of strength has been given by General V.K. Nayar, who has considerable experience at both the operational and political level in the NE.[33] He says that,

> The paradigms of conflict resolution and management relevant to the situation in the NE are Ideal Politik and cooperative approach. The present environment in the country is that of Real Politik and a competitive one. . . . While talking of peace and resolution of conflict . . . the government's approach is faulty. They have essentially fallen back on their intelligence personnel and the bureaucracy as negotiators. Both are seen as an extension of the establishment and as such suspect. . . .[34]

There is a need here to underline that political resolution be handled by those with moral capital. They should preferably be from the same area having political credibility and civil society support, such as the interlocutor Dr Indira Goswami with the ULFA in Assam[35] and the Committee of Concerned Citizens in

Andhra Pradesh.[36] That these initiatives did not proceed to the logical conclusion indicates that a realist mindset must first be overcome.[37] Risking transformative 'Ideal politik' would require insights from peace studies discourse rather than the realism dominant tradition of security studies. Since eventually it is a political call, accountability of politicians, both at the centre and the state requires to be exacted on this score. Thus the political prong appears to be limited by its chosen paradigm of realism which being power-oriented and state centric has its limitations when applied in conditions of internal conflict.

Another reason for persistence of disturbed conditions owes to the assumption that tackling insurgency is 'prolonged'.[38] This assumption is explicated in the Army doctrine:

> LICO will generally be prolonged and will see a large number of changes in policy and directional imperatives. Commanders and troops executing the mandate will move on after completing their tours of duty during the conduct of such operations to be replaced by others. . . . CI operations are seldom time-bound.[39]

This is a sensible approach in terms of depriving the insurgent a major weapon—time—which in insurgency theory is meant to work in favour of the insurgent. This expectation is true in case the counter-insurgent is an external power. In India this is patently not the case.

The doctrine advises that time, not being a constraint, operations should bring about an 'agitational fatigue' in supporters of the insurgency and a 'realization that fighting the government is a "no win" situation and their anti government stance will only delay the restoration of peace and normalcy'.[40] The Army feels this change of attitude may take 'from a couple of years to decades'. This attitude begets what could be termed a 'strategy of exhaustion'—one that does not rely on opening up political possibilities for resolution.[41]

This may be an acceptable situation from the state's point of view in that maintaining national integrity and not compromising the political system is its principle function. This is understandable for bureaucrats in the national security system and for national level politicians. Misplaced enthusiasm can prove detrimental to the national interest. Prudence is expected of those charged with the nation's decisions.[42] However, this need not be the case with effected people in the insurgency area.

People have agency and cannot submissively expect the state to deliver. V.K. Nayar describes the situation in the NE as one in which,

> The core of insurgents will remain separatist and anti-establishment and ethnic . . . the politician-bureaucrat-elite-insurgent nexus . . . , unless checked, will continue to provide support to the insurgency to achieve their diverse aims and further intensify deprivation and alienation of the people. . . . Insurgency in the NE has become an industry . . . in this struggle common people remain poor and the security forces are the 'fall guys'.[43]

Such 'normalcy' should logically be unacceptable. Since the insurgency impacts people and so do counterinsurgency operations, getting the bureaucrat-advised politician to privilege the political prong is necessary through concerted civil society action. Such action would also discredit the 'industry' that vested interests have acquired in the insurgency. It would help the state arrive at creative solutions. It would enable reaching out to insurgents. These organizations could play a 'watchdog' role with respect to preventing a degenerative spiral in actions of both insurgents and the state. The momentum of their action, visibility, wide presence and alliance with the media would be their best security, in that though vulnerable to intimidation by both the state and insurgents,[44] any such action would prove counter-productive. The role of Asom Sahitya Sabha, the All Assam Student's Union, the Asom Jatiyatabadi Yuva Chatra Parishad and in the Bodo case, the Bodo Sahitya Sabha and the All Bodo Student's Union has legitimacy among the people and therefore command credibility both with the insurgents and the state.[45]

The doctrine in treating civil society as an object without agency does not harness its energy and good offices for political resolution. This owes to the belief that political resolution would be the effort of the policy making establishment. This is seldom the case. Therefore there is a need for civil society to bridge the gap autonomously, irrespective of state initiatives. This would supplement state effort and the state should reconcile to perceiving the effort positively and not as a subversive threat as is its wont.

According to the doctrine the prongs of a national counter-insurgency strategy are: 'Creating of a secure environment'; 'Isolation of the Conflict Zone'; 'Addressing local aspirations and winning hearts and minds'; and 'Public information and perception management'.[46] These are to be applied in an orchestrated, centrally-directed manner.

As part of the national strategy, it would appear that the Army has repeatedly managed to recreate a 'secure environment'. Post *Operations Bajrang* and *Rhino*, the MHA Annual Report stated, 'These have improved the law and order in the state. The ULFA camps have been dismantled and their activists apprehended. All these measures have generated public confidence.'[47] Midway through the conflict later, General S.K. Sinha, earlier Governor of Assam, appreciatively said, 'A special word of praise needs to be given to the Army. . .'.[48] A textbook approach to counter-insurgency—an odd 'ketchup Colonel' incident apart[49] —is being practised with the Army mindful of the need to 'win hearts and minds' through an 'iron fist with velvet glove'. The experience over the past two decades, in Assam and elsewhere, has honed the Army's counter-insurgency skills. The earlier method, borrowing from the experience of 'sweeping the Valley floor' in J&K has largely been replaced with intelligence-led small team operations. Thus the declared doctrine is being applied in Assam which, on this account, can be taken as its test bed.

However, the resulting draw down in the conflict has not brought to fore other prongs of the doctrine. For 'Addressing local aspirations and winning hearts and minds', the doctrine requires 'developmental initiatives and restoration of full liberties along with effective functioning of various institutions' to be supplemented by 'a political dialogue accompanied by suitable political initiatives'.[50] In accordance with the tenets of the doctrine, a national level ministry on the NE, the Ministry of Development of North Eastern Region (DoNER), is in place.[51] The Planning Commission, the North East Council, the Cabinet

Secretariat and the Ministry of Home Affairs through its Internal Security, Policy Planning and North East Division are attentive to Assam. At Dispur is the two-tier Unified Command comprising the Strategic Group and Operations Group.[52] Developmental initiatives are underway in particular with respect to infrastructure and connectivity, as is upgradation of policing capabilities under various schemes such as the Central Modernisation of Police Forces scheme, raising of eight India Reserve Battalions, etc.[53]

However, to push the situation decidedly in the direction of peace, the contradiction between the Army preferring to operate in Aid to Civil Authority situations under the cover of the Armed Forces Special Powers Act (AFSPA) and its advocacy in the doctrine of 'restoring full liberties' to generate a 'groundswell for peace' needs to be resolved. It is possible that withdrawal of the AFSPA could catalyse the peace process.[54] The relevant Code of Criminal Procedure articles are in any case covering Army actions.[55] That this has not happened indicates an imbalance between the military and political counter-insurgency prongs in that the political prong not having kept pace, there is a hesitation in taking the initiatives necessary to bring about a qualitative improvement in the situation.

It is not as if political initiatives have not been tried, such as Hiteshwar Saikia's effort at inducing surrenders.[56] That having proven a 'disaster' (to quote General Sinha[57]), the effort has been to engage with extremist leadership. The prime minister's invitation remains open. Lack of coordination between the 'carrot and stick' is also evident in case of J&K and Nagaland.[58] This can regrettably be taken as a dispensable characteristic of India's approach to countering insurgency. It is here that civil society groups need to make a difference with both the insurgent and the state by keeping up the pressure for peace. Society is not inert, but has agency that it must exercise. Attempts to marginalize or deter these groups by the state or the insurgent would lose the side doing so democratic space and credibility.

In case of Assam, and indeed also in J&K, there is little effort to progress the second prong, that of 'Isolation of the conflict zone'.[59] While the Army can apply itself to the internal dimension of such isolation, the external dimension requires other elements of national power, in particular the diplomatic dimension. In the case of Assam this implies getting Bangladesh on board. Home Secretary level annual talks and biannual Joint Working Group (JWG) meetings are available. The instrumentality of the SAARC exists. However, ambivalence between a liberal-rationalist and conservative-realist approach to neighbours exists. The reluctance of Bangladesh to help ameliorate India's NE problem, through enabling connectivity, access to ports, trading links, acknowledging its role in ending illegal immigration, etc., also owes to a like realist world view held in Dhaka. Such an effort had succeeded in case of friendly Bhutan when the Royal Bhutanese Army cleared out its territory of Bodos, ULFA and the KLO camps in 2003.[60] This time round, however, the Bangladesh angle looks very promising since the Awami League is now in power. However, possible movement of the groups to Myanmar may require to be preempted. Dispur needs to prevail on Delhi to activate the diplomatic prong in earnest involving both the Ministry of External Affairs and the Ministry of Home Affairs (MHA).

The diplomatic prong is at a premium with respect to Assam dimension on account of its centrality in addressing the 'root cause'.[61] The ULFA has declared in its mouthpiece, *Freedom* (17 December 2006),

> ULFA is determined to uproot those illegal migrants who threaten Asom's existence, create chaotic situations in its social formation and occupy the political and economic space by making indigenous people homeless. . . . In Asom, the principle illegal occupational forces are the Indian Army. Those who illegally trespassed from Bangladesh and Nepal must be identified and driven away. But before that the Indian occupational forces must be expelled from Asom.

There appears to be a sequencing of its objectives, with the Army being first disabled before it turns its attention to illegal immigrants. Illegal immigration being an emotive issue in Assam, and elsewhere in the country, requires prioritizing. This necessitates a more urgent approach to the *political problem* posed by the ULFA.

According to two NE watchers little has been done on this score:

Even after 23 years of the signing of the Assam Accord, the fence has not been completed. Both the Central and state governments have failed to check the flow of illegal migrants, upgrade the National Registrar of Citizens. . . . India has also been unable to sustain a dialogue mechanism with Bangladesh for resolution of the issue of illegal migrants. Unless the core issues are settled and the root causes addressed through a well formulated strategy and with political conviction, bringing stability to this part of India is not going to be easy.[62]

Thus it is evident that the military prong of counter-insurgency, even if in line with doctrine, can prove inadequate. In the debate between 'security and development', the lack of development cannot solely be attributed to inadequacy of security. A truism, voiced by General S.K. Sinha, has it that, 'There can be no military solution to insurgency. It has to be a political solution. Ideally dialogue with militants and a political settlement should bring about an end to insurgency.'[63]

In this case, a political understanding with respect to illegal immigrants issue needs to be arrived at. This can only be in line with a non-violent approach advocated by Ved Marwah involving strong physical and legal means to end further immigration as against forcibly sending away those who are already here.[64] Moderation of the threat perception is in order in light of a sobering perspective that has it that,

The facts, however, as borne out by the Census report, are that in Assam and in Tripura, the growth rate of the Muslim population is the same and not higher than the national average for the community. And in West Bengal, it is below the national average. Hence the infiltration theory is simply not corroborated by the figures.[65]

An insurgency situation in the conditions of India's fissured social reality lends itself to political manipulation by interested political forces and, perhaps, even by elements of the state. In Assam, this could be in the form of the illegal immigrant being posed as the 'Other' for transforming the insurgency problem of a kind requiring a nuanced approach (against an ethnic-based insurgency) to one making for a simpler force-dependent counter (Bangladesh-aided illegal immigrant as terrorist front of proxy war). The national security angle to the Assam insurgency has already entered into the security discourse.[66] Moderation of the threat perception is in order in light of a sobering perspective that has it that,

> The facts, however, as borne out by the Census report, are that in Assam and in Tripura, the growth rate of the Muslim population is the same and not higher than the national average for the community. And in West Bengal, it is below the national average. Hence the infiltration theory is simply not corroborated by the figures.[67]

The people of Assam cannot allow the insurgency to continue indefinitely since the future has unthinkable possibilities.

An expeditious approach is a difficult proposition in face of an apparent lack of the need for urgency in a militarily favourable counter-insurgency circumstance. However, the threat of an uncertain future should act as a spur. Take for instance a future possibility of a Chittagong arms haul levels of armament infusion into terrorist ranks. In the Chittagong case of 2004, up to a brigade worth of armament was fortunately recovered timely.[68] This could have lengthened the insurgency by at least half a decade. The same is the case with ethnic clashes adding cumulatively to inter-ethnic misperceptions.[69] In case of transforming perception of the problem from one of insurgency to proxy war, by concentrating on the aid and abetement from Bangladesh and at one remove Pakistan, could push any resolution further away.

Clearly, even if the state were to be complacent under the mistaken impression of occupying a position of strength, civil society cannot afford to be likewise. The society cannot with any sanguinity be held hostage to pathologies that can come plague apparently interminable counter-insurgency operations, namely, bureaucratic inertia, the Army's institutional interests, political calculations and vested interests of insurgents. Future threat of cataclysmic events, undesirable trends and unpredictable outcomes should energize civil society initiatives to bridge the gap produced by inordinate political prudence that attends conflict resolution. Therefore, governmental efforts notwithstanding, resolution efforts from within civil society should persist and the 'vote' be used as an instrument to pressurize the government at the state and centre.

ACKNOWLEDGEMENTS

The author would like to thank Dr Namrata Goswami and Mr. Mirza Zulfiqur Rahman for their comments on the previous drafts of this paper.

NOTES

1. In the earlier MOD Annual Reports, the engagement was covered under the heading 'Cooperation between Armed Forces and Civil Authorities'. Now it forms a part of the section 'Counter Insurgency Operations and Internal Security Situations' in the MOD Annual Report chapter 'Indian Army'. This indicates how the military engagement in such situations has moved centrestage over the years.
2. For instance, *Operation Bajrang* was called off in April 1991 and *Operation Rhino* was launched on 15 September 1991.
3. The *MOD Annual Report 2007-08* says, 'In Assam, operations by the Security Forces since the beginning of this year have dealt a severe blow to the ULFA. Major successes have been recorded in ULFA strongholds in Upper Assam and the Lohit district of ALP.'
4. IHQ of MOD, *Doctrine for Sub-Conventional Operations*, HQ ARTRAC, Shimla, 2006.
5. For an excellent overview of the evolution of the counter-insurgency doctrine, see Rajesh Rajagopalan, *Fighting Like a Guerrilla: Indian Army and Counter-insurgency*, New Delhi: Routledge, 2007.
6. This pamphlet had originally been authored by the then Brigadier S.K. Sinha after his three year command of a brigade in Nagaland (Interaction with author, 28 March 2009).
7. Also see, R. Rajagopalan, 'Restoring Normalcy: The Evolution of the Indian Army's Counterinsurgency Doctrine', *Small Wars & Insurgencies*, 11(1), Spring 2000, pp. 44-68.
8. The IAF doctrine was released in 1995, followed by that of the Indian Army in 1998. The Indian Army's Cold Start doctrine was released in April 2004, while the doctrine of the Navy was released in October of the same year. The Joint Doctrine for

Defence Forces and Joint Amphibious Warfare Doctrine have already been released whereas the Joint Special Forces Doctrine, Joint Psychological Operations Doctrine, Joint Sub-conventional Warfare Doctrine and Joint Space Doctrine are in advance stages of preparation at the HQ IDS.

9. An influential sub-conventional warfare doctrine was also drafted in the other democracy over the same time period by Lt. Gen. Petraeus, later chief of US Central Command operating in Iraq and Afghanistan.
10. In this doctrine the Army makes a specific reference (and reproduces) to the Group of Ministers report on internal security (Chapter IV, Paras 4.62, 4.63 and 4.64) which require the chief minister to chair meetings of a body comprising ministers of key ministries and senior civil servants, the senior Army officer and the police and paramilitary heads. When more than one security service is involved, then clear operational authority should be laid down, with the senior Army officer having authority for planning and executing operations.
11. See Chapter 2, *Doctrine for Sub Conventional Operations*, pp. 14-22.
12. For a chronology of events in Assam, see University of Maryland's Minorities at Risk Project: http://www.cidcm.umd.edu/mar/assessment.asp?groupId=75015
13. In contrast to the situation in the NE, the approach to Left Wing Extremism in central India is to avoid deploying the Army and relying instead on capacity building of police forces.
14. See Eastern Command website: http://indianarmy.nic.in/ec/index_ec.htm
15. *Doctrine for Sub Conventional Operations*, p. 17.
16. The military end state is to 'facilitate initiation of a political dialogue for a negotiated settlement'. See, *Doctrine for Sub-Conventional Operations*, p. 20.
17. *MHA Annual Report* for the relevant year.
18. *MOD Annual Report 2007-08.*
19. 'Two companies of ULFA battalion declare ceasefire', *The Hindu*, 25 June 2008.
20. M. Amarjeet Singh, 'Changing Face of Bodo Insurgency', *Strategic Comments*: http://www.idsa.in/publications/stratcomments/AmarjeetSingh120109.htm
21. Memorandum of Settlement was signed in 2003 with BLT leading to creation of Bodo Territorial Council in BTAD. The Bodo

language was included in the Eighth Schedule. Financial assistance of Rs. 100 crore per annum for five years was promised. DoNER has sanctioned 39 projects of Rs. 419 crore and recruitment into CRP of 1,000 cadres of BLT is required to take place. This is the manner the government has approached the problems politically. This indicates that the same approach can be adopted to address the core insurgent group in Assam, ULFA.

22. See *MOD Annual Report 2003-04*. Lt. Gen. S.K. Sinha's strategy when Governor in Assam is described in his 'Transregional Movements of Population', *USI Journal,* July 2000. He writes: 'We crafted a three pronged strategy to deal with the situation. The first prong was intensified and coordinated operations under a Unified Command. The second prong consisted of psychological initiatives . . . the third prong was economic development . . . the impact of the three prongs has brought out a sea change . . . I can say with confidence that Assam is now emerging out of a dark tunnel towards bright sunshine of peace (p. 625).'
23. *MHA Annual Report 2003-04.*
24. Ali Ahmed, 'Understanding Internal Security', *The Infantry (India)*, Autumn 2008.
25. The Army website refers to 'mainstream' indicating the dispensable persistence of the concept: 'The veritable flood of Hindi movies and their popularity in the region have also assisted in no small measure in this slow but sure process of absorption in the Indian mainstream.'
26. 'North-eastern Dream', *Frontline*, 7 June 2008. The *North Eastern Vision 2020* document was released by the prime minister on 2 July 2008 (http://pmindia.nic.in/speech/content.asp?id=693).
27. Namrata Goswami and Dilip Gogoi, 'The October 30 Terrorist Attacks in Assam', *IDSA Strategic Comments,* http://www.idsa.in/publications/stratcomments/NamrataGoswami141108.htm. See also, Sreeradha Dutta, 'Security of India's Northeast: External Linkage', *Strategic Analysis*, November 2000.
28. Lyla Bavadam, 'At the Receiving End', *Frontline,* 22 December 2007.
29. 'Operations Other Than War', Section 14 – 'LICO and CI Operations', *Indian Army Doctrine*, HQ ARTRAC, Shimla, October 2004.
30. Conflict management is a 'situation where a conflict continues but where its worst excesses are avoided or mitigated' (Graham Evans and J. Newnham, *Dictionary of International Relations*,

New York: Penguin Books, 1998, p. 94). Conflict resolution has been defined as 'the search for an outcome that, at a minimum, represents for some participants an improvement from, and for no participants a worsening of, their present situation' (Thomas Saaty and Joyce Alexander, *Conflict Resolution: The Analytic Hierarchy Approach*, New York: Praeger, 1989, p. 43). Conflict termination can be defined as a lasting end to the militarized engagement.

31. *Doctrine for Sub Conventional Operations*, p. 17.
32. Ibid.
33. Lt. Gen. (Retd.) V.K. Nayar has been Governor in Manipur. See his conceptual approach to the solution in his *Crossing the Frontiers of Conflict in the North East and Jammu and Kashmir: From Realpolitik to Idealpolitik,* Delhi: Shipra, 2005, pp. 134-6.
34. Nayar, *Crossing the Frontiers of Conflict,* pp. 140-1.
35. See 'Time for Talks', *Frontline*, 8 October 2005 and 'Pushing the Peace Process', *The Hindu*, 29 June 2007. For a survey of peace initiatives in Assam and the NE, see Ajai Sahni, 'Survey of Conflicts & Resolution in India's Northeast', *Faultlines*, vol. 12, available at http://www.satp.org/satporgtp/publication/faultlines/volume12/Article3.htm.
36. See http://www.mainstreamweekly.net/article337 and htmlhttp://www.pucl.org/Topics/Human-rights/2002/pwg.htm on the concerns of the CCC in AP.
37. PCG set up in September 2005 held three rounds of talks with ULFA resulting in suspension of operations from 13 August 2006. No direct response from ULFA and reports of regrouping led to resumption of operations on 24 September 2006. GOI indicates that it is open to talks provided leaders of ULFA abjure violence and come forward directly for talks without any preconditions. Dr. Indira Goswami, civil society group Citizen's Peace Forum and the People's Consultative Group were key players.
38. The Doctrine for Sub-Conventional Operations uses the term 'long haul'. The *Indian Army Doctrine* terms it 'prolonged'.
39. 'LICO and CI Operations', *Indian Army Doctrine*, Para 5.2.
40. Para 11, 'People Centric Operations', *Doctrine for Sub-Conventional Operations*, p. 21.
41. Firdaus Ahmed, 'Midyear Chakravyuh', indiantogether.org, http://www.indiatogether.org/2008/aug/fah-chakra.htm
42. M.S. John, 'Realism, Neorealism and Critical Theory', in Kanti Bajpai and S. Mallavarapu (eds.), *International Relations in India:*

Bringing Theory Back Home, New Delhi: Orient Longman, 2005, p. 496.

43. Nayar, *Crossing the Frontiers of Conflict*, p. 118.
44. The cases of imprisoned Dr Binayak Sen and murdered Abdul Ahad Guru are examples of the vulnerability of civil society activists.
45. The insight owes to input of Mirza Zulfiqur Rahman, research scholar at SIS, JNU.
46. 'Various Prongs of National Initiative', *Doctrine for Sub-Conventional Operations*, pp. 17-19.
47. *MHA Annual Report 1990-91*.
48. S.K. Sinha, 'Trans-regional Movements of Population', *USI Journal*, p. 437.
49. 'Army sacks "ketchup" colonel', *Times of India*, 26 November 2004. In this incident, the officer splashed ketchup on locals posing dead so as to provide photographic proof of killings of militants in the (fake) encounter so as to gain awards.
50. *Doctrine for Sub Conventional Operations*, p. 19.
51. See website of the DoNER Ministry for its developmental activities: http://mdoner.gov.in/.
52. This was established in 1997 by Lt. Gen. Sinha after taking over as Governor.
53. See for counter-insurgency initiatives being undertaken with respect to NE and elsewhere in India, *Status Paper on Internal Security Situation* (September 2008) of the Internal Security Division of the Ministry of Home Affairs at http://mha.nic.in/pdfs/STTSPPR-IS171008.pdf
54. The AFSPA is a particularly unpopular legislation and has consistently come under criticism by both activists and people in troubled regions. See the Justice B.P. Jeevan Reddy Committee to Review the AFSPA report at http://www.hindu.com/nic/afa/.
55. Code of Criminal Procedure, Section 197, Para 1 states, 'When any person who is or was a Judge or Magistrate or a public servant not removable from his office save by or with the sanction of the Government is accused of any offence alleged to have been committed by him while acting or purporting to act in the discharge of his official duty no court shall take cognizance of such offence except with the previous sanction—(a) In the case of it person who is employed or, as the case may be, was at the time of commission of the alleged offence employed, in connection with the affairs of the Union, of the Central Government. . . .'

And Para 3 (A) states, '. . . no court shall take cognizance of any offence, alleged to have been committed by any member of the Forces charged with the maintenance of public order in a State while acting or purporting to act in the discharge of his official duty during the period while a Proclamation issued trader clause (I) of Article 356 of the Constitution was in force therein, except with the previous sanction of the Central Government.' This provides adequate cover for forces to conduct operations.

56. The SULFA, Surrendered ULFA was formed from those who surrendered in the wake of *Operation Bajrang* and *Operation Rhino*. India's experience with such 'pseudo groups' has been dismal, be it in Sri Lanka, J&K with the Ikhwan and in Assam. These groups lend themselves to manipulation by the intelligence arm of the State. In case of Assam the most inglorious episode has been the 'secret killings' in which relatives of ULFA cadre were killed by unknown killers ('Gogoi's charge against the NDA's regime', *The Hindu*, 29 May 2009). This is another facet of India's counter-insurgency experience that does not have doctrinal sanction, but is nevertheless evident across the troubled landscapes, be it one time Punjab or present-day Kashmir. The 'watchdog' function of civil society organizations becomes more critical in such circumstance.
57. S.K. Sinha, 'Insurgency in Assam', *USI Journal*, p. 433.
58. In J&K, there was no movement on the political report called for by the prime minister as one of four Round Tables Working Group reports. The central interlocutor, Mr. N.N. Vohra (now Governor) did not make any appreciable headway. Likewise, a former Union Home Secretary has headed the central team at the talks with the Naga insurgent groups without any gain other than extension of ceasefire.
59. Though in J&K, the Line of Control fence called the 'Vij' line was set-up in record time, it is a physical barrier. The point at issue is that the measures necessary to prevent Kashmir becoming a magnet for Islamist interest are not being taken with adequate dispatch, despite the people and political parties being in favour of these, such as steps towards demilitarization, withdrawal of AFSPA, greater autonomy, etc.
60. 'Bangla, Myanmar Next after Bhutan, Says Army Chief', *Indian Express*, 3 January 2003.
61. *MHA Annual Report 2002-03* reflects on the causes of insurgency in the NE in the following manner: 'Militancy in the NE is one

of the oldest in India . . . the region is geopolitically sensitive and has tenuous surface link through the Siliguri Corridor. . . . The armed hostilities have been consistently fuelled from across the border. . . . Propaganda of militants has been largely drawing its sustenance from influx of illegal immigrants, perceived or actual demographic distortion of tribal communities in their homelands, disruption of natural trade routes following Partition, poor social and physical infrastructure, relative economic deprivation and weak emotional and cultural links with Indian mainstream . . . the modern forces of social and economic change have been contributing to unrest in certain segments of tribal communities . . . ISI has also been pursuing its evil designs . . . due to agricultural, industrial and infrastructural backwardness the level of unemployment remains high. The frustrated and unemployed youth becomes victim of the militant outfits. . . .' See, Sinha, 'Transregional Movements of Population', pp. 614-19 on effect on Assam.

62. Namrata Goswami and Dilip Gogoi, 'The October 30 Terrorist Attacks in Assam', *IDSA Strategic* Comments, http://www.idsa.in/publications/stratcomments/NamrataGoswami141108.htm
63. S.K. Sinha, 'Insurgency in Assam', *USI Journal,* July 2001.
64. Ved Marwah, 'Demographic Imbalance and Implications on National Security: A Management Challenge for India', *USI Journal,* April 2006.
65. For details see, 'The Population Bogey', *Frontline*, 25 September 2004.
66. 'Illegal Immigration Biggest Threat to India: LK Advani', *Indian Express*, 26 July 2009. The Army in Assam has redeployed with the 4 Corps, earlier conducting operations across the state now confined to Lower Assam, while Upper Assam has been taken over by 3 Corps. This testifies to the threat from Muslim Fundamentalist Organisations (MFO) being taken seriously and the state appears to be gearing up for its future manifestation. There are conventional operational reasons for this redeployment also such as a future threat from China, increasingly being discussed in strategic circles. This is further testimony that procrastination over the resolution would imply future vulnerability for India. The possibility of 'self-fulfilling prophecy' in both approaches is intrinsic.
67. T.K. Rajalakshmi, 'The Population Bogey', *Frontline*, 25 September 2004.

68. Sreeradha Datta, 'Complicity of State Actors in Chittagong Arms Haul Case Revealed', *IDSA Strategic Comments*, March 2009. An estimated $4.5-5.7 million of arms were intercepted in the seizure of 10 trucks comprising rocket launchers (150), rockets (840), over a million rounds of ammunition, grenade launchers (2000), grenades (25,000) and over 1,700 assorted assault weapons. http://www.idsa.in/publications/stratcomments/*SreeradhaDatta090309.htm.*
69. Earlier ethnic clashes have taken place in 1983, 1993, 1994, 1996, 2004 and 2008.

CHAPTER 8

Political Reorganization of Assam in the Wake of Insurgency

H.N. Das

INTRODUCTION

The geographical entity of Assam consists of two valleys—the Barak Valley and the Brahmaputra Valley. The Barak Valley in the south has three overwhelmingly Bengali-speaking districts with some immigrant labourers in the tea plantations and some scattered tribal populations mainly in the foothills. The Brahmaputra Valley in the north never had a homogeneous population or society. From time immemorial different tribes and ethnic groups have lived in the Brahmaputra Valley and the hills surrounding it. Immigrants have come from outside the area throughout the past. They brought their own culture and language. Some retained these, albeit in modified forms, but others got merged into a nebulous ethnic mainstream. In my view three major events which took place in the Brahmaputra Valley in the past two thousand years are noteworthy—the Hindu-Aryan immigration, Tai-Ahom assimilation and the Bangladeshi Muslim infiltration.

HINDU-ARYAN IMMIGRATION

The first major event was the Hindu-Aryan immigration from north India during first to fifth century AD, which continued thereafter. This brought a highly cultured, educationally advanced and socially active group, which in course of time came to dominate the Brahmaputra Valley. It is they who developed the

Assamese language, which is derived from Sanskrit and belongs to the same sub-group as Bengali, Oriya, Maithili, Bhojpuri and the other Aryan languages of eastern India. The Kamakhya Temple is the most important visible monument of those times. Worship of mother goddess was one of the characteristic features of the people of old Kamarupa or Pragjyotishpura. They also built scores of other temples. The sculptural and architectural remains all over the Brahmaputra Valley indicate clear and close linkages with north India. It was in this age that the Assamese literature was initiated. Much later, beside poetry, prose literature was written and composed in Assamese by Bhattadev and others. The Assamese tried to get most of the other tribes and ethnic groups of the Brahmaputra Valley absorbed into their fold. They partially succeeded in this effort.

TAI-AHOM ASSIMILATION

The second major event was the conquest of upper Assam by the Tai-Ahoms, a Shan ethnic community, who came from the China–Myanmar border in the thirteenth century. They got themselves merged into the Assamese mainstream abandoning their own culture and language. They adopted the Hindu religion. Sukapha, the Ahom conqueror and their first king, is reputed to have adopted this policy of assimilation and thus helped the formation of the Assamese sub-nationality as it exists today. Then, in the fifteenth-sixteenth centuries the greatest Assamese of all times, Sri Sankardeva, started life as a Sanskrit scholar and writer, composed his *Kirtanghosha* in Assamese and introduced far-reaching reforms in the Hindu religion. It is Sankardeva who introduced the Vaishnavite cult in Assam. He and his principal disciple, Sri Madhabdeva, who wrote the *Naamghosha*, developed Assamese literature, music, drama, painting, dance and society into very high standards. Their *bargeets* are some of the finest nuggets of Indian classical music. The *sattriya* dance form they developed is recognized as one of the seven national classical dances of India by the Sangeet Natak Akademi. They taught the Assamese how to live hygienically and neatly in cottages built around a courtyard for each family. The Assamese lived a far better, more meaningful and spiritually richer life than most other communities in India till about the 1950s. The per capita income was also higher than the national average. The Assamese *naamghars* (prayer halls) are the centres of social life in the villages even today. The 914 *satras* (large monasteries) and the thousands of *naamghars* are the institutional and structural frameworks of the Assamese society. To quote S.K. Bhuyan, 'though the network of *Sattras* and *Naamghars*, spread all over the country, knowledge permeated to the masses of Assam'. The liberal reforms of Sankardeva and Madhabdeva attracted many more ethnic groups to adopt the Assamese language, the Hindu religion and the socio-cultural milieu which Sankardeva had initiated. In fact, an innovative Saraniya system was introduced in order to make gradual absorption of tribals into the Assamese mainstream possible and easy.

BANGLADESHI MUSLIM INFILTRATION

The third major event was the continuous and unrelenting immigration of Bengali Muslims from East Bengal (present Bangladesh) since the beginning of the twentieth century in the wake of the British Indian government's policy of 'grow more food' campaign. Later, the speed of immigration was stepped up and such immigration was supported and encouraged by the Bangladeshi intellectuals in search of a Lebensraum.

Muslims, the vast majority of whom are of Bangladeshi origin, now form more than one-third of Assam's population. Muslims were 16.23 per cent of Assam's population in 1911. They formed 30.92 per cent in 2001. They have achieved majority in terms of population in 6 out of 23 districts of Assam. Again, illegal Bangladeshi migrants hold sway over 40 out of Assam's 126 legislative assembly constituencies according to an Internal Security Report of the Union Home Ministry. Surprisingly, the Bangladeshi Muslims proclaim Assamese as their 'mother tongue'. They have nominally adopted Assamese as the medium of instruction in schools. However, they never got culturally absorbed into the Assamese mainstream. When the time comes they will probably repudiate both the subterfuges mentioned above. This will happen when the Bangladeshi Muslims became a majority in Assam which seems imminent. The former Governor of Assam, Lt. Gen. S.K. Sinha (Retd.), in his report to the President of India, submitted on 8 November 1998, expressed the fear that unabated influx of Bangladeshis can lead to a severing of the entire land mass of the North-East, with all its rich resources from the rest of the country. This will have disastrous strategic and economic consequences.

The Muslims of north Indian origin, who came to Assam earlier with the Mughal invading armies during the long 600 years of Ahom rule from 1228 to 1826 and remained behind in the Brahmaputra Valley, fully adopted the Assamese language and culture, although retaining the Muslim religion. Some of them were conferred Ahom titles which they use in place of surnames even today. They got some indigenous people also converted into Islam. Their religious leader, Azan Phakir, taught them tolerance towards other religions. Their martial hero, Bagh Hazarika, fought side by side with the Ahom warriors. Their freedom fighter, Bahadur Gaonbura, was banished to *Kalapani* by the British rulers. One President of India (Fakhruddin Ali Ahmed) and one member of the drafting committee of the Indian Constitution (Sir Muhammed Saadullah, who was earlier Prime Minister of British Assam) belonged to the Assamese Muslim community. Similarly, a small number of Sikhs came with the Mughal invaders in the seventeenth century. More Sikhs came to help the Ahoms in their fight against the Burmese invaders in the 1820s. They also remained behind. These Sikhs fully adopted the Assamese language and culture while retaining their religion. They forgot their native Punjabi language.

IMMIGRATION DURING BRITISH DAYS

During the British occupation of Assam in the nineteenth and the twentieth centuries, the British brought some highly educated urban Bengali Hindus to work in their offices and in the educational institutions. When the tea industry was started in the 1830s thousands of indentured labourers were brought from Bengal, Bihar, U.P., Madhya Pradesh and Orissa by the British tea planters to work in the plantations. They now form a sizeable proportion of the state's population and are also politically very active. A small number of Rajasthani traders, Nepali milkmen and Bihari labourers also came in the past two centuries.

CURRENT DEMOGRAPHIC PROFILE

The demographic profile of Assam today presents a mosaic which is rich in cultural diversity and in the profusion of languages, music, dance, drama and the fine arts. Out of the 130 known languages of North-East India the majority are extant in Assam. This amalgam is difficult to comprehend unless the three major historical events I have described above are properly stated and appreciated. In fact, the process of demographic fusion and cohesion which was brought about by Sukapha and Sankardeva continued unabated till the British occupation of Assam in 1826. The process became slow thereafter. But the process has been reversed since 1960s in the wake of Assamese being declared as the state language.

LINGUISTIC STATES

Soon after the new Constitution was promulgated on 26 January 1950, there were agitations in many places for reorganization of states. Potti Sriramulu died in 1952 while on hunger strike demanding formation of Andhra Pradesh. This and a few other incidents led to the appointment of a Boundary Commission in 1952. This Commission, with Sarder K.M. Panikar as the most active member, recommended radical redrawing of state boundaries on the basis of language. Their recommendations were implemented through the States Reorganization Act of 1956. While the Boundary Commission was grappling with its gigantic task, in Assam considerable heat was generated against the demand for transfer of the erstwhile Goalpara district which then consisted of the present districts of Goalpara, Dhubri, Kokrajhar, Bongaigaon and Chirang to West Bengal. Led by Sarat Chandra Sinha (later Chief Minister of Assam) along with Rupnath Brahma, Prakritish Chandra Barua, Khagen Nath, Muhammed

Umaruddin and others a big movement was mounted against this demand. Ultimately, the erstwhile Goalpara district was retained in Assam. When I joined as a young Deputy Commissioner of that huge district, with headquarters at Dhubri, in 1967, the embers of the fire stoked by the movement of a decade ago had not fully died down. Meanwhile, in the process of reorganization of states on the basis of language, the pent up feelings and grievances of ethnic and tribal groups and sub-groups were unleashed. This happened all over India. But it happened in a more intense manner in Assam which was then the only state encompassing the entire North-East (NE) barring Tripura and Manipur which were earlier princely native states and had become union territories after Independence. Later they achieved full statehood.

INSURGENCY AND NEW STATES

In the 1960s far-reaching political changes were made in Assam. Prolonged insurgency in the Naga Hills district, since Independence, led to its separation from Assam and formation of the union territory of Nagaland. Similarly, insurgency in the Lushai Hills district led to its separation from Assam and formation of the union territory of Mizoram. Both these territories achieved full statehood later. In the 1970s the Khasi and Jaintia Hills district and entire Garo Hill district of Assam were joined together to form the autonomous state of Meghalaya, under Article 244A (1) of the Indian Constitution. It achieved full statehood within a short time. The erstwhile North East Frontier Agency was only formally with Assam. It had a separate existence, very strangely, under the Ministry of External Affairs. The Government of India made it into a union territory and later transformed it into the full state of Arunachal Pradesh. In order to achieve co-ordination among the federating units of North-East, the North-East Council was constituted in 1972.

SOCIAL CHANGES

At the same time that the political reorganization was enacted, certain far-reaching changes became discernible in the social sphere. For example, the Assamese language, which had served as the link language for the entire region for centuries, was edged out of this position. Even Nagamese and Arunachalis, which are actually broken Assamese, are being neglected except probably by the All India Radio.

Central financial assistance to Arunachal Pradesh, Meghalaya, Nagaland and Mizoram were stepped up substantially after their separation from Assam. The tribal leaders assumed importance and started enjoying all the constitutional powers and the strappings of office. This was perhaps a historic necessity. But this aroused aspirations in the minds of the other tribal and ethnic groups. The Bodos, for example, organized Plains Tribal Council of Assam (PTCA) and started a movement for a separate state. Some of the Bodo factions became insurgents and started fighting for secession and independence. The Bodos now harbour ill feelings against the ethnic Assamese and do not learn the Assamese language any more. The tea labourers have started abandoning the Assamese language and reviving the Sadri language aided mainly by the Christian missionaries and the NE TV channel. They are also fighting for tribal status. The other tribes and ethnic groups demand separate state or area and have started agitations and even insurgencies. Dima Halongs and Karbis demand upgradation of their autonomous districts into states. Some even demand independence. Several insurgent outfits have surfaced in recent times and hundreds of people have been killed in bomb blasts and grenade attacks in Karbi Anglong and North Cacher Hill districts. Smaller tribes and ethnic groups make similar demands.

The tribal and ethnic groups of Assam have achieved various levels of progress in different spheres. The ethnic Assamese, including Hindus, Muslims, Christians and Sikhs, have also achieved fair to high levels of education and general prosperity. The wealthiest by far, however, are the Marwaris or the Rajasthanis who control the wholesale trade, the tea industry and a sizeable number of private industrial units. They now own most of the prime real estate in Guwahati and other urban centres. The urban Bengali Hindus are as literate and prosperous as the Assamese. But their rural counterparts are not at all well off. Similar is the case with the large communities of Bangladeshi immigrant Muslims and tea garden labourers. Both these communities have low rates of literacy, low landholding and generally low prosperity. Literacy and prosperity rates vary among the other tribal and ethnic groups. At the lowest rung perhaps are the tribes of Karbi Anglong and North Cachar Hill districts. Insurgency also is most virulent and most intense in these two districts.

SPECIAL FINANCIAL ALLOCATIONS

Special efforts have been made by the central and the state governments for the upliftment of the downtrodden communities. Assam's Five Year and Annual Plans, for example, have Hills, Tribal and Scheduled Castes components with separate pre-fixed ratios for weightage to different sections of people. This has been done because according to officials estimates 12.41 per cent of Assam's population belong to the Scheduled Tribes, 6.85 per cent to the Scheduled Castes and approximately 27 per cent to the other backward classes. Large sums are allocated to the Autonomous District Councils and the tribal and ethnic councils, both under Plan and under Non-Plan heads. Development Corporations have been established for the Minorities, Scheduled Castes, Scheduled Tribes and Other Backward Classes. However, the results have not been commensurate nor have the targets been achieved. There are clamours for more funds while allocated funds are not properly utilized.

POLITICAL REORGANIZATION (1990-2009)

Assam after separation of Nagaland, Mizoram, Meghalaya and Arunachal Pradesh, resulted in a series of agitations, disturbances and destructions which rend asunder the cohesion and unity among different sections of society in the state. With the object of quelling such disturbances, innovative but mind boggling political and administrative arrangements have been arrived at in the past two decades. This has resulted in a decentralization of power in a rather peculiar and haphazard manner. These arrangements came in several doses of ad hoc political decisions without any general debate on the issues concerned or examination of the pros and cons of the solutions evolved. In the process even the recommendations of the Bhupinder Singh Committee appointed in this behalf were ignored. Actually these ad hoc decisions were taken to subserve political expediency. Since their implications were not properly studied or discussed before implementation certain inscrutable problems have now surfaced. In fact, units have come up with disputed jurisdictions and varied configurations of financial, legislative and administrative endowments. This has been done through constitutional amendments in some cases and statutory enactments in others. Even executive orders have brought about such units. The pattern that has emerged consists of the following:

(1) The two autonomous districts of Karbi Anglong and North Cachar Hills were formed in stages since 1950 under the provisions of the Sixth Schedule of the Indian Constitution. They have wide administrative and some legislative powers. But law and order remained with the state government. It may be recalled that the process of recognition of sub-nationalism in the NE started with the drafting of the Indian Constitution. On the basis of the recommendations of the Committee, appointed by the Constituent Assembly and headed by Bharat Ratna Gopinath Bordoloi, the Sixth Schedule was incorporated in the Constitution with the object of protecting the tribal people, their rights and their particular way of life. To these two hill districts, the third addition has been the Bodoland Territorial Autonomous Districts (BTAD), formed in stages during the past few years, with powers exercised under the Sixth Schedule of the Constitution by the Bodoland Territorial Council (BTC). It has jurisdiction over the four administrative districts of Kokrajhar, Chirang, Baksa and Udalguri. BTC has wide executive and some legislative powers, except for law and order.

(2) Six tribal councils were formed for the Mishings, Rabha-Hasongs, Tiwas, Deories, Sonowal Kacharis and Thengal Kacharis along with the non-staturory council for the Barak Valley tribes. Recently an eighth tribal council for the Amri

Karbis, who live in the periphery of the city of Guwahati and who are not recognized as tribals in the plains, has also been announced.

(3) Seven ethnic development councils are presently in the process of formation. These will be for the Morans, Motoks, Ahoms, Chutias, Koch-Rajbongshis, Adibasis (also called Tea Tribes) and Gorkhas. These ethnic groups have been demanding tribal status for a long time. In fact, the Koch-Rajbongshis were once declared as tribals by an ordinance. But the ordinance was allowed to lapse. It never became an Act of Parliament. The demand for tribal status to any of these groups has not been agreed to by the Government of India as yet. Only Sarania Kacharis have been newly included in the list of tribes. The state government has promised a new council for the Saranias.

KACHARI LAND AND TRIBAL STATE

On 19 February 2009 a significant event took place when a number of organizations and tribal and ethnic students' unions congregated in Guwahati's ITA Auditorium and passed a resolution demanding a tribal state by carving out certain Assam territories to be named as Kachariland. They claimed to represent 18 tribes. This was indeed a momentous resolution in which all tribals are supposed to have united. Another development has been the demand for a 'tribal state'. This concept has not been defined properly. But the Communist Party of India in their 2009 election manifesto have included this demand reportedly because if Assam is declared as a tribal state, the people of the state would have reservations in the State Assembly and Parliament. More autonomy for Assam has been demanded in the same line as Jammu & Kashmir under Article 370 and Nagaland under Article 371A of the Indian Constitution.

CONSEQUENCES OF REORGANIZATION

The persistence of tribal, ethnic and linguistic differences and the coming into existence of so many tiers of governmental organizations have really complicated the political scene in Assam. In most other states of India at least the overwhelming majority of population belongs to one group. This facilitates political cohesion and economic development. The absence of such integration in Assam has been a cause of concern.

The latest estimates show that the Assamese Hindus comprise only 29.30 per cent of the state's population. This has serious implications. To quote Ishani, a news magazine published by Nagaland Gandhi Ashram, 'the threat perception for the Asomiyas in Assam is that from time to time some of the ethnic communities of the state exclude themselves from the unofficial term "indigenous Asomiyas," and if this alienation of the groups cannot be erased, the future of Asomiyas will be bleak in Assam'. The Muslims, including both Assamese and Bangladeshi Muslims, form 30.14 per cent of the population. The rest of the population consist of 13.19 per cent Bengali Hindus, 5.16 per cent Bodos, 9.58 per cent Adibasis, 1.53 per cent Karbis, 1.76 per cent Nepalis, 1.70 per cent Mishings, 2.07 per cent Koch-Rajbongshis, 0.35 per cent Dimasas and 4.95 per cent others. The existence of so many tribes and ethnic groups and their unfulfilled political aspirations has led to unrest and insurgency. Even the grant of autonomy at sub state level has not fully satisfied the tribal and ethnic leaders. The minor party *apparatchiks* and political agitationists seem to have a vested interest in keeping the tribal and ethnic groups isolated mainly for their own political ambition and monetary gains. Some of these groups, specially the Bangladeshi Muslims, are used as 'vote banks' by the political party in power.

The tribal and ethnic councils demand more power and more money. Already media reports suggest rampant misuse of grants, non-maintenance of accounts and siphoning off of funds by politicians, bureaucrats, contractors and their cohorts. It is also alleged that substantial funds are diverted to insurgent outfits. In April 2009, police arrested a couple of persons carrying Rs. 1 crore to a Dimasa insurgent outfit which the Chief Executive Member (CEM) of the North Cachar Hills Autonomous District Council had drawn from the government treasury and had sent to the insurgent outfit. The CEM is now absconding. Meanwhile, the administrative control and decision-making processes have been complicated by the existence of so many units of different types with varying powers and confusing jurisdictions. This has adversely affected the delivery system for economic development. Actually the system itself has become fragmented.

ISSUES AND PROBLEMS OF REORGANIZATION

The political reorganization of Assam with autonomous, tribal and ethnic councils cannot be considered to be final because in the present arrangement many problems have been left unresolved. These are now begging for solution. In Bodoland, for example, many villages have been included where there is no or little Bodo population. These areas have been included only in order to achieve four territorial contiguity. Moreover, non-Bodos are in majority in three out of Bodoland's four districts. There is considerable resentment among the non-Bodo inhabitants of Bodoland. Again, the reservation of seats in the BTC does not reflect the population pattern of Bodoland. The 40 elected seats in BTC, out of a total of 46, are distributed as follows: 30 for tribals, 5 for non-tribal communities and 5 open for all communities. The remaining 6 seats are filled up by nomination by the Governor. This arrangement is not democratic because it debars non-Bodo communities from proportionate representation. This apparently undemocratic arrangement had to be resorted to in order to satisfy the Bodos. There are a large number of Bodos who live outside Bodoland. They have no special rights or benefits unlike their compatriots inside Bodoland. What irks the Bodos most is the fact that Bodos living in Assam's hill districts are not recognized as tribals. This is anomalous.

There have been many cases of attempted ethnic cleansing inside Bodoland. The victims are the indigenous Koch-Rajbongshis and the immigrant Bangladeshi Muslims who form large groups of Bodoland's population. The legitimate question that is being asked is: How can the indigenous people be uprooted from their own homeland? Where will they go? And, why will they go? These are questions which will have to be answered clearly. In the case of Bangladeshi Muslims it is true that they illegally migrated to the areas, which now form Bodoland, in the past few decades. They are apprehensive about eviction from land which they have occupied for long. Many of them have encroached upon government land including land in the reserved forests and the national parks. Some of them have bought land in tribal belts and blocks. Such transactions are illegal, being prohibited by law. Several thousand Bangladeshi Muslims from BTAD are in relief camps. These people were uprooted following ethnic violence. Their problems need to be addressed boldly.

The Koch-Rajbongshis are the unhappy lot. They are indigenous Hindu people of lower Assam. Their language is Assamese. A Koch dynasty ruled in lower Assam and north Bengal for centuries. The Koch King, Naranarayana, gave shelter to Sankardeva and helped the great saint to spread his religion and culture. Naranarayana and his brother, General Chilarai, rebuilt the Kamakhya Temple about five hundred years ago. The stone statues of the two brothers adorn the ante chamber of the temple. Chilarai married Sankardeva's niece. The Koch-Rajbongshis have two main demands: tribal status and Kamatapur state. As has been already stated they had been given tribal status by an ordinance. But curiously enough the ordinance was allowed to lapse and never became an Act of Parliament. Their demand for a Kamatapur state has equal weightage as the demand for a state of Bodoland. But if Kamatapur is conceded the present boundaries of Bodoland will probably undergo a change.

The total population of Scheduled Tribes in Assam, in the 2001 census, has been estimated to be 33,08,570 forming 12.41 per cent of the state's population. This is wrong. The actual tribal population will be much more because lakhs of Bodos in the hills and Amri Karbi and other such groups in the plains are not considered to be tribals and are left out. Moreover, the demands of Ahoms, Motoks, Adibasis, Morans, Chutias and Gorkhas, beside Koch-Rajbongshis, for tribal status will also need to be seriously considered. This will increase the number of tribals.

PANCHAYATI RAJ INSTITUTIONS

At the grassroots, the autonomous tribal and ethnic councils seem to be in conflict with the Panchayati Raj Institutions (PRI) in the plains and certain traditional tribal councils in the hills. In the hills the traditional councils used to wield considerable power. These are extra-constitutional and extra-statutory bodies. But some intellectuals and tribal experts have romantic ideas about them. There is also an attempt to see their continued existence to be sanctified by the provisions of Article 40 of the Constitution. But it is forgotten that there is no express provision in the Constitution, neither in any of the main Articles nor in the Fifth or the Sixth Schedules, which would allow continuance or revival of these tribal councils. These councils are not democratic but feudal, hereditary and oligarchic institutions. They exclude women, tenant farmers, wage labourers and poor people. They are an anachronism in a democratic country. Again, under normal circumstances neither the tribal councils nor the ethnic councils should be allowed to replace or substitute the PRIs which are democratic entities under Article 243 in Part IX of the Indian Constitution. PRIs never existed in the hill districts of Assam and have been recently abolished from Bodoland areas. The leaders of tribal and ethnic councils do not want PRIs in their jurisdiction. In the Rava-Hasong area, for example, tribals prevented election to PRIs. This led to riots in which several people were killed. How to reconcile the aspirations of tribal and ethnic groups and the necessity of PRIs at the grassroots level is a moot question which must be addressed in the proper perspective and a solution evolved for maintaining unity of the people and integrity of the state.

It may be appropriate to recall here that taking advantage of the ethnic and sub-national grievances, a very large number of insurgent outfits have made their appearance in Assam. The political reorganization of the state as described earlier has been made with a view to curb such insurgencies. However, further administrative reforms will be necessary to take care of the problems which have been mentioned in this paper. Political acumen in bringing about reforms in the structures of the sub-federal and sub-state units, which have been constituted recently, and their integration with PRIs, will determine whether long-term peace and tranquillity can be achieved. A considerable amount of fine tuning will be absolutely essential. Meanwhile, more problems have been created by appointment of executive councils with members who support the political party in power. Elections have not been held. There is no indication when elections would be held and who would form the electorate. The preparation of electoral rolls itself will be a difficult exercise. Finally, there is a proposal to have a legislative council at the apex level representing all tribal and ethnic groups in the state beside the usual special interest categories of citizens. This proposal was opposed by many experts on the subject. I feel, however, that it needs to be examined with special reference to the ethnic problems.

CHAPTER 9

Development of Assam: A Strategic Perspective

Rangan Dutta

The meaning of the word 'strategy' originated from the Greek word *strategos*, which signifies the art of planning and directing military activity in war. It also came to mean a plan designed to achieve a particular aim or objective. The current usage of the word 'strategy' in corporate affairs is unfortunate because, 'strategy' relates essentially to statecraft/statesmanship. Therefore, it is appropriate to consider some developmental issues as 'strategic' for analytical and prescriptive purposes. On the other hand, the word 'development' has always been more problematic. It is now agreed that 'development' does not only mean material development in terms of growth of income, gross domestic product or even by quality of life measured by indicators such as life expectancy at birth, health care, education facilities, job, income security, and access to clean water and air. Behind all efforts to secure these components for citizens, as Amartya Sen aptly suggested, enhancing human capabilities and human entitlements should logically become the overriding developmental objective of any polity committed to democracy, social justice and equity. Amit Bhaduri's idea of development with dignity with provision of gainful employment as the main objective of management of the economy goes hand-in-hand with Sen's concept of development as freedom. Though these ideas may first appear somewhat esoteric, this paper contends that in the context of Assam's huge diversity, geo-strategic position, natural resource endowments, ecological and environment challenges, the concept of 'development' has to be viewed in a broadest sense possible. Development should be seen as a product and an 'inclusive process' with an objective of raising human capabilities. Development should also enhance skill-set of people and empower them to confront the diverse challenges that Assam confronts today.

The initial two sub-sections of this paper deal with the geo-strategic position of Assam in the post-1971 period, and the state's development experience in the context of numerous opportunities and challenges. The remaining three sections will identify strategic issues of development including institutional reforms, which are essential to raise the human capabilities. The enhancement of human capabilities will ensure that development process becomes inclusive, endogenous, and sustainable with knowledge and capacity building acting as engines of growth.

GEO-STRATEGIC POSITION OF ASSAM

Assam is often lyrically described as that part of India through which the mighty river Brahmaputra flows down to Bangladesh. The mighty river does not flow quietly, as during floods it submerges annually 3.15 million hectares of land threatening over 90 per cent of seasonal crops, mainly rice. The floods have many negative consequences such as changing the courses of the tributaries and eroding vast tracts of fertile land estimated annually at 15,000 hectares (3.86 lakh hectares of agricultural land has been eroded so far). Flanked by Eastern Himalayas, Naga Hills, Khasi-Jaintia Hills and Karbi Anglong district, the Brahmaputra Valley has large tracts of land found suitable for tea plantation in the foothills and uplands. The three Barak Valley districts in south-east Assam also have similar agro-climatic situation and substantial tea plantation. Rich in biodiversity, the population density is low by Indian standards (340/sq km) though the two valleys are thickly populated. Geography, history and more significantly politics of the twentieth century have given Assam its unique geo-strategic position in South Asia. This unique geo-strategic position has also thrown up enormous challenges to the development and security. These are summarized below.

Independence and Partition of India in 1947 left the erstwhile province of Assam truncated. The major portion of the rich and populous district of Sylhet was transferred to Pakistan and creation of Pakistan robbed Assam of its traditional rail–road links to Calcutta and Chittagong ports. Overnight Assam and the entire North-East region became 'land locked' and its security became critically dependent on Indo-Pak relations. Partition converted obscure district boundaries into international frontiers and gave inevitably some leverage and opportunity to Pakistan to meddle with ethnic problems of the North-East. Pakistan's support to Naga and Mizo insurgencies in the 1960s became a recurring feature. Unfortunately, some elements in Bangladesh seem to be keen to continue this hostile attitude.

The twentieth century was in several ways unkind to Assam. The Partition of Bengal in 1906 caused loss of her political identity as it became a part of the larger province of Eastern Bengal and Assam with its capital at Dacca. The annulment of the Partition in 1911 restored her status as a Chief Commissioner's province, which was upgraded subsequently to a regular province. The events following independence brought about significant changes with the creation of North East Frontier Agency (NEFA) in 1954 and separation of Naga Hills District from Assam in 1962. The reorganization of North Eastern Region under the North East Areas Reorganisation Act 1971, led to upgradation of the sub-state of Meghalaya created in 1969 into a full-fledged state and separation of the Mizo Hills district which was accorded union territory status under this Act and later in 1986 granted full statehood. The NEFA which was taken out of Assam was formally severed from Assam under the aforesaid Act as a union territory and granted full statehood in 1986. After the reorganization of North-East, Assam became the only state in India that shares borders with six states of the union. To complicate matters, Assam's borders with neighbouring states are largely undemarcated with attendant problems and grounds for misunderstanding, often obstructing cooperation for development.

The other momentous event for Assam's security and development was occupation of Tibet by China in 1950 and the flight of Dalai Lama to India in 1959. The 1962 border conflict with China and the persistent Chinese claims to Arunachal Pradesh have created an uneasy border. The extension of rail link to Lhasa and its proposed extension to a location close to Sikkim is being viewed by experts as a Chinese strategic initiative which has considerably reduced the Chinese response time to deploy forces and armour to India's border area. This development has added a new dimension to the security scenario.

ETHNIC POLITICS, INSTITUTIONAL FRAMEWORKS AND FRAGMENTATION

As if all these were not enough, the simmering inter 'ethnic and linguistic' conflicts in post-1971 Assam saw no signs of waning. The Bodoland Territorial Council (BTC) was created under the Sixth Schedule of the Constitution and further enhancement of its powers was done in 2003 to deal with 40 subjects. Constitutional changes were made to enhance the powers and responsibilities of the existing autonomous Hill District Councils of Karbi Anglong and North Cachar Hills which empowered them to deal with 30 subjects. All these measures made these three Autonomous Areas *de facto*, sub-states and in effect political entities practically freed from any control of either the state government or the state legislature. The crucial amendments which brought about this transformation have been either ignored deliberately in the media or have passed unnoticed. For instance, the implications of the dilution of the word 'district' by a constitutional amendment in defining Karbi Anglong and North Cachar Hills Autonomous Councils has removed the subordinate tag of being one among other districts. This underscores the autonomous character of these districts and it has gone unnoticed. Similarly, the grant of power of 'Superintendence and Control' to the Chief Executive Member (CEM) of BTC in respect of law and order responsibilities discharged by the deputy commissioners of districts under BTC areas has placed the CEM at a level which would in practice preclude any direct issuance of the order of the state government to the District Officers in law and order matters.

This ensures a role for the CEM in what is essentially a substantive function of the state.

In this background, creation of five autonomous councils under the state laws, mentioned below, for ethnic groups like Rabha Hasongs, Mishings, Thengal Kacharis, Sonowal Kacharis, Tiwas and Deuris would appear to support forces inimical to the growth of a composite Assamese socio-political identity.

The Assam State Law for creation of 5 Autonomous Councils are:

1. The Mishing Autonomous Councils Act, 1995.
2. The Rabha Hasong Autonomous Councils Act, 1995.
3. The Lalung Tiwas Autonomous Councils Act, 1995.
4. The Deuri Autonomous Councils Act, 2005.
5. The Sonowal Kachari Autonomous Councils Act, 2005

There is strength in the demand for an institutional framework for preservation of socio-cultural identity of tribal or other such ethnic groups. However, measures like autonomy go further and recognize them as 'geopolitical minorities'—defined as groups which are minorities in the state but 'majorities' in areas where they primarily inhabit. Demands for a Sixth Schedule status would logically follow with recognition of 'geopolitical minorities'. As of now, these initiatives have deepened the existing divisions in the civil society and created a feeling of insecurity among those who do not belong to the dominant ethnic group in a council area. The economic role of 'the other people' as consumers, investors and taxpayers and therefore, as contributors to the local and state economy cannot be brushed aside for the progress and well-being of the region. Thus policies and actions are warranted to harmonize the interests of all groups which in practice is easier said than done. This is because the urge to monopolize power and privileges has been always proven to be irresistible. The continuing ethnic unrest in Bodoland proves this point and the reported assertion of H. Mahilari, CEM, that 'the BTC model should be the first step towards formation of separate state' is only adding to the feeling of insecurity among the 'non-Bodos' an unhappy term though, as it reflects neatly the status of 'the other' people.

The impact of all these political experiments made Assam a deeply fragmented state. Even after the 1971 reorganization, Assam is the only state with three autonomous councils under the Sixth Schedule of the Constitution and five other autonomous councils. Given the ethnic, religious and linguistic divisions existing in areas outside these councils, at least three groups would qualify for recognition as geopolitical minorities. These are the immigrant Muslims in west and central Assam districts of Nagaon, Morigaon, Barpeta and Dhubri, the Tea Labour Community in parts of Upper Assam and three Bengali-speaking districts of Barak Valley. Though the political and administrative power rests with the Assamese Hindu elite, the Assamese language has ceased to enjoy the absolute majority status in 2001 census. This naturally entails a complex act of balancing the interests of all diverse groups without upsetting the apple cart. This paper tries to argue that given the history of ethnic conflicts in the state, since the early 1960s, any further political division in any form would render Assam ungovernable. Further political division of Assam would raise the costs of the union government in terms of various subventions, grants, etc., to an unacceptable level and may eventually turn the entire North-East Region (NER) into another 'Balkan Peninsula'. This fear and argument have some basis. With eight states including Sikkim, nine autonomous councils under the Sixth Schedule and scores of other autonomous councils vying for statehood like the Darjeeling Gorkha Hills Council, the North-East is indeed a deeply divided region. Being flanked by China, a great power, populous Bangladesh and unstable Myanmar, the region is prone to interference from neighbouring countries, as they will be keen to capitalize on internal differences and weaknesses. Since Assam is the lead state in the region on which the regional economy and communication systems depend, a strong and a developed Assam is a strategic requirement for India's progress. A strong and developed Assam will not only stabilize India but will enhance its capability to play a significant and a decisive role in South-East Asia and the Bay of Bengal region. This imperative calls for a complete stop to further political break-up of Assam either directly by grant of statehood or indirectly by grant of autonomy. This is not difficult and indeed perfectly feasible. There is a need to de-incentivize such demands, because grant of statehood or even autonomy means huge financial costs for the centre, as it involves attractive pay packages, perquisites, posts and privileges for the new political classes. These new job opportunities not generally related to the workload, as the minimum size of a state legislature or the administrative set-up has been laid down either in the Constitution or by conventions. In fact, such deconstruction of existing states and grant of statehood to small states that was allowed in the North-East since 1971 has triggered such demands elsewhere and more stridently in the North-East. This must stop now in the larger interest of the country because it takes away scarce central revenues for unproductive expenses. The deconstruction of existing states, as recent history shows, creates dissensions among ethnic groups, fuels demands for autonomy from smaller ethnic groups unhappy with the treatment meted out to them by the politically dominant ethnic group and 'generates refugees' as in Bodoland. Thus, a firm declaration from the central government that no such demands would be entertained might bring about an environment congenial to stability and even cooperation among the North-East states and communities.

RESOURCES, TRADE AND DEVELOPMENT

The strategic importance of Assam is based on three crucial factors. First, it is a resource rich state, as it is endowed with roughly 10 per cent of India's hydrocarbon potential (oil and gas), coal, limestone, forest resources notably bamboo (13.41 per cent of total stock). Second, it is the facilitating state for exploitation of huge hydel potential estimated at 40,000-50,000 MW in the mountains of Arunachal Pradesh and minerals in other Hill states, as the transport/transmission lines for movement of end products have to necessarily pass through Assam. Third, its landmass is critical for ecology and environment of sub-Himalayan and Ganga-Brahmaputra-Meghna basin cutting across state and national boundaries. The flood mitigation efforts in Brahmaputra and Barak Valley or reduction of forest cover in upper reaches of Brahmaputra or construction of large hydel projects in the hills produce environment threats to Bangladesh. Conservation of biodiversity and forests in Assam and Meghalaya, therefore, directly bring about manifold benefits to Bangladesh. As the world grapples with challenges of climate change mitigation, the prospects of earning carbon credits in Assam from developing forests in waste or fallow lands as an alternative to unviable, flood prone seasonal cropping may be seen as highly practicable. This may with some planning, put Assam in a high priority area for ecological security in the sub-region and to attract 'carbon credits' on a large scale.

The Eleventh Plan document of the Planning Commission on the NER observed that 'the development efforts of the States have to be supplemented in order to minimize certain distinct geophysical and historical constraints'. This observation is in broad agreement with the approach mentioned here. However, political sensitivity and complexity of development challenges of Assam has stood in the way of frank appraisal of certain irreversible geographical disadvantages being faced by Assam. The preferred euphemism is 'isolation'—of Assam and the rest of North-East which inadequately states the constraint. The fact is that Assam is not just 'Bangladesh locked'. Except its south-west part, the rest of Assam is geographically far away from the sea coast. It must be stressed here that 75 per cent of the earth's population lives in the area within 200 miles of the sea coast. Since the beginning of mercantile period, port cities and towns along the coast had the most advanced centres of commodity trade, exchange, institutions of higher learning and therefore were instrumental in spread of ideas. As a consequence, since the mercantile period the port cities and towns tended to be power centres. Even today, thanks to development of highly cost-efficient shipping technology, 90 per cent of global merchandise commerce and 65 per cent of oil move by merchant navy. Therefore, it is dirt cheap sea-transport, not just jet or information technology, which has brought about 'globalization'. In the post-liberalization period, states along the east and the west coast of India have achieved consistently high growth rate which goes to support this point. Such locational disadvantage and the fact that the cost of sea transport is a fraction of road or rail transport, rules out any labour-intensive low-cost and export-oriented industrial growth model for Assam and the rest of the North-East. No amount of subsidies in this region could ever create or sustain a model for faster economic growth. The prospects of an agricultural surplus led prosperity are not discernible due to adverse and recurring natural calamities like annual flooding, adverse agro-climatic conditions, increasing fragmentation of farm operational holdings and sadly, lack of technological solutions to many pressing problems of crop growth, plant diseases and post-harvest technology.

Since trade and development are integrally connected, the availability of economic space is crucial. Historically, 'surplus' generated in any economy is meant to be sold where it fetches the highest price. The level of the local demand and the size of external market determine the surplus. Therefore, the small size of regional and local markets have forced Assam's economy to export surplus produce like tea, jute, plywood, and horticultural produce to neighbouring markets in eastern India and overseas. Denial of access to Chittagong port after Partition was damaging since it substantially raised the cost of transport of tea and other export commodities. Equally harmful was the loss of a natural Eastern Bengal market for Assam's horticultural and other merchandise. Search for an alternative and easily accessible market has not been easy. The entire scheme of transport subsidy for moving inputs and outputs has not been able to neutralize the adverse effects of market losses or high transport and associated costs in this region. Despite massive central support, the roots of stagnation in Assam and the rest of North-East economy can be traced to this reality. The North-East Vision 2020 document prepared by the North Eastern Council and the Ministry for Development of North-East Region (DONER) gives the impression as if the region stands by itself as an economic zone and opening up of the trade-transit-rail-road communication links through Bangladesh would remove obstacles to development. This is a delusion, because Bangladesh in her present mood, considers grant of transit facility as her trump card. Bangladesh's relations with India and her past refusal to allow construction of a pipeline for transporting Tripura gas through Bangladesh is indicative of her policy to use such moves as leverage against India to extract some advantages. However, if South Asia Free Trade Association (SAFTA) materializes, things may change. Till then, strategically positioning Assam's economy in the Eastern region continues to deserve a higher priority. This is all the more important now, because since the 1990s economies of West Bengal and Orissa have been making rapid progress. While Orissa surged from 2.1 per cent growth in the Eighth Plan to 5.1 per cent in the Ninth and 9.1 per cent in the Tenth Plan, West Bengal registered a steady growth at 6.3, 6.9 and 6.1 per cent in the Eighth, Ninth and Tenth Plan periods respectively. Bihar also seems to be getting out of low growth trap and achieved 4 and 4.7 per cent growth in the last two plans. Markets in the east are therefore, expanding offering opportunities for all states especially the neighbouring Assam and rest of the North-East. Equally significant has been the success of Bangladesh in climbing what Jeffrey Sachs called 'the ladder of development' by raising agricultural output and successfully adopting a labour-intensive export-led growth model especially in the garments industry. Bangladesh, perceived as a poverty-stricken country in Assam, now enjoys a per capita income of US$ 460, which is well ahead of Assam. This, however, shows an expanding market in Bangladesh for possible exports from Assam and therefore must be strategized in policy formulation for integration of Assam economy into the broader regional economy. This has been stressed emphatically in the strategy report of the World Bank on North-East (2006), where it states that 'geography is economic destiny'. The World Bank highlights the imperative of resumption of durable economic ties and cooperation of NER with Bangladesh and other neighbouring states.

In this environment, examination of Assam's development experience from the 1970s till the Tenth Plan has been disquieting, characterized by continuity with little structural changes. Assam entered the plan era during the Second World War, and initially it experienced economic growth, infrastructural boom, productive agriculture, a per capita income well above the national average, and a flourishing tea and jute trade. However, economy of Assam started to lag behind from the 1960s as the 'partition effect' came to be increasingly pronounced, which was compounded by floods, erosion, poor governance, and tribal unrest. Further, failure to introduce either 'Green Revolution' or industrial development to meet the demands of Assam's increasing youthful population had a negative impact on the economy of Assam. However, the need for creation of a local middle class, professionals, civil servants and improvement of physical and social infrastructure like roads, electricity, flood control, and educational institutions were critical to counter such economic downturn. Given such constraint, the economic resurgence of Assam should come from the tertiary sector by strengthening its population through knowledge skills. Even in 2001, urban areas contained only 12.4 per cent of population against the all-India average of about 28 per cent. A fairly high literacy rate of 64 per cent (Male 72 per cent and female 56 per cent) despite the state's high percentage of Muslim and SC/ST population shows success in the literacy drive. However, while the Indian economy moved on to a higher growth path in 1980-2000 at an annual growth rate of 6 per cent, Assam's GDP grew only at 3.3 per cent. In the Eighth and the Ninth Plan, Assam's economy grew at measly rates of 2.8 and 2.1 per cent respectively, hardly exceeding the population growth. Agriculture stagnated as the actual average farm operational holding came down below 1.31 ha as against the all-India average of 1.71 ha due to increase in sharecropping and tenancy. The prolonged agitation on the 'foreigners' issue must have adversely affected the Plan implementation, but the fact remains that Assam has missed two decades of growth opportunities even though it had received generous grant of central support in all forms such as central assistance on 90 per cent grant and 10 per cent loan basis as a 'special category state' and other dispensations from the Government of India and the Planning Commission. Restoration of political stability and initiatives of the state to recover the lost ground yielded positive results in the Tenth Plan as the state could achieve 6.1 per cent annual growth rate missing the 6.2 per cent target by a whisker.

A remarkable achievement of the state has been in the area of poverty reduction both rural and urban. According to the Government of India (GOI) economic survey data of 2007-8, the percentage of population Below Poverty Line (BPL) in Assam was 19.7 per cent well below the national average of 27.5 per cent. The BPL population in Assam is also comparatively lower as compared with other leading states such as Maharashtra (30.7 per cent), Tamil Nadu (22.5 per cent), Karnataka (25 per cent). The proportion of BPL is the lowest in Assam among the major eastern states. Assam has been able to reduce the urban poverty to 7.47 per cent. That the recent development efforts have made some impact and it is reflected in human development indicators of the state. According to the Planning Commission, human development indicators of Assam are comparable with the rest of the country.

The per capita Gross State Domestic Product (GSDP), however, continues to be low at Rs. 18,172 (2004-5 prices) and Assam holds 15th position among 18 major states. This is not surprising, as the 'lost' development decades caused stagnation in all sectors as evident from the following facts:

1. The primary sector grew at 1.2 per cent during 1993-4 to 2002-3 much below the national average of 3.6 per cent and agriculture, the mainstay of the rural economy, grew marginally at 1 per cent.
2. Sluggish growth of agriculture is seen in low rice yield (1.3 MT/ha from a gross cropped area of 22 lakh ha compared to the national average of 1.9 MT/ha), low fertilizer use (28 kg/ha of NPK against the national average of 113 kg/ha; these figures for Bihar and U.P. are 105 and 188 kg per ha). Though cropping intensity, thanks to high soil moisture is 146. Only 14.3 per cent of the net cropped area is irrigated, which limits the application of Green Revolution technology. The rural incomes both from farm and non-farm sectors have thus remained low, which constrains growth of rural demand-driven industries that took place elsewhere particularly in U.P., Punjab and Haryana. And this has restricted the growth of the service sector as well as development of urban areas.

The state is thus unable to participate in urban led growth strategy that has transformed north-west India and enabled some regions to move to high growth path. The composition of GSDP thus shows the profile of a state struggling to make a beginning towards 'modernization' with a high share of Primary Sector (38.5 per cent) against 18 per cent share of agriculture and allied sector in the national economy (which fell from 26 per cent at the beginning of the Tenth Plan). Assam's economy has a low of share of secondary sector (15 per cent) including 9.4 per cent of manufacturing compared to 26 per cent of the national economy. The tertiary sector in Assam provides the balance 46.5 per cent of state GSDP. Public administration, banking and insurance contribute about 12 per cent of the service sector which indicates the dominance of state or state-led services in the economy. Growth rate of registered manufacturing in Assam, in the above period, was 1 per cent though the average growth of small-scale industry (SSI) was 5.93 per cent. The base is still small as the value of total out put of SSI was Rs. 3302 crore, and the SSI employed about 4.29 lakh workers. Assam has 1.20 per cent of all registered factories in India.

3. Flow of institutional credit to the Assam economy has been static, fluctuating between a credit-deposit ratio of 33 per cent in 1997-8 and 35 per cent in 2004-5. In 2007, Assam received Rs. 9,461 crore bank credit from public sector banks as per the Economic Survey of Government of India (2007-8), which is the lowest among major states, and even Jharkhand (10,560 crore) and Chhattisgarh (11,099 crore) received a larger bank credit than Assam. This explains the slow growth of the private sector, state's own revenues and total dependence on the central government for development finance. Without going into the details of central funding of the state plan, the fact is that the per capita central assistance for Assam in the year 2006-7as a special category state was Rs. 1,130.83 in the Tenth Plan as against Rs. 570.40, which is the average for non-special category states in the same year.*

* *Eleventh Five Year Plan*, vol. 1, Chapter 7, Annex. 7.2, GOI, Planning Commission.

The total Central Assistance (CA) to Assam in the Tenth Plan was Rs. 12,842.93 crore which confirms critical dependence on the centre. The centre also annually funds the state for implementation of Central Sector Schemes in the state. In 2007-8, Assam received about Rs. 1,983 crore for implementation of five such schemes—Prime Minister's Gram Sadak Yojana (PMGSY), Sarba Shiksha Abhiyan (SSA), National Rural Health Mission (NRHM), Indira Awas Yojana (IAY) and Supplementary Nutrition.

In the aforesaid position, the outcome of five decades of development experience reflects the stark reality—Assam stands excluded from real growth process because it still lacks the physical, institutional and knowledge base on which to build the new economy. There is an inadequate appreciation of structural deficiencies and geo-strategic realities. Therefore, there is a need to identify the core strategic issues, if unaddressed will keep Assam in a state of delusion—that is growth without development and worse still growth with 'path dependence' defined brilliantly in the strategy report of the World Bank as 'the tendency of a community or a region to continue along the path it is already following'.

ECOLOGY, EDUCATION, TECHNOLOGY AND ECONOMIC TRANSFORMATION

The Eleventh Five Year Plan document contains some new features. The first volume of the Plan document is devoted to enunciation of the concept of inclusive growth in the Indian context, spatiality and the need to institutionalize and build spatiality into development programmes. Chapter 7 of this document dealing with 'spatial development and regional imbalances, which recognizes possibly for the first time, what foreign and Indian analysts have been mentioning for quite some time—the growing regional divide in economic and social development. The section on NER of this chapter has laid strong emphasis on the following three aspects of North-East development (as Assam is the anchor state of NER, all these points are relevant to Assam).

1. The NER forms an area of low per capita income and requires major growth impetus.
2. The region is deficit in physical infrastructure, which is having a negative multiplier effect on economic development.
3. Growth in social infrastructure through national programmes must be complemented by development of physical and economic infrastructure.

The first point is contradicted elsewhere in the chapter which shows that the per capita GSDP of all seven Hill and smaller North-East states has been well above the GSDP of a number of major states. The overemphasis on infrastructure gives an impression that in the planners' view, infrastructural growth means development. This is not borne out by experience because it imposes a huge maintenance cost on the states and therefore unless it is backstopped by economic growth which depends mainly on the creation of growth-inducing institutions and not just sound policies, the infrastructure will not pay for itself. The poor state of major roads in Assam constructed with central funds bears testimony to this fact. The strategic development issue, therefore, is how to get 'value for money' from investments made. In this pursuit, the 'human capital' is most important in terms of capability enhancement. This major growth factor is reflected in many ways—entrepreneurship development, quality of products and service delivery which together generate a multiplier effect on Assam's development processes. There cannot be any set pattern for all these to happen to lift Assam from the clutches of underdevelopment. However, the Indian growth story since opening up of the economy in 1990s indicates that urbanization and rapid diffusion of scientific and technological entrepreneurship and management skills have enabled much of peninsular India, coastal states, National Capital Region and its adjacent territories to attain a high growth path. The infrastructure base created on a special footing has been self-sustaining and played a critical role in the above regions. Keen observers of Indian development have pointed out that under typical patterns of economic development, countries or areas tend to go through labour intensive manufacturing cycles before they specialize. But in India, some fast growing states or areas have skipped this stage and moved 'directly to skill and capital intensive industries (within manufacturing) or in services where they appear to have a comparative advantage'. According to a 2006 IMF working paper, Delhi, Karnataka and Maharashtra have in this way quickly moved with the information technology wave in their cities and realized faster growth. This has been possible because, these areas enjoyed a headstart in science and technology and management education. A good number of world class S&T and R&D institutions of India have been functioning in these states. It must be mentioned here that the crucial decision of the central government to establish, on strategic grounds, nuclear facilities, space research facilities, aircraft industries, electronic industries, heavy industries in defence related activities, and associated scientific research and educational institutions in a big way have contributed significantly to this growth process in peninsular India. Delhi and neighbouring areas have been also the preferred location for national S&T institutions, seats of learning and management skill development. The Eleventh Plan has recognized this reality by stating emphatically that 'scientific knowledge and expertise, innovation, high technology industrial infrastructure and skilled workforce are the currencies of this new era'.

The strategic issues for development of Assam are emerging from national perspectives, which narrow down to urbanization, science and technology capability and conservation of ecology and environment. When put together, these efforts essentially mean enhancement of human and institutional capabilities to meet the challenges. And in these vital areas, Assam has a long way to go as explained in the succeeding paragraphs.

Marx noted 'commodity fetishism' as integral to capitalist mode of production. In a similar way, development efforts in Assam and the rest of the North-East are characterized by 'infrastructure fetishism' and reliance on central funding. In this process, the crucial role of dissemination of science and technology and the S&T system as the engine of growth has been ignored and the prevailing mantra seems to be that financial investment plus infrastructure add up to development. This is a fallacy because S&T inputs are critical for every activity or scheme in every sector such as education, industry, agriculture environment and urban development. The point made by Jeffry D. Sachs that 'technology has been the main force behind the long-term increases in the income of the richer world' must be noted here and also his view that the 'transition of modern economic growth involved urbanization, changing gender roles, increased social mobility changing family structure and increasing specialization'. Education, especially science education, has a vital role in bringing about economic transformation. Where does Assam stand in the two interrelated fields of science and technology education and scientific research? The available data on Assam on general education presents a dismal scenario which is analysed below:

Gross enrolment ratio

GER (6-14 years)	2004–5 – total	– 92.0 per cent
GER (14-16 years)		– 48.4 per cent
GER (16-18 years)		– 14.4 per cent

Source: Economic Survey 2007-8, Government of India.

This shows that while the enrolment at the primary level was high, close to all-India average of 93 per cent, drop out percentage has been high at the high school level and very high at the class XII level. This is a puzzle, given the fact that Assam has done reasonably well in literacy as noted earlier and calls for a field study because Higher Secondary Education is the threshold level in skill development. The United Nations Programme of Millennium Development Village in sub-Saharan Africa has shown that for adopting modern agricultural practices and inputs, higher secondary level of knowledge is essential for appreciating intricate soil and water management relationships and crop management. It thus appears that the catchment area for technical skill and development in Assam has been very narrow. The position gets worsened when one looks at college enrolment data by subject stream compiled by NEC. Seventy-four per cent of students in Assam go for Arts, 6 per cent for commerce and only 12 per cent for science stream. Manipur on the other hand, sends 35 per cent to science and 5 per cent for commerce streams. This explains why Assam has only three medical colleges with annual intake capacity of 426 seats when the people need expanded medical facilities. This holds good for science and engineering education also. The reasons for continuing narrow base of science education must be explored by looking at the key factors such as standard of mathematics teaching. Unfortunately, social science research in North-East has neglected the vital area of skill development. A 2004 Harvard University-World Bank Field Study of Teacher Absence in India, showed that, in Assam, teacher absence percentage was among the highest—33.8 per cent of teachers were absent, 30.7 per cent of teachers were present but not teaching and 30.7 per cent of teachers were present and teaching. It also shows that incentives like salary increase of teachers do not seem to be associated with lower teacher absence. The weighted national average for teachers' absence was 24.8 per cent. Though this study covered primary school education, the findings might as well be the same if not worse for higher secondary schools as evident from the huge dropout rates. NEC report also shows that only 15.5 per cent higher secondary schools have laboratories and 15.2 per cent have adequate number of computers in Assam.

From 1947, Assam developed a network of five universities, medical colleges, and other technical educational institutions, which constitute an impressive spread across the state compared to its relatively small population size (2.66 crore in 2001 census). This includes an agricultural university, two central universities at Tezpur and Silchar, IIT Guwahati, which is also a deemed university. Regional Research Laboratory at Jorhat under the CSIR and ICAR Research Complex for Hill Areas at Barapani in Meghalaya are designed to provide real time solutions to the technological needs and problems of Assam and its hill areas a part of this charter. There has been a little effort to institutionalize the involvement of this scientific system in the state planning and development process as independent evaluators of state programmes. There has also been a little effort to enhance the involvement of scientific institutions as research centres for referring scientific and engineering problems for location-specific solutions. The S&T capacity of these institutions has thus remained highly under-utilized. This has possibly affected the overall quality of academic and scientific research work also. This deficiency is systemic in the sense that neither the technical departments of the state engaged in development work nor the industry have any worthwhile interaction through industry-academia collaboration, which is now recognized world over as the foundation of technology led growth. These ideas are pushed hard these days, citing the Chinese success in generating larger number of publications in SCI journals than India. Thus, the feeling that China might have gone ahead in science and technology has led to a hard look at the scientific work done at the Indian S&T institutions which is a positive development. It would be useful to look at some of the broad findings of this review pertaining to the S&T institutions of Assam.

A 2006 analysis of the publication output of science and technology made by the National Institute for Science and Technology Development Studies (NISTADS), a CSIR organization, titled 'Measures for Progress of Science in India' identified 24 top high quality institutions with significant impact factor of their research output in terms of citation, etc. No S&T institution or university in Assam is included in the category of top 24 institutions. The report also has brought about a level of distribution of such publications across the country, which showed Assam's share in national publications in the year 2002 was only 1.20 per cent, which has climbed albeit slowly from 0.99 per cent in 1985-6.

In an ongoing NISTADS survey on India's S&T output and patents, Assam has been placed in the category of low productive state as the state's contribution to national publications was found to be 1.53 per cent of the total. In the area of access to international journals using citations, it is reported that in 2007, Indians published 7,726 papers, wherein Assam has only 21 papers amounting to 0.27 per cent of the total. On a positive note, the only positive aspect is the good work being done in Dibrugarh University, which is rated highly among the major active coal research institutions in India. The Central University Tezpur is considered as one of the major active petroleum research institutes in India and has to its credit some good papers in fuel cell research. However, the disquieting fact is that no university in Assam finds place into 43 top universities or in 24 top research institutes of India.

Making the S&T system responsive to state's development needs and raising the capability of scientific institutions has assumed strategic importance because these are the foundations of a 'knowledge economy' or society and the systemic weakness will put severe constraints on Assam's chance of getting into IT or ITES or sophisticated BPO activities. A May 2008 NASSCOM study on the ratings of Indian cities in IT industries placed Guwahati and Gangtok in the last category of aspiring centres as 88 per cent of the work is now confined to nine cities. Nevertheless given the irreversible geographical disadvantages, the economic future of Assam lies only in hi-tech, knowledge-based industries like pharmaceuticals, floriculture, organic farming, high value-low weight spices, processed food, organic and quality tea, and services like eco-tourism and even medical tourism. A coordinated S&T based development strategy is therefore needed to lift Assam from the present central dependency-led growth to an endogenous and sustainable high growth path. The state's diverse pool of talented manpower will certainly meet the challenge.

Application of science is equally critical for conservation of Assam's real strength, which consists of unique wildlife, ecology, flora, evergreen forests, large water bodies and Brahmaputra River system. Lack of awareness of ecological and socio-economic value of these assets and its wanton destruction for short-term commercial gains has been the bane of post-1947 Assam. The silting and drying up of Deepar Beel, a vast water body close to Guwahati airport, is a case in point. It is not known to many that Guwahati has richer wildlife than Nairobi and that Deepar Beel is one of the Ramsar sites—a wetland identified by the 'Convention on Wetlands, Waterfalls and Habitat of International Importance' at Ramsar, Iran in 1972 for conservation of wetlands. Its rejuvenation could bring about a sea-change in tourism prospects of Guwahati. Similarly, Assam's 2.37 lakh ha of wetlands in different districts have enormous potential for fish output and tourism. Conservation of reserve forests, wildlife sanctuaries, and national parks must be seen as foundations of ecological security on which depends the survival of not only human but all other species. Unchecked encroachments on forest lands and diversion of forest lands for non-forest use and construction of projects must be checked and a policy to provide alternatives outside forest area should be adopted. In agriculture, Assam needs rice strategy to raise the yield-per-hectare of its main *kharif* Sali paddy. There is a scientific problem due to a longstanding inability of research to evolve either a new short-duration HYV variety or to improve the existing HYV rice which could withstand submergence, and yet respond to fertilizer use and resist pest attack, as 92 per cent of crop area in Assam is flood prone. Since 15 lakh ha of land is under Sali Rice and to a large extent gives a base to the rural economy, the state cannot lessen priority to the Sali Paddy. On the other hand, the failure to evolve a cold tolerant rice variety, which could be late sown after flood waters recedes is also a technological failure. Assam Agricultural University's Rice Research Programme therefore, needs a closer look to become result oriented. Raising rural incomes by raising crop productivity and expanding rural non-farm sector through technology-based value-addition and application of post harvest technology are thus crucial.

The Indian growth story that began in the 1990s is an urban phenomenon. An urban environment is conducive to technology led growth in manufacturing and services, as it provides cost-effective positioning of the necessary capital, infrastructure, skilled manpower and other management options. This technology growth has by-passed Assam, as it achieved limited urbanization. The urban areas contain only 12.4 per cent population and its urban centres including capital city Guwahati are really overgrown district towns. Assam and the other NE states have really no worthwhile urban development strategy. The North-East Vision 2020 contains no vision for growth of new townships which has changed the urban landscape of much of north-west India, Punjab, Haryana, NCR, western UP and Uttarakhand. The Vision 2020 dwells on J.L. Nehru Urban Renewal Mission, which is a central scheme to upgrade the urban infrastructure of existing urban centres. However, the J.L. Nehru Urban Renewal Mission does not envisage establishment of new towns, which is an initiative entirely left to the states.

Experience elsewhere has shown that only when an IT or bio-tech park is located within a planned city like Gurgaon or Noida, the industry starts moving there because of readymade physical and social infrastructure. Thus provisioning of good roads, public transport, schools, medical facilities, sports and recreation facilities is as much important as power supply for taking an investment decision especially by a foreign investor. These facilities are best developed when the state opens its doors to investment from all—domestic and foreign and also invites expertise and skilled personnel from far and wide. In fact, an ethnic mix is the life blood of a thriving metropolis and a city of indigenous people is indeed a contradiction in terms.

THE WAY FORWARD

The growth model for Assam, for reasons stated in the previous section, has to be what has worked in a landlocked region like her that succeeded in realizing high growth and not that of a coastal state. The high growth quadrant of Delhi and the surrounding National Capital Region comes, therefore, as the only model worthy of emulation for following reasons:

1. A relatively small population but highly skilled due to the fact that over the years, the region has built one of the most extensive and broad-based institutions of learning in science, engineering, finance, computer application, electronics, law and management. It is also the location of a large number of hi-tech, scientific R&D centres, universities, vocational training centres which facilitated growth of biotech, IT, ITES and computer hardware manufacturing and BPO activities. Above all, a fair share of the 1.2 million science graduates and engineering diploma holders made this possible, which is about 20 per cent in the captive area. The output from these industries, mostly in the service sector are high-value and low-weight exports and are therefore largely transport cost neutral—an advantage that should be the cornerstone of Assam's industrial development policy.
2. The region had the benefit of a long-term industrial infrastructure development policy which resulted in emergence of

Okhla, NOIDA, Greater NOIDA or Gurgaon Industrial Area developed by the respective urban development authorities. The emergence of these industrial areas is a consequence of active government intervention and not merely a product of market forces or private land developers. Assam and the rest of North-East, therefore, need a long-term industrial policy and not a five year plan specific to enable her people as in peninsular India, to get infrastructure, mother industries and skill building facilities. This will enable the industry to strike a foothold and propel people to inculcate the industrial culture. Over course of time, people of the region will develop the necessary capabilities in terms of modern skills acquired and entrepreneurship to make their own reasoned choices.

3. To make this development perspective a reality, the state has to adopt a strategic framework with human capability enhancement as its core. There is a need to develop a science and technology policy and new look at educational system to equip the schools with adequate laboratory, library, and computer facilities. There is a need to obtain central support for a long-term industrial policy for growth of knowledge based industry. Along with industrial policy and urban development initiatives, one of the main planks of the state development in the twenty-first century should be a well thought out conservation of ecology and environmental strategy for growth of agriculture.
4. Assam had missed the Green Revolution and IT Revolution for want of a clear direction. She is unlikely to enter into the knowledge economy and develop a knowledge-based society unless its policy makers work out a long-term plan to achieve coherent synergy in these interrelated activities.

REFERENCES

Bhaduri, Amit, *Development with Dignity*, New Delhi: National Book Trust, 2005.

Chen, Andrew and Jennifer Warren, 'Paving the Path for India's Growth', *Far Eastern Economic Review*, 171(2), March 2008.

Gupta, B.M. and S.M. Dhawan, 'Measures of Progress of S&T in India: An Analysis of the Publication Output in Science and

Technology', *National Institute of Science Technology and Development Studies (NISTADS) Report*, Office of the Principal Scientific Advisor, Government of India, 2006 available at http://www.nistads.res.in/index.php?option=com_content&task=view&id=181&Itemid=110

Kaplan, Robert D., 'Center Stage for the 21st Century: Power Plays in the Indian Ocean', *Foreign Affairs*, 8(2), March/April 2009.

Kremer, Michael, Nazmul Chaudhury, F. Halsey Rogers, Karthik Muralidharan and Jeffrey Hammer, 'Teacher Absence in India: A Snapshot', *Journal of the European Economic Association*, 3 (2-3), 2005.

NASSCOM, 'Prospects of 50 cities in ITES and BPO in India', *NASSCOM Report*, May 2008.

North Eastern Council, *The North East Vision 2020: Annexures*, vol II available at http://mdoner.gov.in/writereaddata/sublink images/Vision_2020_ANNEX.pdf

Planning Commission of India, 'Chapter 8: Innovation and Technology', in Planning Commission of India, *Eleventh Five Year Plan, 2007-2012*, Vol. I *Inclusive Growth*, New Delhi: Oxford University Press, 2008, available at http://planningcommission.nic.in/plans/planrel/fiveyr/11th/11_v1/11th_vol1.pdf

Sachs, Jeffrey D., *End of Poverty: How We Can Make it Happen in Our Lifetime*, London: Penguin Books, 2005.

Saikia, Jaideep, 'Periphery in Peril', in J.K. Ray and R. Bhattacharya (eds.), *North-East India: Administrative Reforms and Economic Development*, New Delhi: Har-Anand, 2008.

Sen, Amartya, *Commodities and Capabilities*, New Delhi: Oxford University Press, 1999.

———, *Development as Freedom*, New Delhi: Oxford University Press, 1999.

Sharma, A., 'Not an End in Itself', *The Statesman*, 25 May 2009, available at http://www.thestatesman.org/page.arcview.php?date=2009-05-27&usrsess=1&clid=14&id=288400

World Bank, *Agriculture for Development: World Development Report 2008*, Washington DC: World Bank, 2007.

———, *Development and Growth in Northeast India: The Natural Resources, Water, and Environment Nexus,* New Delhi: World Bank, 2007, available at http://siteresources.worldbank.org/INTSAREGTOPWATRES/eatureStories/21702969/NortheastStrategyReport_20-3-08.pdf

CHAPTER 10

Insurgency in Assam: The Ethnic Dimension

Papori Chetia Phukon

INTRODUCTION

Ethnic aspirations and associated anxieties are not phenomena that are the characteristics of only certain regions of the world. Indeed, there is hardly any region that has not experienced the problem of ethnic conflict. It is generally assumed that ethnic tension is related to traditional societies and education plays the role of a catalyst in eradicating it. However, this is not always the case. With the development of society, the problem of ethnicity has intensified, and tribal culture, religion and language has been utilized for ethnic mobilizations even in the most advanced parts of the world.

Inter-ethnic conflicts and insurgencies are intertwined in the North Eastern region of India. Assam being an epitome of India, it projects several layers of ethnic, linguistics, religious and cultural heterogeneity, which are often superimposed. Further, the complexity of interaction between these different layers of identity is more intense in Assam. Furthermore, the vexed relationship between ethnic identity and national identity as well as political identity is particularly a relevant issue in the North-East, and more so in the case of Assam. The search for ethnic identity is a result of ethnic groups which become minorities, and thereby claim special privileges to safeguard their culture and traditions. E. Hunter and Phillip Whitten[1] are of the opinion that ethnic minorities are social groups that are distinguished from the larger society of which they form a part by certain traits, such as language, origin, religion, race, values or customs. Since ethnic minorities belong to a minority group, the dominant group often subjects them to discrimination. This discrimination ultimately leads to a different kind of assertion from the minority group. The former colonial territories of the world, experienced political problems due to enormous ethnic diversity within their dominions. This is true even for countries like the United States where ethnic aspirations have led to social cohesiveness among the ethnic minorities.

ETHNICITY AND NORTH-EAST

North-East India has a long history of ethnic movements, which can be attributed to the politico-geographical set-up of the region besides the history of political evolution, administrative restructuring and an emergent social system. The geopolitical factors like distance, inaccessibility and backward economy have played a significant role in the emergence of ethnic insurgency in the region. North-East India is sandwiched between China, Myanmar, Bangladesh and Bhutan. Ninety-eight per cent of North-East India's land area has international border with China, Myanmar, Bangladesh and Bhutan. Only 2 per cent of land area abuts the rest of India. The region borders a highly sensitive frontier, like the Myanmar, where insurgent groups like the Shans, Kachins and Chins are constantly at war with Yangon for separate political status. Besides, Bangladesh has emerged as a most favoured safe haven for the Indian insurgent groups. Further, the insurgents have expanded their areas of operations to Cachar plains, extending their areas of operations in the region. The nature of terrain—parallel mountain ranges with their thick vegetation cover—along with isolated settlement pattern provides the necessary conditions for sustenance of insurgency in the region.

There are more than 300 culturally distinct ethnic groups of various sizes and at various levels of development. Ethnically the region is more similar to South-East Asia than South Asia. But this beautiful part of the world has witnessed a sustained low intensity conflict. The assertion of ethnic identity has been a phenomenon that has gone on for several decades. Although the North-East comprises eight states of Assam, Arunachal Pradesh, Manipur, Meghalaya, Mizoram, Nagaland, Tripura and Sikkim, this paper will focus on the ethnic issues that characterize Assam. More specifically, this paper will seek to address the reasons that have led to the violent outburst by ethnic minorities seeking redressal of their grievances. An important aspect that needs to be borne in mind is that this dissonance is not only trained against the Indian state, but also against the socially dominant races of the region. Before delving into the ethnic movements in Assam, it is necessary to understand the historiography of ethnic related violence of the entire North-East region. This is because the seed of ethnic discord has been sowed in the pre-independent India and undivided North-East.

The North-East always had its own identity. Long before the colonization process began in North-East India, the tribals of the plains like the Bodos, Mishings, Tiwas and Deuries were virtually Aryanized. The process got impetus with the assimilation process of the Ahoms to the Aryanization process and introduction of a uniform administration. The assimilation process gained momentum with the rise of Vaishnavism in the fifteenth century, which had welcomed all sections of the people regardless of their caste and class into its fold. However, the traditional elites failed to mobilize the people towards a unifying metaphor and standardized the Assamese language, as the assimilation process happened without an overarching ideological framework.

The changed political and economic conditions with the advent of the British (following the annexation in 1826) had severely affected the natural process of ethnic group formation. The unprecedented change in the demography of Assam due to the state-sponsored migration from different parts of British India made it a fertile ground for persistent ethnic conflicts. The state sponsored migration as part of British economic policies had long-term implications for construction of ethnic identity as well as nationality formation in Assam. The perception of Bengali hegemony resulting from migration threatened the Assamese middle class and elites and remained a major factor in the shaping up of Assam politics in the colonial and post-colonial Assam.

The North-Eastern states were not a part of British India in the beginning. It was much later that they became a part of the colonization process. Many of the ethnic groups of the region in the 1940s opposed the idea of political unity with the Indian state. The Naga people were the first to convey the message that they were never a part of India and they wrote to Nehru seeking a separate state. Others, including the Manipuris, made similar requests. New Delhi refused to accept their requests and by the 1950s the Indian government deployed the army, which used full powers given to it through the Armed Forces Special Powers Act of 1958, to control the growing violence. Mizoram too came to the fore after the formation of the Mizo National Front, which was formed as a protest group against the Indian government's lackadaisical attitude towards the impending famine in the state in the 1960s, which eventually resulted in the death of a large number of people. However, the Mizos signed a peace accord in 1986 after fighting for 20 long years. The Naga and Mizo insurgencies provide glaring examples of ethnic identity assertion that transformed into separatist demands.

Tripura has been a homeland of 19 different tribes, which was ruled for thousands of years by a dynasty of tribal origin. Its ethnic problems started with the Partition of India and with the large influx of East Pakistanis (now Bangladeshis) from the Chittagong Hill Tracts, which threatened their tribal identity.

In case of insurgency in Manipur, the ethnic assertion became more pronounced because of neglect by the centre and lack of economic development. The Meiteis in the plains and the two main tribes of Kukis and Nagas in the hills are continuously waging a war of attrition in Manipur. In the hills, the Nagas and Kukis have their own insurgent organizations and are fighting against 'Indian occupation', and also against one other. In Meghalaya, ethnicity is a dominant factor despite three main tribes—the Khasis, Jaintias and the Garos—agreeing to come together in their fight against the outsiders. The intensity of such violence in Meghalaya is, however, not on the same scale as that of Tripura or Manipur.

Assam is a land of several tribes living in the plains and hills and has a history of numerous problems along ethnic lines.

Separation of Nagaland, Mizoram, Meghalaya and Arunachal Pradesh diminished its land area but not its problems. The Assamese majority remained dissatisfied with New Delhi. The other ethnic communities also have grievances against the Assamese caste Hindus and also New Delhi. This is leading to ethnicization of politics in the region, a phenomenon that is becoming more and more intense with time. Adding to the woes is the influx of millions of foreigners from neighbouring Bangladesh and Nepal, which is generating a 'crisis of identity' among various ethnic groups. It should be remembered that this 'crisis of identity' gave birth to insurgency in Tripura and has also manifested itself in Assam.

Violence was not a part of the post-independent political struggle in this region until 1960. It was the Nagas who resorted to violent activities with the help of China and others followed the same path in the later years. With the change of foreign policy of China in 1970s, the insurgent groups took shelter in neighbouring Myanmar (which is still sheltering major insurgents groups from the North-East). Assam witnessed several ethnicity related insurgencies in the post-colonial era, the seed of which had been sowed by the colonizers with a motive of dominating the region without much resistance from the indigenous people. According to anthropologist D.N. Majumdar,[2]

> During British period, may be due to encouragement from British officers like Charles Pawsey, ethnic identity organisations grew up among many of the major tribal communities of North-East India. In fact, the ground had been already prepared by the feeling among the hill tribes that the ruling class, be it the British or Indian, tended to adopt a policy of ethnic discrimination towards the hill people.

It was the British, who had planted the idea of separatism in the minds of various ethnic communities in North-East India. These ideas ultimately metamorphosed into insurgencies in both Nagaland and Mizoram, which in-turn showed the path of violence to other ethnic minorities in the North-East. After Independence Nehru adopted a policy for the tribals, which was advocated by Verrier Elwin. Elwin had proposed some sort of a 'National Park' for the tribals in his book *The Baiga*. Although he had regretted later for unfortunate connotations of the expression 'national park'[3] but it had a striking effect on public policy. The ethnocentric nature of state-sponsored development after Independence has been an important aspect in creating ethnic rifts in polyethnic Assam and it played an important part in the appearance of the hill state movements. The net result of this discrimination in the pre- and post-colonial era was the assertion of ethnic identity, with individuals taking renewed pride in the traditions and deriving personal identification from their group membership.

However, it must also be stated—and forcefully—that there are ethnic groups in the North-East that have come to the fore by articulating ethnic sentiments but over time have done an about turn. The case of ULFA in Assam is an important case in this regard. Not only is this prominent insurgent group silent on the question of illegal migration from Bangladesh, but the *Prachar Patras* (publicity material) of ULFA has—despite the inherent contradiction[4]—begun to address illegal migrants from Bangladesh as 'people of Assam of East Bengal origin', and have sought to justify the role of the migrants by stating that 'all the labouring masses are our friends and the main motive force of our freedom struggle'. While it seems that the grant of safe-havens by Bangladesh to the leaders of ULFA[5] has been an important factor in its turnaround, the demographic compulsion that presently grips Assam too has forced ULFA to reconsider the proud aims by which it was sired. Indeed, this contradiction in ideology that is being witnessed in ULFA (which is one of the strongest ethnic separatist movements in Independent India) is a signature of the primary phenomenon of abdication of ethnic ideologies that seems to be gaining ground in the region. This aspect is being underscored by the fact that an important section of ULFA—primarily the 'alpha' and 'charlie' companies of ULFA's Upper Assam based 28 Battalion—declared a unilateral ceasefire with the government in June 2008, purportedly because it no longer believes in the 'sovereignty' demand of ULFA. This section of ULFA instead seeks to raise 'real issues' that beset Assam, including the illegal migration from Bangladesh. The issue of ISI-DGFI support to ULFA is also a matter that needs to be taken into account when the question of ULFA's turnaround on its founding ideology is taken into consideration. This abdication of its core-principles that led to the foundation of ULFA in 1979 must be noted.

THE BURNING HILLS

With this brief history of ethnicity of the North-East and its role in ethnic related insurgency, this paper delves into inter-ethnic conflicts that are being engendered in the region. Today the ethnic groups are fighting one another instead of their purported claim of fighting the state. The militant groups of a particular ethnic community attack the member of the other group on the ground that they do not belong to the same community. Thus the outbreak of violent inter-ethnic conflict between the Bodos and the Santhals, Bodos and Koch–Rajbongshis, Karbi–Kuki conflict in Assam, Kuki–Naga in Manipur, Dimasa and Zemi Naga–Hmar tribe clashes in North Cachar Hills and Barak Valley, are some of the examples of inter-ethnic clashes in this region. The Karbi National Volunteers, Tiwa National Revolutionary Force, Kuki National Front, Hmar Revolutionary Front, etc., are some of the names that go by the ethnic community that they represent and are trying to defend their respective communities. This indicates very clearly that some militants are mobilizing along clear ethnic lines resulting in fratricidal struggles. This phenomenon of ethnicity, where rival ethnic groups form the ethnic militias[6] has posed a serious security threat to the region. For the state every such ethnic militia is a threat to the security of the nation. But, for a particular clan, such militias can provide more security than the Indian security forces. The militias of a particular group provide security to their ethnic kin and this can be ascertained from the strong followers of such groups.

The two hill districts of Assam, Karbi Anglong and North Cachar Hills situated in the southern bank of Brahmaputra bear the brunt of inter-ethnic insurgency more conspicuously than any other part of Assam. The Karbi Anglong district located at the junction of Upper Assam and Lower Assam is formed of two discontinuous parts, the Diphu sub-division and the Hamren sub-division. The Diphu sub-division is separated from the Hamren sub-division by a strip of North Cachar Hills and part of Nagaon district. The Karbi Hills and North Cachar Hills were taken over by the British imperialist forces in 1838 and 1854 respectively. The Mikir-Dimasa tract was designated as 'backward' under the provisions of the Scheduled District Act, 1874 and 'Backward tracts' by the Government of India Act, 1919. With the recommendation of the Simon Commission, 1929, the North Cachar Hills were placed in the category of 'Excluded Area' (EA) and Mikir Hills under 'Partially Excluded Area' (PEA) category under Section 92 of the Government of India Act, 1935. The two ethnic communities have justified the demand for autonomy on this historical basis.

The offering of PEA status to the Karbis has augmented the aspirations of the political leaders like Samson Singh Ingti, Khor Sing Terang, Seng Bay, etc. In 1937, a memorandum was submitted to the then Governor of Assam, Sir Robert Neil Reid, demanding a separate hill district for the Karbis. To generate people's support they held two conventions at Kathalguri in 1945 and at Hawaipur in 1947 and in the later convention, Karbi-a-Durbar, a regional political forum was formed to strengthen the movement. This demand for autonomy was the beginning of the movement's demanding union territory status by the two hill districts. The demands of the Karbis during colonial rule had fallen on deaf ears. It was in 1951, that the two ethnic groups, the Karbis and the Dimasas, were given the composite United Mikir and NC (UMNC) Hills district covering the areas of Mikir hill tract and its adjoining Karbi inhabited areas of the then Nagaon, Sibsagar and United Khasi and Jaintia Hills and the North Cachar Hills. The UMNC district got its first Autonomous District Council on 23 June 1952 under the Sixth Schedule, but the search for autonomy continued. The Karbi-a-Durbar, the ruling party in the Autonomous District Council, faced some opposition in 1964 as a section of the Durbaris supported the merger of Naga Hills and the North Cachar Hills and also merger of the Karbi and Khasi Jaintia Hills. This has created a rift between the Karbi-Dimasa communities.

The Karbi and Dimasa leaders demanded an autonomous state under Article 244-A of the Indian Constitution in a memorandum to the prime minister in 1973. On 2 February 1976, the UMNC district was divided into two districts and in October 1976, Mikir Hills was renamed as Karbi Anglong district. Unlike other hill districts, Karbi and Dimasas were deprived of statehood or union territory status and in the 1980 memorandum to prime minister, the leaders complained of their identity crisis as a result of the Assam agitation. A separate State Demand Committee was formed in 1981, which asserted the identity movement. With the formation of Autonomous State Demand Committee (ASDC) in 1986 under the CPI(ML) leadership, the movement for statehood got impetus with mass support. The Karbi Students' Association (KSA) also joined the ASDC and the movement became more vociferous in the post-reorganization Assam. ASDC was more dynamic in the Karbi Anglong district until its split on 25 July 2000. The ASDC attributed unemployment and lack of economic development as the reason behind failure of the Autonomous District Council. But ASDC failed to mobilise the mass support in conducting the movement. The movement for an autonomous state has today reached a turning point in the aftermath of the split in the ASDC in July 2000. Internal conflicts, which once jeopardized the movement altogether, led to the creation of two factions, the ASDC-Progressive (ASDC-P, aligned with the CPI-ML) and the ASDC-United (ASDC-U). The split has also divided the once influential KSA into three units, allied with the two different factions of the ASDC and with the Congress party, which rules the Karbi Anglong Autonomous District Council (KAADC) today.

Violence entered the scene in the mid-1990s with the coming up of Karbi National Volunteers (KNV), a militant organization of the Karbi tribe of Assam, with the objective of using violent means to secure a separate state of Karbi Anglong. KNV activists had been trained by National Socialist Council of Nagaland-Isak-Muivah (NSCN-IM).[7]

In early 2000, this outfit merged with another Karbi militant group—Karbi People's Front (KPF)—forming a new platform called the United Peoples' Democratic Solidarity (UPDS). It has the active support from NSCN(IM). The UPDS and the Dima Halam Daogah (DHD) are the two outfits behind the emergence of violence in the two hill districts with the support of NSCN and other secessionist groups like the ULFA. In the beginning these two outfits were trained by the NSCN(IM) but when the NSCN signed peace with the centre in 1997, the UPDS turned to the ULFA for help. Although there has been several case of violence created by militants in these two districts earlier also, it became threatening to the state security in the year 2000. On 9 April 2000, the UPDS cadres shot dead Hindi-speaking timber workers at Langatso in Karbi Anglong, which set the alarming bell. On 19 April, the UPDS again killed 11 Nepalis with the help of the DHD under Baithalangso police station. Again the target was non-Assamese people and the disastrous ethnic cleansing was in progress. Inspired by the success, the UPDS forced the government of Karbi Anglong and the North Cachar Hills to oust outsiders. The violence carried out by the UPDS brought them to limelight and the ULFA and NDFB also resorted to similar kind of violence in other parts of Assam. The NSCN trained by the UPDS joined hands with ULFA to target non-Assamese Hindi speakers in un-officially declared Hindi belts. The killing stopped immediately[8] for two months when some unidentified ultras killed two senior UPDS leaders. In December 2001, eight persons of a polling party near Langlokso village were killed by suspected UPDS ultras. An overview at the major violence carried out by the ultras in Karbi Anglong since 2003-5 is provided below for better comprehension:[9]

- 29 November 2003—six Karbis were gunned down under Bokajan PS by Kuki Revolutionary Army (KRA)[10] militants and 116 Karbi houses were set on fire.
- 3 December 2003—KRA ultras killed three people and burnt 30 huts in a Karbi village in Menterang.
- 5 December 2003—The UPDS militants made a futile attempt on the lives of DC Anurag Goel and SP Abdul Kuddush at the village of Hidim Terang, Karbi Anglong.
- 19 March 2004—UPDS gunned down six Kukis in a village, 45 km from Diphu.
- 24 March 2004—KRA militants in retaliation killed 34 Karbi villagers in attacks on four villages within 36 hours. This incident was considered an instance of highest civilian casualty in a single day in Assam.

- 29 October 2005—a total of 88 people were killed of whom 76 belonged to Karbi ethnic group, 9 Dimasa, one Bodo, one Nepali and one Assamese.[11]

Besides the UPDS and the DHD, the Karbi Longri North Cachar Hills Liberation Front (KLNLF), a breakaway faction of the UPDS,[12] was formed on 16 May 2004. The split was triggered by a ceasefire agreement, signed on 23 May 2002, between the UPDS and union government. This militant group claims to fight for the cause of Karbi tribes and its declared objective is *Hemprek Kangthim*, meaning self-rule/self-determination of the Karbi people. Ethno-political dynamics and economic resources of the Karbi Anglong play a dominant role in the inter-ethnic violence in the region. The Karbis are the largest tribe in the area and Kukis proclaim to be in majority in Singhason area. The UPDS's fight against the Kukis has brought the KRA into the picture, adding another chapter of violence and ethnic conflict. The group, with a declared objective of protecting the interest of the Kukis, is seen to be a serious contender in engendering violence of Karbi Hills against the UPDS. The growing number of the Kukis is also perceived as a threat to the aspirations of the Karbi groups. While Kukis claim themselves to be the aboriginal tribes of the district (living in contiguous areas in Diphu, Bokajan and Howraghat before the creation of the district), their growing population indicates the essentially mobile character of this tribe. According to the 1951 census, only 15 respondents in Karbi Anglong wrote their mother tongue as Kuki. The number grew to 2,914 by 1961. The 1971 census suggested that there are 21,034 Kukis in Assam. However, by 1991, only 21,883 Kukis were said to be living in the state. Till 1971, Karbi Anglong witnessed an inward migration of Kukis, the 20 years time between 1971-91 points to an outward migration.[13]

The Karbis demand a state to be carved out of Assam and the Kukis demand an Autonomous Council for themselves to be carved out of this state. The approach of the political parties in the district is divergent towards the Kuki population. While the ASDC-U is willing to offer 'son of the soil' status to some of the Kukis, who lived in the district before 1951 (the year in which the Karbi Anglong district was created), the ASDC-P does not accept the same. The result is that the polarization along ethnic lines is appropriately fabricated with political divisions among the communities. In addition to this, the basic issues of livelihood and economic opportunities have also played a role in sustaining the violence, and the subsequent confrontation has benefited the insurgents.

While the hills are reeling under ethnic violence, another factor leading to brutal Karbi-Kuki clash is the struggle for supremacy in the lucrative trade of 2000 MT of ginger that is produced annually in the Singhason Hills. Over the last couple of years, the UPDS has also besieged the ginger-producing Kukis in the Singhason Hill range. Both UPDS and KRA take away their share of production from the local tribal cultivators, and so the rivalry among both the groups has increased. The UPDS in order to prove its control over the area had announced a ban on ginger cultivation, terming it a 'threat to the environment of Karbi Anglong', and it further decided to stop any economic and productive activity by non-Karbis in Karbi-Anglong. On several occasions, armed cadres of UPDS have set signal ginger-laden vehicles on fire. The mode of cultivation being slash-and-burn, it poses serious environmental hazards to the forest cover in the hills. But Karbi cultivators in the lower part of the hills follow the same method of cultivation. This kind of move by UPDS has garnered support from the Karbi organizations, particularly with the ASDC-U, and the section of the KSA aligned with the Congress party. However, the UPDS action against Kukis had brought the KRA into the scene, resulting in violence. This eventually caused a sense of insecurity among all the various other communities living in Karbi-Anglong.

CONCLUSION

This paper has tried to provide an overview of the ethnic situation in the North-East and Assam by concentrating on a few groups that are currently in the news. It has also sought to establish that ethnic aspiration if ignored invariably gives rise to dissonance that transforms into insurgency and separatist movements. It is also no longer a matter of any doubt that both New Delhi and

Dispur have neglected the ethnic communities in the region and the state. It is strongly recommended that the present non-existent policy towards the North-East must be re-examined, and a robust plan of action be set in motion so that the ethnic aspirations of the various communities that dot the region's landscape are respected. Furthermore, New Delhi must realize that setting one ethnic community/group or ethnically based insurgent organization against the other is not a correct strategy. It only leads to greater unrest as is being witnessed in the case of NDFB-erstwhile Bodo Liberation Tigers, NSCN(IM)-NSCN(K), and now Zemi Nagas and Dimasas. Such short-term goals are contrary to the vision of the Indian state. This is important for India to survive as a nation state.

NOTES

1. E. Hunter and Phillip Whitten, *Encyclopedia of Anthropology*, New York: Harper & Row, 1976.
2. D.N. Majumdar, 'Ethnicity and Regionalism in North East India', in B. Pakem (ed.), *Regionalism in India*, New Delhi: Har Anand, 1993.
3. Verrier Elwin, *The Tribal World of Verrier Elwin*, New Delhi: Oxford University Press, 1989.
4. The ULFA spawned the Assam agitation against illegal migrants from Bangladesh. It rose to prominence as the militant manifestation of the movement.
5. Most of the important ULFA leaders, including the Chairman, Arabinda Rajkhowa, the Chief of Staff, Paresh Barua, the Foreign Secretary, Sasadhar Choudhury, the Operations Commander, Raju Baruah (the General Secretary of the organization, Anup Chetia is incarcerated in the country) et al. are based out of Dhaka, Chittagong, Halowaghat, etc., in Bangladesh. The former prime minister of Bangladesh, Begum Khaleda Zia, has also gone on record (during her tenure in the opposition) in calling the ULFA 'freedom fighters'. However, in December 2009 Arabinda Rajkhowa was arrested by Bangladeshi authorities and was latter handed over to India.
6. Sanjib Baruah, 'Historicizing Ethnic Politics in Northeast India' in Girin Phukon (ed.), *Inter Ethnic Conflict in Northeast India*, New Delhi: South Asian Publisher, 2005.

7. 'Karbi National Volunteers (KNV): Terrorist Group of Assam', South Asia Terrorism Portal, available at http://www.satp.org/satporgtp/countries/india/states/assam/terrorist_outfits/knv.htm (accessed on 22 May 2009 at 9.30 a.m.)
8. *Hindustan Times*, 30 December 2000.
9. Col. Ved Prakash, *Terrorism in India's North East: A Gathering Storm*, New Delhi: Kalpaz Publication, 2008.
10. KRA was formed in 1999 with the help of NSCN(IM) for setting up of an Autonomous Kuki National Council for the Kukis in Karbi Anglong district. The outfit based in the Saikal area of Senapati district in Manipur claims to have linkages with both factions of NSCN, NDFB and DHD.
11. A similar pattern is evident in the break-up of people who took shelter at the 55 relief camps set-up in the district in the wake of the violence: of the 44,747 people listed at the relief camps till 24 October 2005, as many as 37,604 were Karbis. There were 5,687 Dimasas, and 1,456 persons belonging to a mixture of communities. But, the same pattern is not evident in the damage of property: as on 19 October 2005, out of a total of 1,014 houses burnt, 534 belonged to Karbis and 469 to Dimasas. Significantly, the Karbis constitute about 40 per cent of the district's population of 812,000, and the Dimasas just 3 per cent.
12. 'United People's Democratic Solidarity (UPDS)', South Asia Terrorism Portal, available at http://www.satp.org/satporgtp/countries/india/states/assam/terrorist_outfits/UPDS.HTM
13. Bibhu Prasad Routray, 'Assam: Karbi-Kuki Clashes', South Asia Terrorism Portal, available at http://satp.org/satporgtp/sair/Archives/2_37.htm#ASSESSMENT3.

CHAPTER 11

Insurgency and Development in India's North-East States: A Study of Assam

M. Amarjeet Singh

INTRODUCTION

For years now, several areas of India's North-East region have been experiencing insurgencies. Close to about 100 separatist or secessionist insurgent groups and subgroups are seeking to achieve a variety of objectives having ethnic and territorial focus. As a result, a large quantity of small firearms, including AK-47 assault rifles, M-16 rifles and rocket launchers, are in circulation in the region. Though the clustering of factors that gave rise to insurgency differs from case to case, the most familiar kind of violence unleashed by the insurgents has been guerilla warfare and terrorism. Since 1979, the state of Assam—the most populous state in the region—has also been experiencing insurgencies, seeking to achieve a variety of objectives ranging from the creation of new state within the Indian Republic to the ultimate independence of the whole of Assam. As a result, the security of life and property is a major problem there. While some of these insurgencies had been resolved mainly through peace negotiations with the government, several others remain unresolved. In response to these insurgencies, the central government has been following two distinct policies. They are: firstly, the creation of small states, such as Mizoram and Nagaland, and territorially-defined autonomous councils such as the Bodo Territorial Council (BTC[1]); and secondly, a large amount of development funds have been earmarked exclusively for the region with the principal motive of buying peace and development. Unfortunately, these policy responses are partly successful in coping with the problem there. Hence, insurgency and counter-insurgency continue to claim several lives. Of late, insurgency is increasingly viewed as one of the principal reasons inhibiting the economic development of the insurgency-ridden states of the region, including that of Assam. Although this issue has received considerable journalistic treatment, there is relatively scant systematic analysis on the impact of insurgency on economic development in the North-East region. The present paper, therefore, attempts to study this crucial subject and thus an attempt has been made at examining 'whether insurgency affects economic development'. Although insurgency cannot be given as an excuse for the lack of development, the paper boldly argues that insurgency and its related activities act as one of the principal hurdles to economic development. The paper concludes with the observation that, at least in India's North-East, the peaceful states (states unaffected by insurgency) have achieved faster as well as higher economic development compared to the other states affected by prolonged insurgency.

ASSAM

The North-East region of India is located alongside four countries: Bangladesh, Bhutan, China and Myanmar, and it comprises eight Indian states: Arunachal Pradesh, Assam, Manipur, Meghalaya, Mizoram, Nagaland, Sikkim and Tripura. The region is connected to the rest of India by just 22 km long land corridor passing through Siliguri town in the eastern Indian state of West Bengal. The region accounts to 8.06 per cent of the country's territory and 3.73 per cent of the total population (*Census of India*, 2001). Characterized by extraordinary ethnic diversity, the region is inhabited by three distinct groups of people: the hill tribes, the plain tribes and the non-tribal population of the plains. This diversity is both the region's most spectacular strength and most formidable challenge too. Further, most states of the region are small in size and population, landlocked and hilly, and have poor communications and transportation infrastructure. Almost all the consumer goods are imported from outside the region; and in all these states, the non-government employment opportunities are minimal, and hence the government is the principal employer. The region also lags behind the rest of the country in terms of key development indicators.

Unfortunately, the entire region is generally viewed to be affected by insurgency. But the reality is otherwise. This is so because there are hardly any insurgent activities in Arunachal Pradesh,[2] Mizoram and Sikkim (see Table 11.1) All of them are some of the most peaceful states in the country. Meghalaya, too, is one of the peaceful states, with a very low level of insurgency. Therefore, insurgency in the region is largely confined to Assam, Manipur, Nagaland and Tripura, and which in 2008, claimed around 1,049 lives. In 2008, as much as 96 per cent of total fatality was reported from Assam, Manipur and Nagaland. Among the various incidents in 2008, nine near-simultaneous bomb explosions in Assam on 30 October killed nearly 100 people and wounded several others. This was the deadliest terror attack in the history of insurgency in the region.

Meanwhile, insurgency in Nagaland is largely confined to the factional rivalries among rival insurgent groups;[3] while insurgency in Manipur is largely due to the criminal activities unleashed by numerous insurgent groups. Insurgency in Tripura is largely under control. But, the insurgency situation in Assam differs from other states and is disturbing mainly due to the increasing external patronage and manipulations. The state has been facing regular violent incidents with active external support. For instance, the Pakistani Inter Services Intelligence (ISI[4]) has been directly assisting some of the insurgency movements, most notably of the United Liberation Front of Asom (ULFA) and the National Democratic Front of Bodoland (NDFB). It is widely held that the ULFA and the NDFB are 'reliable partners' for ISI in its efforts to promote anti-India operations in Assam. For instance, serial bomb explosions of October 2008 were reportedly the handiwork of the NDFB and the ULFA in collaboration with the Bangladesh-based Harkat-ul-Jihad-al-Islami (HuJI). HuJI is a close associate of the ISI. Available evidences indicate that the ULFA-ISI nexus began in the early 1990s, and that since then the ISI had imparted specialized arms training to several ULFA men. The NDFB too followed suit. In due course of time, this alliance grew rapidly. Further, it was through ULFA that the other smaller insurgent groups came into contact with the ISI. One visible impact of the extensive external influence is the erosion of the original objectives which led to the outbreak of these insurgencies in the first place. For instance, illegal migration into Assam was one of the key triggering factors for the birth of ULFA in 1979. However, as most of their top leaders are taking shelter in neighbou ring Bangladesh, the group hardly raised the issue any longer.

TABLE 11.1: MOST ACTIVE INSURGENT GROUPS IN NORTH-EAST INDIA

Name of the Insurgent Group	Areas of Operations	Goal
United Liberation Front of Asom (ULFA)	Assam	Sovereign socialist Asom (or Assam)
National Democratic Front of Boroland (NDFB)	Assam	Sovereign Boroland (or Bodoland) in the areas north of the river Brahmaputra in Assam
National Socialist Council of Nagaland – Isak-Muivah (NSCN-IM)	Nagaland and parts of Manipur	Greater Nagaland (Nagalim), comprising the whole of the present state of Nagaland and parts of Arunachal Pradesh, Assam and Manipur
National Socialist Council of Nagaland – Khaplang (NSCN-K)	Nagaland	'Greater Nagaland' comprising of the Naga dominated areas of the neighbouring states within India, and contiguous areas in Myanmar
United National Liberation Front (UNLF)	Manipur and some parts of Assam	An independent socialist Manipur
People's Liberation Army (PLA)	Manipur	To organize a revolutio-nary front covering the

		entire North-East and unite all ethnic groups, including the Meiteis, Nagas and Kukis, and to liberate Manipur.
Kanglei Yawol Kanna Lup (KYKL)	Manipur	To rebuild the Manipuri society by clearing it of all vices like immoral activities, drug trade and corruption. It stands for 'nationalism' of the entire North-East to be based on the principle of 'all for one and one for all'.

Moreover, insurgency in Assam has been further compounded by growing internal differences within the insurgent groups. In 2008, a section of ULFA, popularly known as ULFA (pro-talk group), declared a unilateral ceasefire with the government, and the NDFB expelled its founder-president Ranjan Daimary, leading to the emergence of two rival factions. Over the years, the internal differences had been primarily responsible for the proliferation of several insurgent groups. There is a widespread apprehension that these developments could escalate the factional rivalries like that of Nagaland. For instance, on 24 March 2009, Robin Gogoi, a senior leader of the ULFA (pro-talk group), was shot dead by suspected ULFA insurgents in Tinsukia district. About a month later, on 26 April again suspected ULFA killed another member of the pro-talk group, Hitesh Rabha, in Goalpara district. So, the division within NDFB has further compounded the security situation in Bodo-dominated areas of the state.

INSURGENCY AND DEVELOPMENT

Despite being endowed with rich natural resources, the North-East region remains economically backward with poor infrastructural facilities. So as to achieve faster economic development of the region, the central government has made special provision by declaring all the eight constituent states of the region as 'Special

Category States'.[5] Besides, various central ministries have been outlaying funds through their respective budget for the development of their respective sectors in these states. These states are also implementing their own development programmes. Furthermore, the North Eastern Council (NEC[6]) and the Ministry of Development of North East Region (MDONER[7]) exclusively handle the developmental need of the region. Despite all these efforts, the economic development of the region is lagging behind the rest of the country.

Of the eight states of the region, Assam is the second largest (78,523 km^2) and most populous state (26,638,407 persons in 2001). The state shares international land border with Bangladesh and Bhutan. At least three North-Eastern states of Meghalaya, Mizoram and Nagaland were once part of undivided Assam. Insurgency in Assam began in 1979 with the formation of the ULFA[8] and subsequently other insurgent groups had also emerged. By now, the ULFA and the NDFB are considered the two most active insurgent groups there. The former seeks to secure a 'sovereign socialist Asom' through an armed struggle, the latter wants a 'sovereign Boroland' in the areas north of river Brahmaputra of the state.

The trend of economic development in Assam is falling behind the rest of the country. Way back in 1950-1, Assam's per capita income was 4 per cent above the national average, and by 1998-9 it was 45 per cent below the national average (at 1980-1 prices). Between 1980 and 1990, its per capita income (at 1980-1 prices) grew by 20 per cent as compared with 40 per cent for all-India. Between 1951 and 1979, Assam's economy grew at more or less the same rate as the rest of India. While the Indian economy grew at 6 per cent over 1981 to 2000, the Assam state GDP grew only at 3.3 per cent. Growth rate of Indian economy accelerated in the 1990s over 1980s, but Assam's economy decelerated in the 1990s.[9]

Prominent factors for poor growth are: firstly, floods have been major source of handicap for the development of Assam causing serious erosion, loss of life and livestock, damage to infrastructure and property, disrupting communications and posing health hazards. At least 92.6 per cent of the cultivated land in

Assam is flood prone. The flood damage to crops, cattle, houses and utilities in the state between 1953 and 1995 was estimated at Rs. 4,400 crore.[10] Floods are also impeding the technological transformation of agriculture. Farmers in Assam are hesitating to apply costly inputs such as fertilizers and high-yielding variety seed, as the fear of floods washing away the costly inputs is ever present. Secondly, with 87.09 per cent of rural population dependent on agriculture, inadequate attention on agricultural sector will have overwhelmingly negative consequences. Thirdly, industrial growth has been very poor.

Apart from the above mentioned factors, one cannot set aside the impact of insurgency. There are different sorts of costs associated with insurgency. At the same time, measuring the extent of its impacts on development remains a herculean task. But the costs can be broadly seen as: loss of human lives, displacement of population, and other social, political and economic costs. In this context, this paper attempts to explore the extent to which insurgency had affected the economic development in areas impacted by it. This is done by comparing the key development indicators of insurgency-affected states of Assam, Manipur and Nagaland with that of the peaceful states of Mizoram, Sikkim and Meghalaya which is evident in the past three decades. Further, despite the growing literature over the past few years on insurgency in the region, very little attention has been paid to the effects of insurgency on economic development. Therefore, there is need for systemic analysis on the impact of insurgency on development. A detailed analysis of how insurgency impacts economic development has implications for the policy makers, as it allows them to understand the subject better.

Manipur and Nagaland have been facing insurgency since early 1950s, and intensified since the 1990s. Insurgency broke out in Assam since 1979. On the other hand, Mizoram is a peaceful state after a 22-year long insurgency (1966-87).[11] Further, Sikkim is unaffected by insurgency. Likewise, Meghalaya is also peaceful.

Almost all the insurgency movements of the region and their insurgent groups do not have sound financial resources. Running an insurgent group requires a huge amount of money. Let's assume, that an insurgent group spends around Rs. 20,000 per annum to take care of a single man/insurgent. How much they must be spending if there are 5,000 such men? It will run into several crores of rupees. Apart from this, they also need costly firearms. Also they have to utilize a substantial part of their funds in the training of their personnel, especially the new recruits. Where from all these funds came from? Not all the insurgent groups are involved in gun running or drug trade. As a result, they resorted to a number of means to raise funds from within their areas of operations. Therefore, the impact of insurgency on economic development could be analysed by examining the following.

1. *Illegal Taxation:* As noted above, running an insurgent group like ULFA requires huge amounts of money, therefore they resorted to illegal taxation and siphoned-off a significant amount of development funds in collusion with officials of the state. Almost all the major business establishments, oil and tea companies were illegally taxed in Assam. This is extended to salaried people, petty traders and villagers, demanding regular payments in small amounts. The ULFA was suspected to be collecting at least Rs. 1.5 crore every month from such micro-collections, and their annual budget was estimated somewhere between Rs. 30 and 35 crore.[12] Likewise other insurgent groups also employed similar tactics to raise funds. As a result, extortion is normally rampant; and it might be difficult for senior leaders of all the insurgency groups to monitor the large-scale extortion that was going on in the name of their group. H.N. Das, the former Chief Secretary of the Government of Assam remarked, 'The major portions of such funds seem to have come indirectly from government sources. The extortionist can easily blackmail corrupt officials because they know the illegal activities of these officials. The same is the case with the unscrupulous businessmen who easily pay up'.[13] Further, rural development, according to H.N. Das, has been identified as a 'lucrative sector' and it is estimated that as much as 70 per cent of all the funds available to the Assam government was systematically siphoned off under a well-organized network of ULFA and surrendered ULFA (locally known as SULFA) cadres,

contractors, civil servants and members of the political elites. Quoting unspecified sources, H.N. Das, estimated that of the total Rs. 11.65 billion made available under various rural development schemes during the period 1992-3 to February 1998, less than Rs. 4 billion went to legitimate schemes. It is also well known that several businessmen resorted to the practice of making up their losses due to extortion by creating artificial scarcities and thus raising the prices of the goods and commodities. Hence, the common men suffer the most.

Further, the insurgents also directly or indirectly interfere in the award of government contracts and execution of developmental projects. In many cases, these contracts were awarded to those individuals loyal to certain insurgent group from which the latter received certain percentage of the funds. This is further compounded owing to the presence of a large number of insurgent groups. In this context, one scholar remarked: 'terrorist organizations have developed a vested interest to work within the existing governmental system by subverting and exploiting the existing institutions for financial gain rather than dismantling them'.[14] Officials of the state heading crucial departments such as Public Works Department or Public Health were regularly intimidated and those refusing to cooperate were either abducted or killed.[15] In order to be on the safe side many officials, under duress, associated themselves with the insurgents and their 'partnerships' grew rapidly. Thus, an uneasy nexus involving the insurgents and the officials had developed. Therefore, insurgency had promoted corruption in the state administration. No doubt, the insurgency affected states of the region are known to be more corrupt than the peaceful ones.

Extensive extortion has adverse impact on people's willing ness to invest in productive activities due to the insecurity. Fear associated with insurgency and counter-insurgency also restricts people's free movement, either for work or leisure, and this in turn affects their work culture and productivity. Mahendra P. Lama, a scholar from the region succinctly argued:

> It is clear that the resources allocated for both plan and non-plan expenditures have not been utilised for the purposes they were allocated for. Even if they were targeted to objectives such as poverty

alleviation, public distribution system, health, education, drinking water and rural electrification, these resources either did not reach the target groups or had a huge leakage in the delivery mechanism. In the absence of any monitoring and evaluation of these projects and related use of resources, the leakage and diversion of funds became a regular feature and gradually became institutionalised. Meanwhile, the resources kept coming in from Delhi regardless of how they were utilised. This continuous flow of resources resulted in emergence and consolidation of institutionalized corruption.[16]

2. *Development Projects*: There are several reasons that impinge upon the timely implementation of development projects in Assam. Insurgency is one of them. In several instances, insurgency delayed the timely execution and completion of development projects leading to escalation of the costs. Sometimes projects had to be abandoned due to insecurity. Clinching evidence to this is the 201-km long Silchar–Lumding Broad Gauge Conversion Project in Assam. The project was sanctioned in 1996 with a budget of Rs. 648 crore. The said project came to a grinding halt due to unabated violence unleashed by Dimasa insurgents—the Dima Halam Daogah (DHD) and its arch rival the Black Widow—who resorted to kidnapping and killing of worker engaged in the project. The project was earlier targeted to be completed in 2006, but the deadline was revised to 2009, resulting in cost escalation to Rs. 1,823 crore. Once the project is completed it would make commuting between Brahmaputra and Barak valleys more convenient. Insurgency, according to Indian Ministry of Railways, has been identified as one of the reasons for the 'very slow' progress of the railway modernization schemes in Assam. Other reasons identified were long and heavy rainy season and non-use of mechanized methods for track renewal.[17]

3. *Ethnic Displacement:* Contesting claims over land and territory by insurgent groups who claimed to represent a particular ethnic/tribal group often led to violent conflict, such as the Kuki–Karbi violent conflict.[18] These incidents not only claimed several human lives but also displaced several thousands from their homes thereby disturbing their livelihood for years. In 2005, clashes

between the Karbi and the Dimasa insurgent groups displaced several thousand people. The largest conflict-induced displacement in Assam occurred due to the fighting between the Bodos and the Santhals which erupted in the early 1990s. Till August 2004, as much as 230,000 people were reportedly staying in relief camps across the state.[19] In all these episodes, insurgent groups claiming to represent a particular ethnic/tribal group played a key role in triggering the ethnic violence.

4. *Loss of Public Property:* Insurgents also caused widespread destruction of public properties including rail infrastructure including numerous violent attacks carried out to passengers' as well as good trains. The oil and tea companies in the state were also repeatedly intimidated and their oil pipelines and installations were regularly blown up, and their officials/personnel were either abducted or killed. The oil majors—the Oil and Natural Gas Corporation Ltd. (ONGC) and the Oil India Limited (OIL)—have suffered the adverse effects of insurgency and terrorism, and their gas and oil installations have been regularly targeted. There had been several instances of attacks against the OIL and ONGC staff, including kidnapping and killing. Oil and gas production and explorations were frequently interrupted. Large-scale destruction has been wrought on public property such as roads, bridges, and schools by different Bodo insurgent groups in the 1990s.

5. *Tourism:* Tourism is yet another victim of insurgency. Although there is no report of any harm being meted out to the tourists visiting the state, but the latter generally felt insecure to visit Assam in view of the existing security situations. Major tourist spots, including the Dibru-Saikhowa National Park and the Manas Wildlife Sanctuary, are known to be safe havens for insurgents. In the past, the security forces had also launched several operations in and around these parks to flush out the insurgents. The Manas Wildlife Sanctuary had been virtually under the control of the Bodo insurgents. In 2007, Assam ranked 22nd as against Sikkim's 21st rank in terms of foreign tourists' arrival in the country.[20] One of the travel advisory of the Australian

government issued to its citizens visiting the North-East region said: 'We advise you to reconsider your need to travel to the North-Eastern states of Assam, Nagaland, Tripura and Manipur because of the risk of armed robbery, kidnapping, extortion and terrorism-related incidents. If you do decide to travel to these areas, you should exercise extreme caution.'[21]

In such a state of affairs, private investments have decelerated in Assam. Several experts have argued that there has been flight of capital from Assam, which is evident from the steadily declining credit-deposit ratio of banks, and the diversion of surplus funds and earnings by industrial establishments outside the state. In the name of diversification some tea companies have taken out surplus funds to units outside the state. The credit-deposit ratio has declined from 50.20 per cent as on 31 December 1991 to 31.00 per cent as on 31 December 2001. Jayanta Madhab, an economist from Assam, noted that

> [T]he credit-deposit ratio being very low in the region, the banking sector transfers something like Rs. 5,000 crore from this region to other regions for investment. Because of prolonged insurgency in the region, despite abundance of natural resources (oil, gas, coal, granite, limestone, water and forest wealth), no outside investment has taken place. Indeed, there was capital flight in the last eight years from the region.[22]

The credit-deposit ratio of all insurgency affected states has declined substantially over the years (Table 11.2).

The Siliguri town (4.7 lakh people in 2001) in West Bengal bordering Assam is located in the narrow corridor connecting North-East region with the rest of the country. Siliguri town has been emerging as a business hub, which is happening at the expense of Guwahati and other towns of Assam from where several traders and businessmen have partially shifted their bases. Similarly, some industrial units have shifted over to Burnihat area of Meghalaya.

As a consequence of insurgency and its related violence, the government attention was often diverted from development activities to maintaining security, and law and order. As a result, large amounts of money, energy and time were spent on non-

TABLE 11.2: CREDIT-DEPOSIT RATIOS IN PER CENT
(FOR SCHEDULED COMMERCIAL BANKS)

States	Credit-Deposit Ratio 2005	Credit-Deposit Ratio 1995	Credit-Deposit Ratio 1985
Assam	35.3	38.7	50.2
Manipur	42.4	58.2	72.4
Meghalaya	43.6	17.0	24.9
Mizoram	47.8	16.5	24.9
Nagaland	22.9	37.8	35.6
Sikkim	29.5	24.0	15.7
Tripura	28.6	47.5	65.4

Source: India Development Report 2008, New Delhi: Oxford University Press, 2008, p. 225.

developmental activities. This was accompanied by a drastic cut in the development expenditure. For instance, the public spending on education and health sectors, is low in insurgency-affected states (see Table 11.3). As long as there is insurgency, there is likely to be a decreased spending in health and education sectors by the insurgency-affected states.

TABLE 11.3: PUBLIC SPENDING ON EDUCATION AND HEALTH AS RATIO OF GROSS DOMESTIC PRODUCT

States	1980-1		1990-1		1998-9	
	Education	Health	Education	Health	Education	Health
Assam	3.46	1.48	4.53	1.32	5.23	1.05
Manipur	8.63	5.57	10.26	2.39	9.00	1.95
Meghalaya	4.83	7.93	7.12	2.78	5.58	2.32
Mizoram	–	–	12.73	4.47	–	–
Nagaland	10.22	12.25	7.83	4.39	–	–
Sikkim	7.59	4.78	11.62	5.14	12.55	4.92
Tripura	5.81	2.38	10.35	3.26	7.58	2.14

Note: Public spending on education includes both revenue and capital expenditure for both plan and non-plan.

Source: National Human Development Report 2001, New Delhi: Planning Commission, 2002, p. 291.

The central government took care of the much of the security-related expenditure incurred by the states of the region. The annual quantum of central assistance released for security-related expenditure to the region (except Sikkim) has gone up from Rs. 104.86 crore in 2000-1 to Rs. 153.44 crore in 2006-7 (see Table 11.4). In 2006-7, over half of these amounts—Rs. 90.86 crore—have gone to Assam alone. An expert committee of the central government found the flight of capital from rural to urban areas of Assam due to threat posed by insurgency. The committee found that an upsurge in insurgency was responsible for practically no developmental activities in rural areas.[23] So much so that the Assam government has sought a special package of Rs. 250 billion over the next five years (2009-13) from the central government to offset the economic damage incurred due to 30 years of insurgency.

In such an environment of rampant extortion, compounded by widespread corruption, development activities have languished. Basic infrastructure facilities like roads, communications, health care and education, all show visible signs of decline. And, innocent civilians suffer the most. With these discussions the following sections examine the growth performance of North-East states in terms of key developmental indicators. Emphasis is given on comparing the growth performance of peaceful states to that of the insurgency-affected ones.

DEVELOPMENT INDICATORS

Having discussed various facets of insurgency on development, this section exclusively highlights the growth performance of key development indicators before and after insurgency broke out in Assam. Hence, efforts have been made to compare the growth performance of key development indicators of the insurgency-affected states and the peaceful states. It is noticed (Table 11.5) that the overall per capita income of the peaceful states is growing at the faster pace in comparison with those of the insurgency-affected states. Just imagine, in 1990-1, Sikkim (a peaceful state) had the second highest average income after Nagaland (an insurgency-affected state), and by 1999-2000, Sikkim had overtaken Nagaland.[24]

TABLE 11.4: CENTRAL GOVERNMENT ASSISTANCE ON SECURITY-RELATED EXPENDITURE (FIGURES IN CRORE)

State	2000-1	2001-2	2002-3	2003-4	2004-5	2005-6	2006-7	2007-8 (up to 29.02.08)	Grand Total
Assam	63.97	92.86	68.01	50.80	75.40	63.91	90.86	53.01	558.82
Nagaland	7.50	12.71	22.42	19.17	26.49	24.83	25.55	7.60	146.27
Manipur	14.18	7.75	7.64	4.00	9.44	33.65	13.60	5.16	95.42
Tripura	15.00	27.70	29.85	34.33	36.17	27.00	18.24	4.44	192.73
Arunachal Pradesh	1.00	1.90	0.95	2.47	1.35	1.35	1.28	–	10.30
Meghalaya	3.21	0.60	8.35	1.92	1.56	13.17	3.91	2.69	35.41
Total	104.86	143.52	137.22	112.69	150.41	163.91	153.44	72.90	1038.95

Source: Annual Report 2007-8, New Delhi: Ministry of Home Affairs, Government of India, 2008, p. 16.

TABLE 11.5: PER CAPITA INCOME IN NORTH-EAST INDIA
(CURRENT PRICES 1999-2000 SERIES IN RUPEES)

State	2001-2	2003-4	2005-6
Assam	13,153	15,687	18,598
Sikkim	17,324	21,476	26,412
Nagaland	18,961	20,821	-
Manipur	12,801	14,728	20,326
Mizoram	19,430	21,963	-
Meghalaya	17,936	20,729	23,420
Tripura	18,368	21,138	24,706

Source: Data compiled from Directorate of Economics & Statistics of respective state governments.

The percentage of people below poverty line in Assam is also one of the highest among the North-Eastern states (see Table 11.6). The percentage of people below poverty line in peaceful states like Mizoram in 1973-4 was 50.32 per cent and it steadily came down to 19.47 in 1999-2000. These imbalances could have been due to serious disruption of life due to insurgency.

In terms of per capita consumption of electricity which is also a good indicator of development, the peaceful states are far better off than those affected by insurgency. Most insurgency-affected states, including Assam, registered low per capita of electricity consumption. As far as hospital beds per million are concerned, Mizoram (1,029.9) and Sikkim (1,192.5) have more than the national average of 665.5 beds per million (Table 11.7). The shortfall is serious for all the insurgency infested states: Assam (472.7), Nagaland (543.1) and also for Manipur (655.3).[25]

Again, almost all the peaceful states have performed remarkably in terms of their literacy, which is also another key developmental indicator (See Table 11.8). Further, according to the *5th Economic Census*[26] of 2005, there were 9,83,693 establishments of which 42,466 were agricultural establishments and 9,41,227 non-agricultural establishments in Assam. When compared with the previous *Economic Census* of 1998, the compound annual growth rate of establishments during the period 1998-2005 was of the order of 7.49 per cent. Employment

TABLE 11.6: POPULATION BELOW POVERTY LINE (IN LAKH)

States	1973-4		1983-4		1993-4		1999-2000	
	No. of persons	% of persons	No. of persons	% of persons	No. of persons	% of persons	No. of persons	% of persons
Arunachal Pradesh	2.66	51.93	2.83	40.88	3.73	39.35	3.98	33.47
Assam	81.83	51.21	77.69	40.47	96.36	40.86	94.55	36.09
Manipur	5.36	49.98	5.65	37.02	6.80	33.72	7.19	28.54
Meghalaya	5.52	50.20	5.62	38.81	7.38	37.92	8.23	33.87
Mizoram	1.82	50.32	1.96	36.00	1.94	25.66	1.85	19.47
Nagaland	2.90	50.81	3.50	39.25	5.05	37.92	5.49	32.67
Sikkim	1.18	50.86	1.35	39.71	1.84	41.43	2.05	36.55
Tripura	8.54	51.00	8.95	40.03	11.79	39.01	13.02	34.44
All India	3,213.36	54.68	3,228.97	44.48	3,203.68	35.97	2,602.50	26.10

Source: National Human Development Report 2001, pp. 164-66.

TABLE 11.7: PER CAPITA CONSUMPTION OF ELECTRICITY AND AVAILABILITY OF HOSPITAL BEDS IN NORTH-EAST INDIA

States	Consumption of Electricity				Hospital Beds* (2002)	
	1986-7	1989-90	1996-7	1999-2000		Ranks
Assam	51	78	104	–	472.7	5
Manipur	48	80	128	69.5	655.3	3
Meghalaya	83	108	135	160.3	485.9	4
Mizoram	26	57	128	120.7	1029.9	2
Nagaland	56	70	88	84.7	543.1	6
Sikkim	57	96	172	192.4	1192.5	1
Tripura	29	51	80	–	446.0	8
All India	191	236	334	354.7	665.2	

Sources: Data compiled from the *Economic Survey 2007-2008*, New Delhi: Ministry of Finance, Government of India, 2008; *National Human Development Report 2001*; and from www.indiastat.com.

TABLE 11.8: LITERACY IN NORTH-EAST INDIA

States	1971		1981		1991		2001	
	Percentage	Ranking	Percentage	Ranking	Percentage	Ranking	Percentage	Ranking
Assam	33.0	2	–	–	52.89	6	64.28	6
Manipur	36.0	1	49.66	4	59.89	4	68.87	4
Meghalaya	–	–	42.05	5	49.10	7	63.31	7
Mizoram	–	–	74.26	1	82.27	1	88.49	1
Nagaland	20.4	4	50.28	2	61.65	2	67.11	5
Sikkim	14.2	5	41.59	6	56.94	5	69.68	3
Tripura	24.3	3	50.11	3	60.44	3	73.66	2

Source: India Development Report 2008, p. 267.

grew at the rate of 0.09 per cent per annum during the period 1998-2005[27] (see Table 11.9). In another insurgency-infested state of Manipur, the compound annual growth rate of establishments during the period 1998-2005 was of the order of 3.83 per cent. Employment grew at the rate of 2.34 per cent per annum during the period 1998-2005.[28] Further, in Nagaland, the compound annual growth rate of establishments during the period 1998-2005 was of the order of 2.70 per cent. Employment

TABLE 11.9: GROWTH OF EMPLOYMENT AND UNEMPLOYMENT IN NORTH-EAST INDIA

States	Growth of Employment[1]			Incidence of Unemployment[2]		
	1983-4 to 1993-4	1993-4 to 1999-2000	1998-2005	1983-4	1993-4	1999-2000
Assam	1.6	2.5	0.09	2.2	5.6	4.6
Manipur	3.3	2.0	2.34	0.4	1.8	3.5
Meghalaya	3.5	2.6	3.98	1.5	0.5	0.9
Mizoram	6.3	4.0	4.68	0.4	0.8	2.0
Nagaland	22.4	8.6	0.04	0.3	2.4	3.5
Sikkim	2.3	3.4	5.33	2.2	1.0	3.4
Tripura	4.3	1.4	7.87	3.9	3.4	1.9
All India	2.1	1.6	2.78	2.0	2.0	2.3

Notes: 1. Growth in employment has been estimated as compound annual growth in persons employed in the age group 15 years and above on the usual principal and subsidiary status.
2. Incidence of unemployment is defined as the percentage of persons unemployed in the age group 15 years and above on the usual principal and subsidiary status to the total number of persons in the labour force.

Source: *National Human Development Report 2001*, pp. 158 and 161; and data compiled from the *Fifth Economic Census 2005*.

grew at the rate of 0.04 per cent per annum during the period 1998-2005.[29]

The situation in other peaceful states is quite encouraging. For instance, in Meghalaya, the compound annual growth rate of establishments during 1998-2005 was of the order of 5.69 per cent. And, employment grew at the rate of 3.98 per cent per annum.[30] Similarly, in Mizoram, the compound annual growth rate of establishments during the period 1998-2005 was of the order of 9.71 per cent. And, the employment grew at the rate of 4.68 per cent per annum.[31] Further in Sikkim, the compound annual growth rate of establishments was of the order of 5.79 per cent. And, the employment grew at the rate of 5.33 per cent per annum.[32]

CONCLUSIONS: WHICH WAY NOW?

This paper has attempted to shed light on the impact of insurgency on economic development in India's North-Eastern states. The paper strongly argued that besides the loss of human lives, insurgency has acted as one of the stumbling blocks to economic development in areas affected by it. The paper clearly underscores the fact that the peaceful states have recorded faster economic development in comparison with other insurgency-affected states. Way back in the 1960s and 1970s, these peaceful states were some of the most backward areas of the region, and now, they have overtaken insurgency-affected states. In such a situation, there is strong evidence to show that insurgency has been a deterrent to economic development. In sum, the impact of insurgency needs to be examined in greater detail with follow-up work in the various areas that have been identified in this paper. Lastly, the paper offers the following policy suggestions:

1. *Need for Focus on Political Dialogue:* It is fashionable to blame the ongoing peace talks, as these processes took several years without much tangible result. However, one should not underestimate its importance as it remains the most effective tool to resolve the grievances of the insurgent groups such as that of the erstwhile Mizo National Front (MNF) and Bodo Liberation Tigers (BLT). Presently, several such groups have entered into temporary ceasefire agreements with the government. Unfortunately, the peace initiative to facilitate direct talks between the ULFA and the government has remained a non-starter. In recent times, this has been manifested by the emergence of ULFA (pro-talk group) and the expulsion of Ranjan Daimary from the NDFB. The ULFA (pro-talk group) and a faction of NDFB are in favour of resolving their grievances within the framework of the Constitution. However, neither of these factions are capable of emerging as suitable partners with whom the government could work for restoring peace in the state. As a result, the unilateral ceasefire by ULFA (pro-talk group) and the ceasefire with a faction of NDFB might not succeed in bringing peace to Assam. Although, conditions for favourable peace talks have

been complicated by the emergence of factions within these groups, we cannot easily set aside the importance of peace talks.

2. *State funding of Ceasefire Group:* One way of containing the extortion practices of the ceasefire bound insurgent groups could be by way of state funding of ceasefire groups such as DHD as long as the peace talks continue.

3. *Involve Civil Society Groups:* As a part of the building confidence building measures the government must open a channel of dialogue with the civil society groups. It is highly necessary that members of the insurgent organization may also be given safe passage during major festivals.

4. *Strengthening the State Police Force:* This has been neglected for years. It is the need of the hour. Instead of the Army or other central paramilitary forces, let the state police handle the insurgency. This will surely help in containing the alienation of the people.

NOTES

1. For details on the creation of new states and territorially-defined autonomous councils, see M. Amarjeet Singh, 'Assam: Challenges before Bodo Territorial Council', *Economic and Political Weekly*, 39(8), 2004, Mumbai, pp. 56-7; and M. Amarjeet Singh, 'Ethnic Diversity, Autonomy and Territoriality in Northeast India: A Case of Tribal Autonomy in Assam', *Strategic Analysis*, 32(6), November 2008, pp. 1103-14.
2. Insurgents from Assam and Nagaland usually took temporary shelter in the deep forests of Arunachal Pradesh.
3. Scc M. Amarjeet Singh, 'The Attempt to Sideline Muivah', *IDSA Strategic Comments*, 2 February 2008.
4. See M. Amarjeet Singh, 'The ISI's Supervisory Role in Assam', *IDSA Strategic Comments*, 7 November 2006.
5. All the states in the North-East are 'special category states' which means the central government funds up to 90 per cent of their capital budget requirements.
6. The North Eastern Council is the nodal agency for the economic and social development of the north-east region. For details, visit http://necouncil.nic.in.

7. For details of the Ministry of Development of North East Region, please visit http://mdoner.gov.in.
8. For a detailed study on insurgency in Assam, see K. Hrishikeshan, 'Assam's Agony: The ULFA and Obstacles to Conflict Resolution', *FAULTLINES: Writing on Conflict and Resolution*, vol. 12, May 2002, New Delhi, pp. 23-37.
9. For a detailed study on the economy of Assam, see *Assam Human Development Report 2003*, Government of Assam, 2004.
10. S.P. Shukla, *Commission, Report of the High Level Commission, Transforming the North-East-Tackling Backlogs in Basic Minimum Services and Infrastructural Needs*, Part I, Planning Commission, Government of India, 1997.
11. Mizo insurgency came to an end following an agreement between the Mizo National Front (MNF) and the central government in 1987.
12. Rahul Karmakar, 'ULFA Extortion goes Micro, EMI', *Hindustan Times*, 18 May 2007.
13. H.N. Das, 'Economic Consequences of Insurgency in Assam', *Indian Police Journal*, January-March 2008, p. 72.
14. Archana Upadhyay, 'Terrorism in the North-East: Linkages and Implications', *Economic and Political Weekly*, 2 December 2006, p. 4997.
15. Abducted Food Corporation of India (FCI) official Dr. P.C. Ram was killed during a gun battle between security forces and ULFA in Kamrup district of Assam on 12 July 2007. Dr. Ram, Executive Director (Northeast) of FCI, and his driver were abducted by ULFA on 17 April 2007.
16. Mahendra P. Lama, 'India's North-East States: Narcotics, Small Arms and Misgovernance', *Ethnic Studies Report*, 19(2), July 2001, p. 244.
17. Ministry of Railways, Government of India, *Rail Network in North East Region: Expansion and Investment* (Sixth Report of the Standing Committee on Railways—2004-05), Lok Sabha Secretariat, New Delhi, 2005.
18. Praveen Kumar, 'Karbi-Kuki Clashes in Assam', *Strategic Analysis*, 28(2), April-June 2004.
19. Internally Displaced Monitoring Centre (IDMC), *India: Large Numbers of IDPs are Unassisted and in Need of Protection*, Geneva, 3 May 2006, p. 5.
20. Ministry of Tourism, Government of India, *Indian Tourism Statistics 2007*, New Delhi, 2008, p. 70.

21. Australian Department of Foreign Affairs and Trade, Australian Government, Travel Advice, India, at http://www.smartraveller.gov.au/zw-cgi/view/Advice/India (accessed on 12 May 2009).
22. Jayanta Madhab, 'North-East: Crisis of Identity, Security and Underdevelopment', *Economic and Political Weekly*, Bombay, 6 February 1999.
23. Ministry of Rural Development, Government of India, '*Report of the Committee on Credit Related Issues under IRDP in North Eastern States*, New Delhi, 2000.
24. Planning Commission, Government of India, *Sikkim Development Deport*, 2008, p. 35.
25. This is for the year 2002.
26. The complete details of the scope and coverage of the *Economic Census* is available at http://mospi.gov.in/4ec_chapter1.htm (accessed on 1 May 2009).
27. Central Statistical Organisation (CSO), Ministry of Statistics & Programme Implementation, Government of India, *Fifth Economic Census 2005*, *Assam*, January 2008, New Delhi, pp. 1-2.
28. Ibid., *Manipur*, January 2008, New Delhi, pp. 1-2.
29. Ibid., *Nagaland*, ibid., pp. 1-2.
30. Ibid., *Meghalaya*, ibid., pp. 1-2.
31. Ibid., *Mizoram*, ibid., pp. 1-2.
32. Ibid., *Sikkim*, ibid., pp. 1-2.

CHAPTER 12

Security-Development Interconnection: The Assam Perspective

M.P. Bezbaruah

INTRODUCTION

In the post-Independence period, the state of Assam has gone through prolonged turbulence originating from both exogenous factors and internal upheavals. In August 1947, when India attained Independence from British rule, the entire North-East region, barring Manipur and Tripura, was the undivided Assam province. The administrative arrangement throughout the then Assam province was, however, not uniform. While the plains were under effective administration of the provincial government, the hills inhabited mostly by tribal people were virtually left out from that system of administration. In fact, the hills were classified as 'excluded' or 'partially excluded' areas depending on 'whether the area was inhabited by a compact aboriginal population or the aboriginal population was mixed with the other communities'.[1] Though the administration of these areas was vested on the Governor, in effect the tribal groups were left alone to continue with their traditional administrative arrangements. After Independence measures became necessary to integrate these areas into the administrative system of the country. The hill tract forming the north-eastern part of the region, which constitutionally remained a part of Assam till becoming the Union Territory of Arunachal Pradesh, was named as North-East Frontier Agency and administered directly by the central government. For the remaining erstwhile 'excluded' and 'partially excluded' areas of Assam, autonomous districts with district councils were provided under the Sixth Schedule of the Constitution. However, the arrangement did not meet the aspirations of the newly emerging political leadership of many of the hill tribes inhabiting these areas and these tribal groups organized movement for greater autonomy and separate statehood. The states of Nagaland, Mizoram and Meghalaya were eventually carved out of Assam in response to these movements. Unfortunately the steps did not succeed in resolving the question of tribal ethnic identity. Instead, formation of the smaller states encouraged other ethnic groups to organize themselves into struggles for more autonomy and separate statehood. As it became clear that creation of newer states in the region was no longer viable, in the more recent period the ethnic aspirations have been sought to be quelled by providing autonomous councils. Besides causing frequent disruptions to normal life through agitations, these movements have also contributed directly or indirectly towards perpetuation of insurgency and bloodshed in the state.

Meanwhile, Partition of the country at Independence virtually disrupted links of the state with the rest of India and the world, raising cost of movement of man and material to and from the state. Further, the wars with neighbouring countries in the 1960s raised security concerns among potential investors in the region. The industrialization of the economy taking place under colonial rule came to a standstill. During the early plan period, when India pursued a public sector led development programme, there was little appreciation of these difficulties faced by the state at the central policy making circle. In consequence Assam quickly slipped from its status of a high per capita income state of India in 1951 to a low per capita income state by 1961.[2] The process fermented a sense of neglect by the centre among the people of Assam. The resulting alienation later contributed in no small measure to growth of separatist movement in the state.

Besides, the state experienced unusually high rate of population growth, especially till 1971, fuelled initially by influx of Partition related refugees but sustained later by inflow of both refugees and economic migrants, legal and illegal. Besides straining the limited opportunities in a period of slow progress of the economy, the influx had an impact on the religious and linguistic composition of the population of the state, arousing a perception of insecurity of identity among the indigenous people of the state.

Marked by relatively slow growth of the economy and frequent breaches of security induced from conflicts related to identity aspirations of groups, the post-Independence history of Assam provides a fit case for exploring the efficacy of various ideas and hypotheses about security-development interconnections. The present paper pursues this exploration and attempts to infer a suitable policy package for dealing with the under-development-insecurity nexus in the state. Before moving forward on this agenda, a conceptual background on 'development' and 'security' is provided here.

THE EVOLVING NOTIONS OF 'DEVELOPMENT' AND 'SECURITY'

Both 'development' and 'security' are almost universally desired, but the connotations of the terms have defied exact delimitation. Development became an important issue in the post-Second World War years as war ravaged economies of the north set out on reconstruction path and countries in the south, having attained Independence from colonial rule, aspired to 'catch up' with the developed north. Broadly, development is understood as a dynamic process resulting in sustained improvement in the quality of life of the people. However, the indicators of the quality of life as well as component of the dynamic process have not been unanimously determined. Initially, i.e. in 1950s and 1960s, development used to be equated with and measured in terms of per capita income. Since per capita income is simply the average income, indicating the average access of the population to goods and services without taking into account the large inequality that may exist in the distribution of that access, the limitation of the measure became readily apparent. Some writers of development economics therefore tried to qualify per capita income as a measure of development with the stipulation that the distribution of income must not become more unequal as the level of per capita income rise.[3] However, more serious limitation of the measure came to be realized in the 1970s as it became clear that mere access to goods and services is not enough to improve the quality of life of people, unless their capabilities are enhanced to make best use of available commodities. Accordingly, the 1970s saw a shift in the measurement of development emphasizing also on attainment of health standards captured in parameters like life expectancy and infant mortality, and educational attainment of society seen in terms of literacy rate. Since 1990 the UNDP has been annually publishing the Human Development Report which has popularized the notion of 'human development'. Combining both the 'commodity' and 'capability' approach, human development has been defined as a process of enlarging people's choice in three essential areas of (1) living a long and healthy life, (2) acquiring knowledge, and (3) having a decent standard of living.[4] While the concept of human develop has largely caught on, its measurement has evolved considerably in the last decade and a half. UNDP's own version of the Human Development Index (HDI) has undergone change over the years as a result of refinement of indicators of components of human development and also due to the practical problem of obtaining reliable data on initially selected indicators. At the national and sub-national levels the HDI have been further adapted to better suit the local context.[5]

Likewise the connotation of security has evolved over the last few decades. Traditionally, security used to be often equated with security of a nation from external threats. Following the end of the Cold War by the end of 1980s, the focus shifted from security of a nation to security of individuals and people, which came to be referred to as 'human security', for which security of the traditional type is only a necessary but not a sufficient condition. Initially human security was viewed as security from bodily threat of being injured, killed and/or robbed from violent acts that may arise from individual or group conflicts. Subsequent literature attempted to expand the notion of human security to encompass security of food and other basic needs. Thus human security came to be thought of as comprising of two components, viz., 'freedom from fear' and 'freedom from wants'.[6] Indeed there has been an argument to expand the concept further by incorporating not only 'basic freedom' or freedom from wants but also 'civil freedom' which includes things like freedom of cultural practices.[7]

DELIMITATION OF 'SECURITY' IN THE PRESENT CONTEXT

For the present context, too broad a notion of security will not be helpful. Since the goal of 'freedom from wants' form a significant part of development aspiration, interpreting security as compressing of both 'freedom from fear' and 'freedom from want' will largely subsume 'development' in 'security' itself. Consequently, a discussion on development-security interaction will not be meaningful. Hence, in the present context, the term 'security' will be limited to its 'freedom from fear' component only. Even within this component, security will be limited to freedom from fear arising from group conflicts, which will encompass conflicts between a group and the state, between two groups and threat from insurgent groups. The other components of fear arising from poor state of general law and order such as fear of theft, dacoits, crime against women and children are on doubt important. But they are not specific to our reference location of the state of Assam.

MANIFESTATION OF THE UNDERDEVELOPMENT-INSECURITY NEXUS IN ASSAM

Since both development process and security situation in Assam have had a marred record in the post-Independence period, a question is often asked if insecurity and underdevelopment in the state have been causally related. More specifically it is questioned whether persistence of underdevelopment has bred the conflicts which subsequently turns violent and often give rise to insurgency. Alternatively it is asked if insurgency has actually kept the development process at bay giving rise to a vicious circle of underdevelopment and insecurity. The questions are not mere academic issues but have important policy implications, and therefore deserve some detailed discussion.

IS UNDERDEVELOPMENT THE ROOT CAUSE OF INSECURITY?

The traditional Marxist view, which gives primacy to economic factors forming the 'basic structure' over cultural and other factors which are supposed to be part of the 'superstructure', holds that underdevelopment has been the root cause of conflict-induced insecurity in the state. The basic argument runs in the following line. When underdevelopment persists, shortages surface everywhere and people have to compete for basic necessities as well as economic opportunities (say jobs). In a climate of shortage it is easy to blame a group of depriving another group. Such blame, real or perceived, has the potency of snowballing into group conflicts. In support of this line of argument, evidence is available in the form of Assam slipping from 'above all-India per capita income state' at the time of Independence to 'below all-India per capita income state' by 1961 and Assam slipping further behind the all-India average in most development indicators including per capita income especially in post-1991 period.

A closer look at the origins of the major group conflicts in Assam in the post-Independence period, however, shows that it would be simplistic to explain the resulting insecurity in terms of underdevelopment alone. The first major conflict taking place in Assam in the post-Independence period was a by-product of the language movement where the main issue was about the choice of a state language—more a cultural factor or identity related issue than a dispute over economic opportunities. The foreign national movement starting in late 1970s was once again triggered off by the fear of being outnumbered by immigrants. Even the Bodo movement, invariably focused on securing a homeland for the Bodo people, a territory the tribe would control politically. In short, all these major conflicts in post-Independence Assam had their seeds in movements launched by groups for asserting their cultural identity. The movements inevitably gave birth to conflict situations as one group's attempt to secure a homeland or a larger sphere of influence inevitably meant a threat for another group, as people of different tribes, religion and linguistic affinity live in the state in a geographically disperse manner, rather than compartmentalized locations. In both the movements against foreign nationals and the Bodo movement, economic issues were no doubt raised. But such issues got added up subsequently to the key issues as the movements acquired momentum. Hence, a safer conclusion seems to be that the failure to accommodate identity aspiration of the groups has been as much, if not more, responsible for the prolonged adverse security situation in the state as the failure to expedite the pace of development.

UNDERDEVELOPMENT-INSECURITY NEXUS

While underdevelopment may not have been at the root of most of the conflict-induced insecurity in the state, it is not difficult to see that there is a strong nexus between underdevelopment and insecurity and the two have been locked up in a mutually reinforcing vicious circle in Assam.

Persistence of underdevelopment has been constantly used by militant groups to whip up a passion of 'neglect' by the state and the central governments and 'exploitation' by other groups. Such passion serves as useful capital for mass mobilization as well as mobilization of insurgent outfit. Moreover, in a situation of dearth of employment opportunities giving reasonable economic returns, insurgent groups find it easy to induct fresh recruits to their cadres.

The state of insecurity has adversely affected implementation of public sector projects for infrastructure development, critical for overcoming the deficiency of social overheads in the state. As it is, infrastructure projects like railway and highway construction is difficult to implement in the region because of prolonged rainy season in the area. Militant activities in the form of *bandhs* and obstructions by insurgent groups compound the problem of implementation of such projects on which the economic development of the region hinges so critically. The railway gauge conversion project in the hill section of NF Railway between Lumding in Brahmaputra Valley and Badarpur in Barak Valley is a classic example. Disrupted frequently by ethnic conflict in the hills, interference by several insurgent groups, kidnapping of project officials and killing of workers; work on the project has been going on for years in an off and on manner leading to enormous cost escalation and time overrun and more importantly missing out on development opportunities.

The climate of insecurity is obviously not conducive for the inflow of private investment. It is therefore little wonder that FDI inflow to Assam till date is virtually negligible.[8] On the contrary, there are reports of serious outflow of private capital from the region. This has severe development consequence in the present paradigm of market-oriented economic system, where commercially oriented units are expected to carry out the major chunk of economic activities and the state is expect to limit itself mostly to provision of public goods.

Moreover, dealing with conflicts, violence and insurgency strains governmental efforts so much that general governance has often suffered. There is ample evidence to show that quality of governance has been a significant factor accounting for differences in development attainment of the states.[9]

Contrasting the spatial variations, development indicators in Assam with the conflict map of the state reveals another dimension of the insecurity-underdevelopment nexus. By almost all indicators such as per capita income, human development index, human poverty index, percentage of BPL households, etc., Dhubri in western Assam bordering Bangladesh and West Bengal is the poorest district of the state.[10] Prior to Independence, Dhubri used to be a gateway of the entire Brahmaputra Valley westward. Partition of the country reduced the area to a peripheral corner. The district has also been bearing the brunt of immigration of poor people from East Pakistan/Bangladesh, which has pushed the density of population to a high level and reduced per capita availability of land in the district. Moreover erosion of the Brahmaputra and its tributaries has over the years displaced a sizeable part of its population. The district is devoid of any large- or medium-scale industry. It is therefore not surprising that people at large are rather poor. But yet economic inequality is also not pronounced. The district is also remarkably free of potentially violent group conflict so far.

By contrast the districts of Dibrugarh and Tinsukia in the eastern end of the Brahmaputra Valley form the most prosperous part of the state. Founded on tea plantation and mining of oil and coal, there is a good concentration of industrial activities. Average size of landholding is larger than the state average and concentration of poverty is also less. However, inequality of income is pronounced and conspicuous, and so is the discontentment with the existing economic status. The separatist ULFA has traditionally had a stronghold in these areas. In recent years other militant outfits have also been active in these districts. This contrast propels us to hypothesize that rather than underdevelopment *per se*, the inequality in the sharing of fruits of development and resultant perception among a sizeable section of being left out of the development process foments discontentment with the potency of steaming up into conflict and insecurity.

CONCLUSION AND POLICY IMPLICATIONS

The underdevelopment-insecurity nexus manifested in Assam over the last fifty years or so has been a complex one. It is difficult to claim that prolonged insecurity has germinated from the slow pace of development of the state. Often the group conflicts contributing to the insecurity have originated from identity questions. Yet it is not hard to see that insecurity and underdevelopment have been locked up in a mutually reinforcing vicious circle, which has been obstructing both peace and the pace of development in the state. The intricacies of the nexus have important bearings for choice of policy package for breaking this vicious circle.

It is obvious that development efforts need to be sustained. The agenda should not be focused merely on a few visible projects, but should include programmes where participation of people can be extensive so that benefits get widely shared. Creation of enclaves of industries with minimal linkage with the rest of the economy can actually make matters worse.

If development initiatives succeed, it will serve to wear down the underdevelopment-insecurity section of the vicious circle, as vested interest will be created in sustaining the developmental activities. However, the chances of success of development initiatives can be bright only if security measures also become more effective. Unless criminal acts like extortion, kidnapping and all forms of physical violence are dealt with firmly and effectively, it will be impossible to make the social environment conducive for productive economic activities to flourish.

However, these two necessary courses of action may not be sufficient to eliminate conflict and insecurity completely if identity issues lying at the root of many of these conflicts remain unaddressed. These issues obviously have no readymade solutions, as conceding the demands of one group often results in aggrieving another. The ultimate solution perhaps may arise from deepening of democracy in the state, which does not merely end at creating a few more autonomous councils, but ushers in a culture of dialogue, interactions, tolerance and trust among groups, in which different groups find the space to pursue and develop their own language, literature and culture so that identity aspirations are fulfilled without posing a threat to the existence of the others.

NOTES

1. S.K. Agnihotri, 'Constitutional Development in North-East India Since 1947', in B. Dutta Ray and S.P. Agarwal (eds.), *Reorganisation of North East India since 1947*, New Delhi: Concept Publishing Company, 1996.
2. M.P. Bezbaruah, 'Assam Economy: Past Trends and Some Future Projections', *Indian Journal of Regional Science*, 31(2), 1999.
3. G.M. Meier, *Leading Issues in Economic Development*, Oxford: Oxford University Press, 1984.
4. UNDP, *Human Development Report 1990*, New York: Oxford University Press, 1990.
5. Planning Commission, *National Human Development Report 2001*, New Delhi: Government of India, 2002, available at http://planningcommission.nic.in/reports/genrep/nhdrep/nhdreportf.htm
6. UNDP, *Human Development Report 1994*, New York: Oxford University Press, 1994.
7. Kanti P. Bajpai, 'Human Security: Concept and Measurement', *Kroc Institute Occasional Paper*, no. 19: OP: 1, August 2000.

8. Out of a total FDI inflow of $19,038 million in the manufacturing sector during April 2000 to December 2007 in the country, inflows in the North-East (including Assam) were merely $1.44 million, North East Development Finance Corporation Ltd., Guwahati, 2008.
9. Montek S. Ahluwalia, 'Economic Performance of States in the Post-Reform Period', *Economic and Political Weekly*, 5 May 2000.
10. Government of Assam, *Assam Human Development Report, 2003*, Dispur, Guwahati: Planning & Development Department, Government of Assam, 2003.

CHAPTER 13

Development-Conflict Interface: Assam in the Context of the North-East

Rakhee Bhattacharya

MOSAIC OF ISSUES: BRITISH INTERFERENCE

Assam was once famous for its southern trail of the historic Silk Route and for its stable and self-sufficient economy. It interestingly also had strong ethno-cultural affinities along with trade and economic links with its neighbours such as Tibet, Bhutan, Burma and China.[1] This vibrant economic and cultural landscape of Assam changed forever when British colonizers set eyes on Assam's vast, valuable and virgin natural resources. They exploited its resources, drove out the profits, and forcibly changed its geo-politics and economic roadmap according to their own interest. The easy movement of people and products between Assam and other parts of North-East India along with its neighbours got truncated as boundaries were drawn to end the free accessibility. This changed the geopolitics of North-East India forever, and brought an end to its socio-cultural and economic links with its neighbours. The British established enclave economies in Assam by introducing tea estates. This absorbed a large number of skilled migrant labourers from different parts of undivided India. People of Assam were unmindful, and gradually became marginalized in various economic activities. The region was re-visited as a 'resource hub' and a 'place of strategy'. The whole of North-East India's connectivity with mainstream India was then established only through Assam by a sole narrow 21 km wide corridor along a small town of West Bengal called Siliguri, often referred to as the 'chicken neck', and by and large the region remained as an isolated periphery of India. This did not change much even after India's Independence. The new set of power centric rulers of the country started re-visioning and re-defining the region without the mandate of the local people. Such economic deprivation and political reconstruction had sown the seeds of anger and grievance among the people of the region.

MUDDLING BY INDIAN ADMINISTRATION

During the post-Independence period, the region was in search of an identity. The new Indian rulers adopted a sympathetic approach to safeguard the people here. The word 'tribal', which was coined by British ethnographers, was then annexed as 'scheduled tribe' under the Sixth Schedule of the Indian Constitution in the 1950s. Henceforth Scheduled Tribes have been identified as one of the backward indigenous groups of India; and special advantage was given under 'protective discrimination'[2] to such tribal communities for preserving their lands, business and culture from the onslaught of outsiders. With the onset of five-year planning, a new era was set to develop these 'weaker sections' emphasizing on education, community development and upliftment. Over a period of time, Assam and its neighbouring states were declared as 'Special Category States' for their economic backwardness, under which substantial central financial assistance were rendered for economic development. These kinds of endeavours have not remained very successful. People of North-East could never accommodate and assimilate with this process of resurgence and never accepted the decisions of 'New Delhi' administration, no matter how welfarist the approach was. Resilience and resentment erupted in the region over a period of time on the issue of identity and demand for political sovereignty.

Movements for sovereignty in North-East India started from Nagaland and gradually spilled over to the other states in the region with a strong manifestation in Assam. As pointed out by Brahma,[3] 'the oft-repeated slogan of the insurgents, that Assam is being used as a colony by the Indian government, appears to have sunk quite deep into the minds of the local populace. This is notwithstanding the fact that during the same period, the central government tried its best to reverse the trend by establishing a number of special institutions'. Though seven states were created on issue of identity and of cultural heterogeneity, where more than 200 different ethno-cultural and linguistic groups co-exist, the Indian administration muddled up such divergent issues of the region by treating it as a homogeneous entity. The proliferation of state structure in the region as argued by Baruah was rather 'cosmetic'[4] given the existence of a *de facto* government structure that controlled the region from New Delhi. The administrative failure to address the economic and political issues of these states increased the grievances 'within' the region and aggravated the fights for identity and sovereignty, resulting in domestic violence and insurgency. As Lt. General Mukherjee[5] argued, 'it is apparent that insurgency occurs in most cases, due to poor governance and neglect of minorities, including the constitutional provision which allows them to air their grievances, and have the same redressed'.

On the other hand, the prolonged political conflicts between India and Pakistan had also worsened the fate of North-East India, more prominently in the aftermath of the 1971 war, which created Bangladesh, the erstwhile East Pakistan. In this process of reconstruction and redrawing of political boundary, India's North-East became security sensitive. Sanjoy Hazarika[6] argues that insurgency in the region has established international connections with various armed groups inimical to India and democratic forces. He also points out the consequences and problems of illegal migration into the region, especially in Assam. The intensity of such challenges is immense, which ranges from ethnic standoffs and struggles for land and space to political rights. North-East India's states became thus 'soft states' in terms of strategic, economic, political and security issues. To encounter the issue of insurgency and conflict, the Government of India had enforced Armed Forces Special Power Act (AFSPA) in 1958 as a 'carrot and stick policy'. Lt. General Mukherjee[7] estimated that in Manipur itself, there were about 6,000 to 8,000 armed insurgents, violating orders, committing murders and widespread extortion. He feels that the AFSPA was necessary to restore peace and stability, and an enormous power given to the army was necessary to deal with the problems of unlawful activities and bloodshed by the insurgent groups, which already had started establishing cross-border linkages, besides receiving training and other assistance from Pakistan. Under AFSPA, the Indian army had received extended powers in the region to shoot, arrest and search, all in the name of aiding civil power. It was initially applied to the North-Eastern states of Assam and Manipur and was amended in 1972 to extend to all the seven states. Under this Act, security forces were given unrestricted and unaccounted power to carry out their operations, once an area was declared as disturbed. Even a non-commissioned officer was granted the right to shoot and kill, based on mere suspicion that it was necessary to do so in order to maintain public order. AFSPA in the region has continued since then though as argued by Hazarika[8] 'many of the security problems of the region can be tackled by the local police and the commando forces with the assistance of the armed forces, where essential'. North-East India eventually became a big challenge for the Indian administration on strategic and internal security issues. These acted as impediments for the region's development. Unrestricted amount of expenditure and central funds have been pumped into the region to restore peace on the one hand and initiate development on the other. That was probably not the right strategy for the region. A 'clinical'[9] approach to 'development' was the necessity of the hour, instead of merely pumping in more funds. The New Delhi administration should have identified the most urgent constraints, which were responsible for the impoverishment and underdevelopment of the region. Thus accessibility, transport network, physical infrastructure, governance, voices of the local people, building good relations and foreign policy with neighbours like Myanmar and Bangladesh—all these were the most important variables that were undermined. This has accentuated the problems of North-East India and inflamed peoples' minds. As argued by Hazarika[10] that representations were made to address the political problems of this region politically but not militarily and the process of development of participatory planning, and involvement of local traditional groups in self-governance are important. He thinks that without the restoration of governance and the faith of the public in the ability of governance to provide security to the citizens, the problem become more acute. A huge financial loss was being incurred over the years to sustain the economy on the one hand, and maintain peace on the other hand, in this problematic region of India. Fund was not the solution, rather leakages in the system and the rampant corruption everywhere caused further damage to the economy. H.N. Das,[11] the former chief secretary of Assam, argued that in every state of North-Eastern region, a plethora of allegations and complaints had surfaced regarding the misuse of funds and rampant corruption. The ground level reality also did not indicate any significant and effectual developmental activity. Media reports indicated that bureaucrats, politicians, bank managers, contractors and their cohorts siphoned-off major portions of the central funds, consequently leaving very little—and at times nothing—for the poor. Thus, despite its rich reserve of natural resources, the landlocked region became an unstable periphery, without many economic opportunities. The plea for sovereignty by the insurgent outfits gradually became a camouflage to destabilize the region for their vested interest. Over the years economic gains had become more important for these outfits than their concept of identity and sovereignty. These 'drain on resources' and eventually 'decline of business confidence and flight of capital'[12] have made the North East India's fortune even worse and its economy extremely vulnerable with Assam at the bottom.

CONFLICT MANAGEMENT AT THE COST OF DEVELOPMENT

Persistent activities of terrorist outfits had forced the Indian administration to enforce and reinforce security measures in the region at the cost of huge unproductive defense expenditure. The various yearly Annual Reports of Ministry of Home Affairs shows that a total of Rs. 1,219.52 crore has been released during the period 1998-9 to 2006-7, with the state of Assam accounting for the bulk—Rs. 636.84 crore followed by the states of Tripura (Rs. 234.37 crore) and Nagaland (Rs. 192.16 crore). Thus Assam shares the maximum of 52.22 per cent of the total security related expenditure in the region and the rest 48 per cent is shared amongst the other states. The total central assistance on security has grown by 3.4 per cent over the last nine years, which is higher than the growth rates of state domestic product of Assam, which is around 2.5 per cent.

The region shelters around 39 million people of India (2001 census), out of which 68 per cent of the population lives in Assam alone with highest density of population with 340 per sq km. Assam is the key state in the region, which connects all the other North-Eastern states, and also has connectivity with the rest of India. This is also one of the most resourceful states in the region, but despite such importance, the state is one of the worst performers as compared to other states in the region. As argued by Brahma[13]

> Assam . . . , started sliding downwards on all parameters of growth and equity. Ranked high among the developed states during the early stages of state formation, Assam at present is among the most backward states on all development indices. In the 1950s, during the formative period of Assam, the per capita income of the state was Rs. 50.4, which was a little higher than the all-India figure. In 2000-01, Assam's per capita income was Rs. 6,157 at constant prices (1993-94) and Rs. 10,198 at current prices, almost 40 per cent lower than the all-India figure. In 2004-05, Assam's per capita income was Rs. 6,756 at constant prices (1993-94), which is still much lower than the all-India figure.

Development in Assam is badly affected due to prolonged and intense security issues and in terms of measures also, it is absorbing highest financial shares to deal with such security problems. Despite AFSPA and its huge powers, the insurgent activities have not shown any drastic decline in the region. Between 2001 and 2006, the total incidents of insurgency reported to have remained same as shown in Table 13.1. Rather the total incidents in Jammu & Kashmir, which is perhaps the worst affected Indian state with sustained terrorism, have gone down over the years from 3,860 to 1,667 during the same period.

TABLE 13.1: A BROAD SCENARIO OF INSURGENT ACTIVITIES IN NER

North-East India	2001	2002	2003	2004	2005	2006
Incidents	1,335	1,312	1,332	1,234	1,332	1,366
Extremists killed	572	571	523	404	405	395
Security forces killed	175	147	90	110	70	76
Civilians killed	600	454	494	414	393	309
Jammu & Kashmir	2001	2002	2003	2004	2005	2006
Incidents	3,860	3,362	3,401	2,565	1,990	1,667
Extremists killed	1,537	1,491	1,494	976	917	591
Security forces killed	433	326	314	281	189	151
Civilians killed	994	753	795	707	557	389

Source: Annual Reports, 2006-07, Ministry of Home Affairs, Government of India.

Deaths and other terrorist incidents had happened regularly in the North-East India, despite the fact that the total number of armed force personnel deployed in the states of North-East India was much higher than that in any other part of India, even compared to the troubled states of Jammu & Kashmir as shown in Table 13.2.

The union budget for North-East India is not only disproportionately high for security-related expenditure, but also receives much higher grants from the centre for being special category states compared to other states of India. Table 13.3 shows that even in 2006-7, the ratio of gross transfer of central resources in all the eight states of this region were higher than the national average, with the highest share claimed by the small state of Arunachal Pradesh (84.04 per cent) and the lowest by Assam (53.34 per cent), the most important state in the region. Here gross transfer refers to the sum of the state's share of central tax and the total central grants and loans. The states are heavily dependent on this assistance due to their economic non-viability.

North-East region shares only 8 per cent of total landmass of India and shelters 4 per cent of India's 1.2 billion people, and contributes 5 per cent to India's gross domestic product. But the region has absorbed 11 per cent (as can be estimated from Table

TABLE 13.2: PERCENTAGE OF POLICE STRENGTH IN NER, 2005

States	% of Armed forces	% of Civil forces	Total forces
Assam	44.55	54.45	52,049
Arunachal Pradesh	44.23	55.77	5,718
Manipur	64.93	35.07	13,596
Meghalaya	36.90	63.07	8,929
Nagaland	54.07	45.93	11,976
Mizoram	55.31	44.69	8,092
Tripura	48.93	51.07	18,369
Sikkim	45.10	54.90	3,501
Maharashtra	9.97	90.03	1,36,106
Uttar Pradesh	21.57	78.43	1,53,179
Jammu & Kashmir	28.39	71.61	65,005
India	22.06	77.94	13,42,858

Source: National Crime Record Bureau, Ministry of Home Affairs, Government of India, 2005.

TABLE 13.3: GROSS TRANSFERS OF RESOURCES FROM CENTRE TO AGGREGATE STATE DISBURSEMENT OF NER

States	1998-9 to 2006-7 (Rs. crore)	Ratio of Gross Transfer 2006-7
Assam	53,669.10	53.38
Arunachal Pradesh	11,230.30	84.04
Manipur	16,407.80	80.56
Meghalaya	10,976.40	81.04
Mizoram	10,458.55	80.86
Nagaland	15,922.90	83.40
Sikkim	6,480.50	43.41
Tripura	17,199.00	72.31
NER	1,42,344.55	72.38
All States	12,53,348.00	33.59

Source: Estimated from the Reports of Finance Accounts of CAG, Government of India and CMIE for respective years of respective states.

13.4) of the total central assistance in terms of gross transfer from centre during the eight years from 1998-9 to 2006-7, more than double the contribution it makes to GDP! Being predominantly an agricultural region, it hardly accounts for even 1 per cent of India's manufacturing sector. The dependency

TABLE 13.4: PER CAPITA CENTRAL ASSISTANCE TO STATES (RS.): 2000-1 TO 2006-7

States	2000-1	2001-2	2002-3	2003-4	2004-5	2005-6	2006-7
Assam	915	1,132	1,299	1,061	1,423	2,314	2,341
Arunachal Pradesh	7,014	8,135	8,282	12,047	9,979	12,097	13,191
Manipur	4,516	6,279	8,616	6,564	9,442	7,898	8,513
Meghalaya	3,838	3,311	4,283	3,962	4,315	5,510	6,895
Mizoram	6,260	9,366	9,844	13,185	13,885	16,068	13,244
Nagaland	6,745	7,080	7,643	7,166	7,097	8,931	8,862
Sikkim	8,867	9,978	11,117	11,139	12,744	13,049	14,725
Tripura	3,958	4,612	4,399	4,690	5,585	6,906	6,967
NER	2,280	2,670	3,027	2,911	3,401	4,313	4,447
All States	557	653	691	695	732	741	1,015

Source: Finance Accounts of CAG, Government of India and CMIE reports, population figures are taken from CSO reports. Per capita central assistance is estimated by adding both grants from centre and loans and advances from centre as the total assistance, which is divided by state-wise yearly population.

syndrome gets clearer if one looks at the per capita central assistance, as estimated in Table 13.4. Per capita central assistance in all these eight states is much higher than the figures for all-states in India.

Thus the region has been absorbing money since Independence, both on account of its economic backwardness and threatened security, which cannot linger for an indefinite period, and therefore needs a future roadmap for its rescue.

THE IMPACT

The former Indian Prime Minister H.D. Deve Gowda[14] commented once on the status of Assam as,

> Assam was in the forefront of the economic development of the country 100-150 years ago. It was a pioneering State and enterprising entrepreneurs invested in the development of tea-plantations, oil, coal mining, forestry, railways and inland waterways. However, in the

recent years investors have shunned these areas, because some of these States turned inward looking, while others have been afflicted by militancy and terrorism. This has set in a vicious cycle of terrorism, discouraging investments and economic development, leading to growing unemployment, which in turn provided recruits to militancy.

The impact of such prolonged underdevelopment and insecurity are briefly discussed into two broad heads of economic performance and economy of insurgency in the region as follows.

ECONOMIC PERFORMANCE

Release of funds has clearly not served the aim to make the region developed, but has actually pampered the region and created a dependency syndrome. On the other hand, over militarization due to AFSPA for last 50 years has cost human life and liberty, accumulated fear, alienation and anger amongst the people of North-East, impeding peace, stability and development. Both insurgency and counter-insurgency have acted negatively in the region for its economic progress. This is clearly reflected in the per capita income levels. For example, the per capita income in Delhi has registered an increase by 160 per cent to Rs. 49,189 in 2006-7 from Rs. 18,942 in 1980-1, whereas in Assam the increase was from Rs. 9,996 in 1980-1 to Rs. 15,624 in 2006-7, i.e. only by 37 per cent.[15]

The growth rates of Per Capita Net State Domestic Product (PCNDSP) for the period 1993-4 to 2003-4 were also at the lower side in the region compared to the other small states like Pondicherry, Goa and Delhi. The last two columns of Table 13.5 have ranked the states in terms of PCNSDP for two years, viz., 1993-4 and 2003-4. Out of 26 states (all states are not shown here) in India, North-Eastern states are placed mostly in the lower side with Assam being 17th in 2003-4. States like Tripura and Sikkim have done well. Sikkim is only one North-Eastern state, which is not beset by insurgency and is doing progressively well with good governance.

A study made by Debroy & Bhandari (2005)[16] for Indian states, categorizing them into big and small groups according to

TABLE 13.5: GROWTH RATES OF NSDP AND PER CAPITA NSDP (1993-4 PRICES): 1993-4 TO 2003-4

States/Regions	Growth Rates of NSDP	Growth Rates of PCNSDP	Rank (1993-4) PCNSDP	Rank (2003-4) PCNSDP
Assam	2.53	1.08	16	17
Arunachal Pradesh	2.92	0.93	7	14
Manipur	6.42	4.28	15	15
Meghalaya	7.16	4.73	11	11
Nagaland	7.86	2.77	6	9
Tripura	8.50	7.39	17	12
Sikkim	8.31	5.72	10	7
Delhi	8.33	4.71	1	1
Goa	7.77	6.14	2	2
Pondicherry	13.52	11.65	5	3

Source: NSDP and Per Capita NSDP data are taken from CSO reports, Government of India. Growth rates are estimated by fitting log linear trend to NSDP and PCNSDP and are tested at 5 per cent and 1 per cent level of significance.

their populations and areas, shows that in general the overall performance of the latter group was better. This is because governance is easier in smaller states and due to their manageable population. But North-East India is an exception; the authors felt that though the environment was gradually changing with relatively better investment in infrastructure, yet it remained substantially dependent on government support and suffers from some major economic stagnation even in the post-reforms period. As Hazarika[17] rightly mentioned that 'the North-East must strengthen their own systems of governance, restoring the confidence of the people and providing the basics of governance.'

Table 13.6 has ranked the big states in India with different socio-economic indicators, amongst which Assam ranked 16th, just above UP, Jharkhand and Bihar!

It is unfortunate to see such a dismal scenario in the region. Even within the region, the rural urban disparity across the population is widely prevalent, and the fruits of development are not percolating to the rural sector. A report of a committee on Integrated Rural Development Programme (IRDP)[18] in the

TABLE 13.6: BIG STATE PROFILE RANKING IN INDIA: 2005

States	Over all rank	Law & order	Primary health	Primary edu-cation	Infra-structure	Consumer market	Agri-culture	Invest-ment	Budget & prosperity
Punjab	1	12	7	7	1	1	1	3	1
Kerala	2	1	1	2	6	4	10	16	9
Himachal Pradesh	3	6	2	1	2	2	16	4	2
Gujarat	7	7	8	12	7	6	5	1	4
Assam	16	18	15	6	15	16	19	19	16
Uttar Pradesh	17	20	18	19	16	15	7	15	15
Jharkhand	19	16	16	18	19	17	18	12	19
Bihar	20	19	20	20	20	20	12	20	20

Source: Debroy and Bhandari, 2005.

Assam mentioned 'an upsurge in insurgency in Assam' as responsible for 'practically no developmental activities in rural areas' and a simultaneous 'flight of capital from the rural areas to urban areas as the former were less secured than the latter'. Such an observation would also indicate that there has been an increase in impoverishment in the rural areas and a greater lag *vis-à-vis* developmental activity.

ECONOMY OF INSURGENCY

The above indicators reflect that development in this region, especially in Assam is lagging far behind the national average. One can categorically relate to insurgency, bad politics and administrative failures as factors responsible for this. Government of India has been trying to address these through two diverse approaches, viz., ushering development with financial resources under the special category states and restoring security with military forces under the armed forces special power act, but both have actually intensified the problems. While action under armed force special power act has led to increasing violence and resilience, and assistance under the special category states has aggravated dependency and opportunism.

An easy flow of money from the centre has rather established and entrenched moneylaundering corrupt class.

> There is, however, overwhelming evidence of a complex 'web of collusion' between insurgent groups, politicians and political parties. A large amount of the North-Eastern states' revenues is siphoned off and distributed to a well-established nexus of politicians, business and insurgent organizations. Sources estimate that of the Rs. 11.65 bn made available in Assam for rural development from 1992 to February 1998, less than Rs. 4 bn went into legitimate schemes. This criminalization of politics and crisis of governance is a significant obstacle to peace.[19]

Despite security measures, North-East India is highly exposed to a parallel insurgent economy, where huge money is drained off to the coffer of insurgents through extortion mechanisms. The report of Centre for International Cooperation and Security[20] says that 'ULFA alone has collected more than Rs. 5 billion through extortion, abduction and kidnappings. . . . This is common throughout NEI.' As argued by Brahma,[21] in Nagaland and Manipur, almost parallel governments are being run by insurgent groups. There exists a collusive arrangement where group of legitimate power elites facilitate to transfer resource to the underground economy. A large sum of money goes to insurgents in the form of protection money, professional tax and various other dues. Thus the militants are earning easy money by creating threats and destroying the economy of the region. The AFSPA, which gives the security forces excessive powers has actually helped to foster a culture of violence and impunity and has failed miserably even to curb the illegal mobilization of money, leading to further impoverishment of the people in this region and their greater insecurity, displacement and disparity, alienating the region ever further from the mainstream of development.

CONCLUSION

A fresh look at the region with different structural paradigm is the need of the hour. Strategies for rebuilding North-East India need to understand and respect the rights of the people on one hand, and initiate the process for integrating and uniting its people into the mainstream on the other. Many of the armed groups here are in the process of negotiation and dialogue, which in the long run probably can 'restore dignity to the civil society and the rule of justice and law'. In words of Hazarika,[22] a process of reconciliation and democratization in the North-East can create space for dialogue and discussion, can reduce conflicts and would help the region to write a new chapter of peace, change and happiness in its troubled history. Also, sixty years of 'close door' and 'protective' policy in the region needs to be replaced by a meaningful economic reforms and integration with the mainstream economy. Awareness of civil society for economic realism needs to be improved to boost local initiatives and capabilities for an endogenous growth. Call for political action on the other hand, can establish the necessary economic infrastructure and harness various economic potentials. In this process, Assam being the key state needs to play a dominant role.

NOTES

1. Sanjib Baruah, 'Between South and Southeast Asia: North-East India and Look East Policy', Ceniseas Paper No. 4, Centre for North-East India, South and Southeast Asia Studies, Guwahati (2004), cited by Sushil Khanna, *Economic Opportunities or Continuing Stagnation*, Manipur Online (2005), paragraph 6, online. http://www.manipuronline.com/Economy/November 2005/stagnationoropportuny18_1.htm.
2. Sanjib Baruah, 'Nationalizing Space: Cosmetic Federalism and the Politics of Development', cited in Sanjib Baruah, *Durable Disorder: Understanding the Politics of Northeast India*, New Delhi: Oxford University Press, 2005, p. 51.
3. H.S. Brahma, 'Ensuring Peace through Development in the North-East', *ASCI Journal of Management* 37 (2), March 2008, p. 37.
4. Baruah, op. cit., p. 53.
5. Lt. General J.R. Mukherjee, *An Insider's Experience of Insurgency in India's North-East*, New Delhi: Anthem Press, 2005, p. 105.
6. Sanjoy Hazarika, *Writing on the Wall: Reflections on the Northeast*, New Delhi: Penguin Books, 2008, pp. 4-5.
7. Mukherjee, op. cit., p. 114.
8. Hazarika, op. cit., p. 3.
9. Jeffrey Sachs, *The End of Poverty: How Can We Make it Happen in Our Lifetime*, London: Penguin Books, 2005, p. 78.
10. Hazarika, op. cit., pp. 4-5.
11. H.N. Das, 'Insurgency and Development: The Assam Experience' (2006): 4 online http://www.satp.org/satporgtp/publication/faultlines/volume10/Article4.htm.
12. Mandy Turner and Binalakshmi Nepram, *The Impact of Armed Violence in Northeast India*, Centre for International Cooperation and Security Report, Bradford: University of Bradford, 2004, pp. 30-1.
13. H.S. Brahma, 'Ensuring Peace through Development in the North-East', *ASCI Journal of Management*, 37 (2), March 2008, p. 35.
14. H.N. Das, 'Insurgency and Development: The Assam Experience', (2006): 3 online http://www.satp.org/satporgtp/publication/faultlines/volume10/Article4.htm.
15. Estimated from the Data of Central Statistical Organization, GOI at 1999-00 price. The Data for Mizoram at constant prices are not available.
16. R. Saran, 'The Best States to Live in', *India Today, Special Issue*, 15 August 2005, cited by Rakhee Bhattacharya, 'Indian Divide

on Economic Growth: Northeast India in the Perspective of Globalization', *Asia Annual*, New Delhi: Standard Publishers, 2007, pp. 73-4.

17. Hazarika, op. cit., p. 4.
18. H.N. Das, 'Insurgency and Development: The Assam Experience' (2006): 3 online http://www.satp.org/satporgtp/publication/faultlines/volume10/Article4.htm.
19. Turner and Nepram, op. cit., p. 5.
20. Ibid., pp. 20-1.
21. Brahma, op. cit., p. 39.
22. Hazarika, op. cit., p. 6.

CHAPTER 14

Searching through Theories: Developing a Human Security Paradigm for the North-East

Binoda Kumar Mishra

INTRODUCTION

North-East India has remained a hotspot within the Indian Union. The region comprising eight states, precariously connected to the Indian mainland by the chicken's neck, borders the not so friendly neighbours of India. From the time of India's Independence, the region is experiencing political instability owing to the problem of insurgency. Violence related to insurgency that started with the Nagas has been resorted to by more and more groups in the North-East taking the number of insurgent groups operating in the region to above 30. The Indian government has not stopped from formulating region-specific policies over the last 60 years but all of them seem to have failed in curbing the problem of insurgency. The rise in insurgency has created such a situation that now it is not feasible to delineate various movements as causes or effects of the socio-political and economic condition of the region. Of all the problems that always bothered the Indian government, security was the primary problem and continues to remain so even after Indian army operating within the region with special powers for over 50 years. Considering the failure of all government initiatives, one is compelled to think of an out-of-the-box approach to solve the security situation of the region. Secondly, all the previous initiatives to tackle security being one-dimensional, i.e. treating security as a military phenomenon, may have missed the nonmilitary nuances of the region that gets manifested in the form of violence often directed against the state. May be it would be useful to develop a broader understanding of the concept of security and one such way of doing it is to relate the term 'security' to development. Instead of debating if security is a prerequisite of development or development leads to security, this paper tries to combine the two concepts. In the absence of such ideas in the discourses that deal with domestic security problems, the paper searches through some ideas developed within the discipline of international relations.

The concept of 'security' is undergoing a paradigm shift in international relations. Traditionally it simply meant protection of the interests of a nation state. The interests of the nation state were generalized as 'power'. Thus, it referred to protection of the power of the nation state to protect itself *vis-à-vis* other similar units in the international system. Defined thus, security had a characteristic that was primarily militaristic and was related to the geographical integrity of the nation state. Such simplistic and narrow conception of security has, of late, proven to be inadequate in understanding and providing solution to the multi-dimensional problems that the human race collectively face today. The problems of modern day includes over population, over-heating of the planet, inter-state and intra-state conflicts, terrorism, extremist ideologies, tyranny, unstoppable technological momentum leading to production of weapons of mass destruction, imperialism of economic, political and cultural hues, growing economic disparities, religious bigotry, etc.[1] These multiple threats have led to a growing despair among scholars of international relations about the usefulness of the traditional understanding of security. A section of the academia has tried to reformulate the concept of security to make it relevant for the security threats that are real than the perceptual threats to the security of the nation state.

A plethora of literature is being produced critiquing the traditional notion of security that identifies nation state as the only reference point of discourse on security. The new understanding tries to bring to the fore issues that were never part of the security discourse. Issues such as environment, food, social, political and cultural rights of individuals are tried to be included within the security discourse and arguments are being articulated to expand, deepen, and widen the scope of security to make the discourse of security responsive to the many realities of the contemporary world. It is essential to discuss briefly these various attempts of reformulating the concept of security.

BROADENING SECURITY

This effort is attributed to the Copenhagen school influenced by Barry Buzan's work entitled, *People State and Fear*.[2] Buzan and his companions have argued for broadening the scope of security by including issues such as politics, economy, society and ecology within the scope of security studies. Buzan argues that the issue of security is better appreciated if a holistic approach is adopted reintegrating the three levels, i.e. international system, the nation state and the individual.[3] He coins the term *systemic security* to include all the security concerns at all the levels of social existence.[4] Thus, the scope of concern for security is broadened by inclusion of three levels of international relations. The second important aspect of Buzan's argument is to concentrate on the interaction among the various sources of insecurity and take a broad view of security and develop a long-term outlook.[5] Thus, the call is not only to increase the application of security analysis to a broad category of population but also to broaden the scope of the subject matter of security to include the sources of multidimensional security problems that are in operation at various levels. Though Buzan argues for appreciating security at an integrated level, he does not advocate replacement of the state as the principal actor in ensuring security. Later his advocacy for emphasis on societal security as the most effective way of understanding the emerging security agenda in the post-Cold War scenario started a debate whether the point of reference for security studies should move away from the state. But there are others who categorically oppose the state being the reference point of security and also as a body responsible for ensuring security.

DEEPENING SECURITY

Some argue that such an attempt of broadening security is secondary, and what is primary is deepening the concept of security.[6] Scholars like R.B.J. Walker and Ken Booth put more emphasis on the relationship between notions of security and deeper assumptions about the nature of politics and the role of conflict in political life.[7] They consider the notions of security to be derived from these deepseated assumptions. The core of security in the deeper sense is argued to be 'emancipation'. Booth describes the interrelationship between security and emancipation in the following words:

> Security means the absence of threats, Emancipation is the freeing of people (as individuals and groups) from those physical and human constraints which stop them carrying out what they would freely choose to do. War and threat of war is one of those constraints, together with poverty, poor education, political oppression and so on. Security and emancipation are two sides of the same coin. Emancipation, not power or order produces true security.[8]

The primary concern for those arguing for deepening the concept of security is to think of world politics in terms of alternative institutions and practices wherein the state is not necessarily the only actor. Rather the focus should shift to individuals and groups who are at the core of social existence of human beings.

EXTENDING SECURITY

Those who advocate extending the concept of security, primarily talk of shifting the level of security analysis away from the state. They offer different focal points of security analysis. Scholars like Ken Booth emphasize the need to bring the individual to the centre of any security analysis on the ground that state being the means to ensure individual security should not be the primary referral point of security discourse. He argues, '[i]t is illogical . . . to privilege the security of the means as opposed to the security of the ends'.[9] Thus, to him, the individual should be the ultimate reference point for any security analysis. Some others have suggested society, some notion of civil society, should be the reference point of security.[10] There are also suggestions to concentrate on ethno-national and religious identities while conceptualizing security. This is implied in Huntington's *The Clash of Civilizations* and is also present conspicuously in the arguments of Waever.[11] There are internal differences among scholars regarding the reference point for security analysis but there is no ambiguity in the subject matter of security for those who want to deepen, broaden or extend the concept of security. The intention is to emphasize the corporeal, material existence and experiences of human beings without denying the importance of any form of human collective such as community and state.[12]

SECURITY IN THE NORTH-EAST

The rationale for discussing the various formulations of security is to underscore the changing nature of contemporary security and security understanding. In a non-partisan manner, one can argue that the scenario in the North-Eastern Region (NER) of India cannot simply be defined and addressed within the traditional definitions of security. The region remains in a relatively impoverished state in comparison to most other regions of the Indian Union. The security issues of the region are multi-dimensional and have strong extra-territorial connotations as well, thus making it too complicated for the traditional understanding of security to comprehend the security issues and address them. Before applying any particular notions of security to understand the security scenario of North East, it is essential to have an understanding of the security scenario in all its forms.

The noticeable security issue related to North-East is insurgency. More than 30 insurgent groups are operating in the region with varied agendas ranging from separatism to autonomy. Waves of migration from Tibet and Burma for over a long period and the resultant incomplete ethnic assimilation have created a mosaic of ethnicities. Therefore, there is bound to be claims contradicting each other in terms of belongingness to the region and relationship with the larger Indian political space. However, the insurgencies manifested in NER over the years, have become causes of other forms of problems.

The second important feature of the problem of insurgency in NER is the international connections of these problems. In combination with domestic aspects of insurgency, these extra-territorial connections give many colours to insurgency such as, ethnic, ideological, religious and separatism.[13] The mosaic of ethnicities in North-East India has turned into an ethnic mine-field keeping the region always on the boil through insurgency against the Union of India and inter-ethnic rivalries. Some of the insurgencies have retained their basic demands with which they started their movements but some of them have also degenerated into pure criminal activities. The involvement of foreign powers (neighbours) has complicated insurgency-related security situation in the region. The role of Myanmar, Pakistan and Bangladesh have been very conspicuous. Barring Chinese stamps on some of the weapons seized from the region, currently one may not find evidence of direct Chinese involvement in the insurgency situation in North-East, but it was a fact till early 1980s that China used to supply direct and indirect assistance to most of these insurgency groups operating within North-East India. The selective actions by the military Junta in Myanmar and the constant denial by Bangladesh of the presence of Indian insurgents have made the task of handling the insurgency issue in the region more complicated and extra-national. The current nature of conflicts in the region has ethnic, ideological and religious dimensions and trans-border linkages.

Whatever may be the causes of insurgency in the region, it is evident that most, if not all, have developed means other than ideology and ethnicity to survive. Financing insurgency activities in the region through illegal income from trade in contraband through the porous borders of India and her neighbouring countries has been one of the main activities of the insurgents. Thus, the insurgents try to establish control over this contraband trade to the keep the insurgency machinery running.

Apart from insurgency, illegal migration to this region from the poor areas of Bangladesh has emerged as one of the prime security concerns for the state of India. Apart from putting financial pressure on the thin currently usable resource base of the region, migration into the region affects the social and political landscapes of the region. Added to these, an environment of antagonism between the population of the region and its neighbours (other Indian states) has developed. This antagonism gets manifested in periodic xenophobic activities in the region adding to the insecurity complex of the region. Latest in the list of security concerns related to violence in the region is the rise of terror having a particular religious character. The rise of Islamic terrorism in the region is often related to the large-scale illegal migration of Muslim population from the relatively poor Bangladesh. The role of hostile powers in the past was proven to be active and there seems to be no development to believe in the reduction of that role of the hostile powers, such as Pakistan, who keep hobnobbing with forces acting contrary to Indian interests. The migrant Muslim population is being used as a conduit in the terror network in and around India. According to Indian security agencies, in Assam alone there are about fifteen Islamic organizations operating, some of whom are believed to have links with the Inter-Services Intelligence (ISI) of Pakistan.[14] Demands such as creation of 'Islamistan' or 'the United States of Bengal' comprising the border districts of Assam and Bangladesh pose serious and real challenges to the ideological basis of the Indian Union.[15]

The insurgency situation in the region is often made to look too simple as reactions against the state of India. But in reality there are numerous fissures within the various tribal groups that erupt into violent conflict on issues of resource possession. Apart from the identifiable security problems of insurgency, and of late terrorism of a religious nature, the region has remained in a state of relative underdevelopment in comparison to many other Indian states. Despite natural resources and immense economic potential, the region lags behind most other states in almost all developmental indices. The per capita income in the region is Rs. 12,918 (as per state domestic product) in comparison to the national average of Rs. 17,823 (at current prices of 2001-2). The other ironical fact is that the region has a literacy rate higher than the national average but the unemployment rate is higher in comparison to the national average. Assam has 36 per cent of its population below poverty line. Barring Mizoram all other

North-Eastern states have people below poverty line much above the national average. Other developmental indices such as industrial development in the region also remain minimal in comparison to other states or regions of India. The industrial output of the region is only 2.16 per cent of the Gross Domestic Product in comparison to national figure of 27 per cent.[16]

All these poor indicators show that the region has not managed to register faster growth rates. A general sense of deprivation looms large in the psyche of the people of the region. The poor economic development, diverse and often competing ethnic and social groups, visible non-functioning of the state, and the interference of an unfriendly neighbourhood has created a security complex that is beyond the scope of the traditional security approach to comprehend and address.

NEED FOR A NEW PARADIGM

It is a cliché to say that the North-East has remained an area of neglect for more than five decades. But a look at the present state of indulgence of the region by the Government of India, it can be said that the region figures very high in the priority list of the central government. Since Independence, the central government has adopted a paradigmatic approach towards the region. These paradigms have changed in accordance with the changing perception of the central government towards the region. Jairam Ramesh presents an apt classification of these paradigms.

The first of these paradigms is 'Culture Paradigm'. According to this paradigm the North-East is phenomenally diverse and has a mosaic of cultures which have to be preserved and enriched. This paradigm was preponderant largely in the 1950s and in the 1960s. North-East cultures were seen as exotic, endangered which needed to be kept in museums and protected from the 'big bad' wolf called 'economic development' and 'germs' called mainland Indians. This was followed by the security paradigm that identified NER as strategically important to the security of the country and called for enhanced presence of security forces. This was followed by the politics/representation paradigm. The rationale was the assumption that if the diverse communities and sub-national identities of NER were allowed greater representation in the mainstream political process, the divisive tendencies would turn into assimilative ones. This was followed by the latest, i.e. developmental paradigm. Develop the region and this would make the people happy. Once the development processes gain momentum, the people of the region will move away from identity-based politics. Given the historical and contemporary circumstances, one can only say that there existed only an imagined correlation between these initiatives and the desired results. For example, it was simplistically assumed that 'development initiatives' would 'develop' the region, which would ultimately lead to solution of the problems arising out of sub-national assertions.[17]

Paradigms may prove to be wrong and statesmen cannot be faulted for acting on a particular paradigm. But the pertinent question is—whether the actions of New Delhi yielded the immediate results? By any analysis it is a big 'no'. Enhanced presence of security forces has not made either the region or the country secure; development initiatives have not effected development, let alone making the people happy and solving all the problems of the region and for the country.

Is there a problem of understanding the region and its dynamic underpinnings? Views vary regarding the reasons for the chronic underdevelopment of the region but the factor that has a definite influence on the economic condition of the North-Eastern states is its exclusion from its surroundings. For long, natural interaction of the region with the subcontinent mainland has been prevented in the name of protecting the identity of the people of NER. India's neighbourhood policy, particularly South-East Asia policy, was anything but active, and hence prevented NER from interacting with culturally similar neighbouring countries. North-East India remains in the periphery for Indian leadership's thinking, though the centre spends roughly Rs. 20,000 crore annually for the region.[18]

It has taken policy makers a while in identifying the factors that are proving to be strong impediments and derailing all the initiatives for developing the region. The desperation of the government is evident from the fact that it tried to add urgency to India's 'Look East' policy on the grounds of developing the North-East region of the country. It seemed as if North-East India is the central focus of 'Look East' policy. However, India's reluctance to open up the region to its natural neighbours has proven beyond doubt that India does not feel comfortable in allowing greater interaction of the region with its neighbouring countries. The Government of India may have her own perception of interest and security that prevents her from opening the region to the outside world. But the problems of the region—both traditional and non-traditional security problems—have clear cross-border connections. Therefore, a workable paradigm towards ensuring security in the region must take into account the region and its neighbourhoods. Some emerging paradigms within the field of international relations may be searched in order to develop such a workable paradigm. Taking an extended and deepened view of security, the section below discusses some alternative approaches towards ensuring security in the international system.

ALTERNATIVE APPROACHES TO SECURITY

In response to the failure of realism in explaining and providing solutions for the changing nature of security scenarios in various parts of the world, a plethora of literature has developed on alternative approaches to security. All these approaches may differ in their prescriptions but one point they all agree on is the futility of realist paradigm in addressing the emerging security threats that do not have a military character and are not necessarily overtly inter-state affairs. All the alternative approaches support the idea of shifting the focus of the security from the state to individuals—either alone or in within its basic community. The definition of security provided by these alternative approaches varies from each other but a consensual definition can be drawn. In the words of Bill McSweeney:

> Security only makes sense if individual human beings are seen as its primary referent, or subject. . . . The basic need for security . . . is that which expresses itself as such in everyday life and in all social

actions. It is the security of social relations. . . . It is from this elemental experience, by definition common to all individuals, that we derive the social order as the general condition of ontological security.[19]

It has to be realized that security is a matter of choice by individuals and thus one has to choose one model over the other considering the particularities of the security nuances of a specific area. Some of these major approaches that attempt to address security defined as thus and provide solutions are: cooperative security, comprehensive security and human security. Cooperative security is advocated as an effective method for dealing with the non-traditional security issues that affect a region in common. It attempts to deepen the understanding of the mutuality of security as to broaden the definition of security beyond the traditional military concerns. Cooperative security defines security in terms of social, economic and environmental issues.[20] The target of cooperative security is to change the attitude of the state policy makers towards the neighbours who suffer similarly or are part of the same insecurity scenario. It calls for transcending the barriers of narrowly defined national interest and promotes the idea that no single state could address the wide range of security concerns facing the world community. It calls for multilateral collaboration and a collective response towards the problems a particular region faces.[21] The most striking feature of cooperative security approach is to allow active non-state actors to play a role in the management of regional security and the final objective of cooperative approach is to ensure the dissolution of compound states. It wishes to set in motion a process within which the present sub-state groups would peacefully attain independence and would become part of the regional arrangements to solve the various security problems of the region.[22] This approach may be useful in understanding the security situation of a region in a deeper and extended manner but is useful only to regions that comprise 'simple states'.[23] In a region like South Asia and particularly the north-eastern part of India, one cannot think of setting the motion of dissolution of compound states. This is because, the bases of identity of most of the present sub-national assertions are overlapping and one cannot ensure that the process of fission would stop at any point as bases of identity formation may shift fast for a region like south Asia and a sub-region like India's North-East.

The second alternative advanced towards ensuring security in its expanded and broader form is comprehensive security. Comprehensive security became the official policy of Japan and has also been adopted by regional groupings in Asia like ASEAN. It takes a broadened definition of security to include principles of 'balanced national development through endeavours in every aspect of life: ideological, political, economic, socio-cultural and military'.[24] The method prescribed under the comprehensive security is 'national resilience', an inward-looking strategy whereby a state strengthens its resilience to security threats by developing a stable political and economic international environment.[25] The logic is if a nation is internally resilient and the region has political and economic stability, no outside power can interfere in the internal affairs and destabilize the state, therefore, states can pursue the goal of comprehensive security. There is an inherent disadvantage in the prescriptions under comprehensive security when it places emphasis on political stability in the regional and international context. In the context of the security situation in North-East India and its neighbourhood, national resilience would mean different things to different nations in the neighbourhood. Secondly, there being no clear provisions to measure accountability of the regimes, national resilience along with political stability may tend to legitimize the use of excessive force and the concerns of an authoritarian regime that happens to be the most important neighbour of (India's) North-East.

DEVELOPING A HUMAN SECURITY PARADIGM

The last in the long list of alternative approaches towards security is 'human security',[26] a concept that seems to be stretching the meaning of security virtually to the level of vagueness. It is said to be asking for inclusion of everything that a human being requires in his daily life, into the list of items to be covered by the security discourse. The idea of human security became part of security discourse by its inclusion in the United Nations Human

Development Report of 1994. This, is the most often cited source of the concept of human security though the term had an existence before that. In quantifiable terms human security seeks to address security from two perspectives namely: (1) freedom from fear; and (2) freedom from want. This is based on the argument of the US Secretary of State as far back as 1945. In his report to the Government of United States, the then Secretary of States argued:

> The battle of peace has to be fought at two fronts. The first is the security front where victory spells freedom from fear. The second is the economic and social front where victory means freedom from want. Only victory on both fronts can assure the world of an enduring peace. . . . No provision that can be written into the Charter will enable the Security Council to make the world secure from war if men and women have no security in their homes and their job.[27]

This notion of security was brought into the discourse on national security by Kofi Annan when he related human security to national security. According to him:

> Human security in its broadest sense embraces far more than the absence of violent conflict. It encompasses human rights, good governance, access to education and health care and ensuring that each individual has opportunities and choices to fulfil his or her own potential. Every step in this direction is also a step towards reducing poverty, achieving economic growth and preventing conflict. Freedom from want, freedom from fear and the freedom of the future generations to inherit a healthy natural environment—these are the interrelated building blocks of human—and therefore national security.[28]

The most interesting aspect of human security is the argument that security has to be analysed from the perspective of individual as an entity. There are differences in determining the core values of human security but it is not that important so far as the idea is concerned. The analytical core of human security is its emphasis on the individuals. The idea of human security becomes clear when the objective of human security is taken into account. It tries to eliminate conditions that give rise to conflict and insecurity. Secondly, it tries to change aims, identities and aspirations. Thirdly, it ensures livelihoods opportunities for individuals. Given these core concepts of human security, its plausibility of being applied to the security scenario of North-East is evident.

The brief discussion on the security situation in the North-East points to the fact that the insecurity situation in the region not only has military dimensions but also has economic and socio-political connotations. The core of the insecurity situation in the region is related to the sense of relative deprivation *vis-à-vis* the other parts of India. The violent manifestations in the form of insurgency are most often related to real and at times imaginary deprivations. The paradigmatic approach adopted by the Indian Union has failed to assure the people of the region of the intent of the nation to assimilate them in the national mainstream, though it has succeeded in improving some of the development indices for the region. The new approach must address the issue of 'sense of relative deprivation' and the issue of non-functionality of the state. To succeed in implementing the human security agenda the state must functionally disinvest itself in the North-East. It should create institutions involving stakeholders in various issues related to the human security needs of the general population of the region. Some scholars doubt the validity of human security approach precisely on the ground that the list under human security is unending and thus unusable. But a list of human security issues can be prepared that would narrow human security to workable levels. The *Human Development Report* of 1994 itself identifies seven dimensions of human security: personal, environmental, economic, political, community, health, and food security. Scholars like Gary King and Christopher Murray advance the idea of preventing the population from slipping into the condition of generalized poverty.[29] Further, they have identified five indicators to measure human security for the individual and the group. These are: poverty, health, education, political freedom and democracy.[30] Kanti Bajpai proposes a 'Human Security Audit' to measure the '*direct and indirect threats* to individual's physical safety and *freedom, and the capacity to deal with threats*, namely, the fostering of norms, institutions, and democratization/representativeness in decision-making structures' (emphasis original).[31]

While King and Murray provide a fair list of issues to be addressed under the agenda of human security, Bajpai provides a useful tool to implement the agenda of human security. A human security audit would not only help identify all the issues that are perceived to be threats by the population but would also provide flexibility to accommodate emerging human security issues and to eliminate the addressed issues. In the context of the North-East, the perceived victims can be made part of the process of addressing their grievances. Every issue identified through periodic human security audit must be addressed through an institution created specifically for that purpose. Such institutions would be known as 'functional institutions'[32] involving not only government but also non-government stakeholders. In the present context, Vision 2020,[33] a document prepared by the North-Eastern Council, can be used as the first human security audit report. The priorities identified in the report must be addressed through creation of specific institutions around each priority involving representatives of the states, technocrats and civil society representatives. This will address the prime problem of erasing the idea that the state is not functioning, and most importantly the sense of relative deprivation could be arrested from getting manifested in more and more ways. Real participation in the process of amelioration of grievances would reduce the incentive to participate in activities that may derail the developmental process in the region. Further, by reducing the sense of relative deprivation the chances of external forces operating in the region will be minimized as the external forces take advantage of the dissatisfaction of the general masses against the state and turn it into rebellions/movements against the state. The institutions created on specific issues will be secular (not based on primordial identities) and temporary and thus never jeopardize the legitimacy of the state. Further, accountable functioning of the functional institutions would add strength to the delivery ability of the state and would thus facilitate the integration of the region to the national mainstream.

NOTES

1. Ken Booth, 'Critical Explorations', in Ken Booth (ed.), *Critical Security Studies and World Politics*, New Delhi: Viva Books, 2005.

2. Bill McSweeney formulated the term 'Copenhagen School'. Bill McSweeney, 'Identity and Security: Buzan and the Copenhagen School', *Review of International Studies*, 24(1), 1998, pp. 137-40.
3. Barry Buzan, *People State and Fear*, Sussex: Wheatsheaf Boos, 1983, p. 247.
4. Ibid.
5. Ibid., pp. 252-3.
6. Booth, 'Critical Explorations', in Ken Booth (ed.), *Critical Security Studies and World Politics*, pp. 14-15.
7. Cited in Richard Wyn Jones, *Security Strategy and Critical Theory*, Boulder, London: Lynne Rienner Publishers, 1999, p. 102. For details see, R.B.J. Walker, 'Security, Sovereignty and the Challenge of World Politics', *Alternatives*, 15(1), 1990, pp. 3-27; R.B.J. Walker, 'The Subject of Security', in Keith Krause and Michael C. Williams (eds.), *Critical Security Studies: Cases and Concepts*, Minneapolis: University of Minnesota Press, pp. 33-59. Ken Booth, 'Security and Emancipation', *Review of International Studies*, 17(4), 1991, pp. 313-26; Ken Booth, 'Security in Anarchy: Utopian Realism in Theory and Practice', *International Affairs*, 63(3), 1991, pp. 527-45.
8. Booth, 'Security and Emancipation', p. 319.
9. Ibid., p. 320.
10. Martin Shaw, *Global Society and International Relations*, Cambridge: Polity, 1994. Christian Reus-Smit, 'Realist and Resistance Utopias: Community, Security and Political Action in New Europe', *Millennium: Journal of International Studies*, 21(1), 1992, pp. 1-28.
11. Samuel Huntington, 'The Clash of Civilizations', *Foreign Affairs*, 72(3), 1993, pp. 22-49. Ole Waever, 'Insecurity and Identity Unlimited', *Working Paper 14*, Copenhagen: Centre for Peace and Conflict Research, 1994.
12. Richard Wyn Jones, *Security Strategy and Critical Theory*, Boulder, London: Lynne Rienner Publishers, 1999, p. 115.
13. Separatism is treated as a form of insurgency because all the insurgency movements do not necessarily have a separatist agenda.
14. Samir Kumar Das, 'Ethnicity and the Rise of Religious Radicalism: The Security Scenario in Contemporary North-Eastern India', available at, http://www.apcss.org/Publications/Edited%20Volumes/ReligiousRadicalism/PagesfromReligiousRadicalismandSecurityinSouthAsiach11.pdf

15. Ibid.
16. The data in the paragraph are taken from, 'Economic Overview', Centre for Development and Peace Studies, available at, http://cdpsindia.org/ne_economy.asp.
17. The paradigms are derived from Jairam Ramesh's formulation of paradigmatic approach of Government of India towards the North-East India. For details on the paradigms discussed here, see Jairam Ramesh, 'North-East India in a New Asia', *Seminar*, no. 550, June 2005, online version, http://www.india-seminar.com/2005/550.htm.
18. Ibid.
19. Bill McSweeney, *Security, Identity and Interests: A Sociology of International Relations*, Cambridge: Cambridge University Press, 1999, p. 208.
20. Craig A. Snyder (ed.), *Contemporary Security and Strategy*, London: Macmillan Press Limited, 1999, p. 114.
21. K.R. Nossal, 'Seeing Things? The Adornment of "Security" in Australia and Canada', *Australian Journal of International Affairs*, 49 (1), 1995, 39.
22. Craig A. Snyder (ed.), *Contemporary Security and Strategy*, 1999, p. 117.
23. The term 'simple states' is used here to connote states that are mono-ethnic, mono-language and mono-religious character or in other words states that do not have any form of heterogeneity.
24. ASEAN-ISIS, *Confidence Building Measures in South-East Asia*, 1993, p. 17, cited in Craig A. Snyder, op. cit., p. 113.
25. Snyder, ibid.
26. The idea of human security has been articulated in the Human Development Report of United Nations, 1994. For a critical discussion on human security, see Roland Paris, 'Human Security: Paradigm Shift or Hot Air', *International Security*, 26 (2), Fall 2001, pp. 87-102, Des Gasper; 'Securing Humanity: Situating "Human Security" as a Concept and Discourse', *Journal of Human Development*, 6(2), July 2005, pp. 221-45; Kyle Grayson, 'Human Security as Power/Knowledge: The Biopolitics of a Definitional Debate', *Cambridge Review of International Affairs*, 21(3), September 2008, pp. 383-401.
27. United Nations Development Programme, *Human Development Report*, New York: Oxford University Press, 1994, p. 3. Cited in Sabina Alkire, 'A Conceptual Framework for Human Security', CRISE Working Paper, No. 2, 2003, p. 13.

28. The definition based on Kofi Annan's Millennium Report to the United Nations General Assembly, 2000 and is articulated by Sabina Alkire, ibid., p. 14. For details on Kofi Annan's discussion on human security, see Kofi A. Annan, *We the Peoples: The Role of the United Nations in the 21st Century*, available at http://www.un.org/millennium/sg/report/full.htm.
29. The concept of 'generalized poverty' include not only income but also the deprivation of any basic capabilities. For details, see Gary King and Christopher J.L. Murray, 'Rethinking Human Security', *Political Science Quarterly*, 116(4), 2001-2, pp. 585-610.
30. King and Murray, ibid., p. 598.
31. For details on Human Security Audit, see Kanti P. Bajpai, 'Human Security: Concept and Measurement', *Kroc Institute Occasional Paper*, no. 19:OP:1, August 2000. Available at http://www.nd.edu/?krocinst/ocpapers/po_19_1.pdf.
32. The idea of functional institutions has been advocated by scholars like David Mitrany, Ernst B. Haas, and B. Rosamond. To some extent Robert O. Keohane and Stanley Hoffman have also contributed to this literature. Ernst B. Haas, *The Uniting of Europe: Political, Social, and Economic Forces, 1950-1957*, Stanford: Stanford University Press, 1958; Haas, *Beyond the Nation-State: Functionalism and International Organization*, Stanford: Stanford University Press, 1964; David Mitrany, *The Progress of International Government*, New Haven: Yale University Press, 1933; Mitrany, 'The Prospect of European Integration: Federal or Functional', *Journal of Common Market Studies*, IV (2)1965; Mitrany, *A Working Peace System,* Chicago: Quadrangle Books, 1966; Mitrany, *The Functional Theory of Politics*, New York: St. Martin's Press, 1976; B. Rosamond, *Theories of European Integration,* New York: St. Martin's Press, 2000; R.O. Keohane and S. Hoffmann, *The New European Community: Decision-making and Institutional Change*, Boulder, Colorado: Westview Press, 1991; Inis L. Claude Jr., *Swords into Plowshares*, New York: Random House, 1964.
33. North Eastern Council, *North Eastern Region: Vision 2020*, May 2008.

CHAPTER 15

North-East India: A Photo Essay

Dilip Banerjee

Dilip Banerjee in this photo essay chronicles the usual and the unusual aspects of North-East India. These photographs were taken by the author during his extensive travel of North-East India. Apart from recording the breathtaking beauty of North-East India, Dilip Banerjee's photographs capture the security-development interlinkages. His photographs portray the dilapidated infrastructure, challenges to development and insurgency that one confronts in North-East India.

Instead of taking the usual approach of focusing merely on the violent aspects of insurgency, Dilip Banerjee's photographs humanize the life of an insurgent. By focusing on the daily chores, his photographs depict the 'ordinariness' of an insurgent's life. However, the author's photographs also demonstrate that the 'ordinariness' happens in the shadow of the gun. His photographs also bring into relief the human costs of the unending spiral of violence in North-East India. For instance, the photograph of a Chakma mother with her kid, waiting for rations at a refugee camp is indeed poignant. Dilip Banerjee has taken these photographs over a span of two decades, during which the region witnessed large-scale insurgencies. One can see in these photographs, the many phases of insurgency, counter-insurgency operations, and also the attempts to kick-start the democratic process in various states of North-East India.*—*The Editors*

* The captions for the photographs were given by Antara Mitra, Fellow, MAKAIAS.

Plate 15.1: Enchanting North-East India: Meandering road from Lunglei to Aizawl.

Plate 15.2: Infrastructural setback: A collapsed railway bridge due to floods in Assam.

Plate 15.3: An aerial view of an oil field in Assam: Despite being the major source of state revenue, lack of infrastructure, industrialization, and inaccessibility have remained major hurdles for optimum exploration of such oil fields. Also, these oil fields have been the major targets of the ULFA factions operating in the Upper Assam stepping up periodic attacks since the late 1980s. All the routes connecting Lakhipathar, a major ULFA operational base, with Digboi (10 km east of the Lakhipathar forest) and the Dibrugarh oil fields (60 km from the forest) were completely sealed off during Operation Bajrang in 1990.

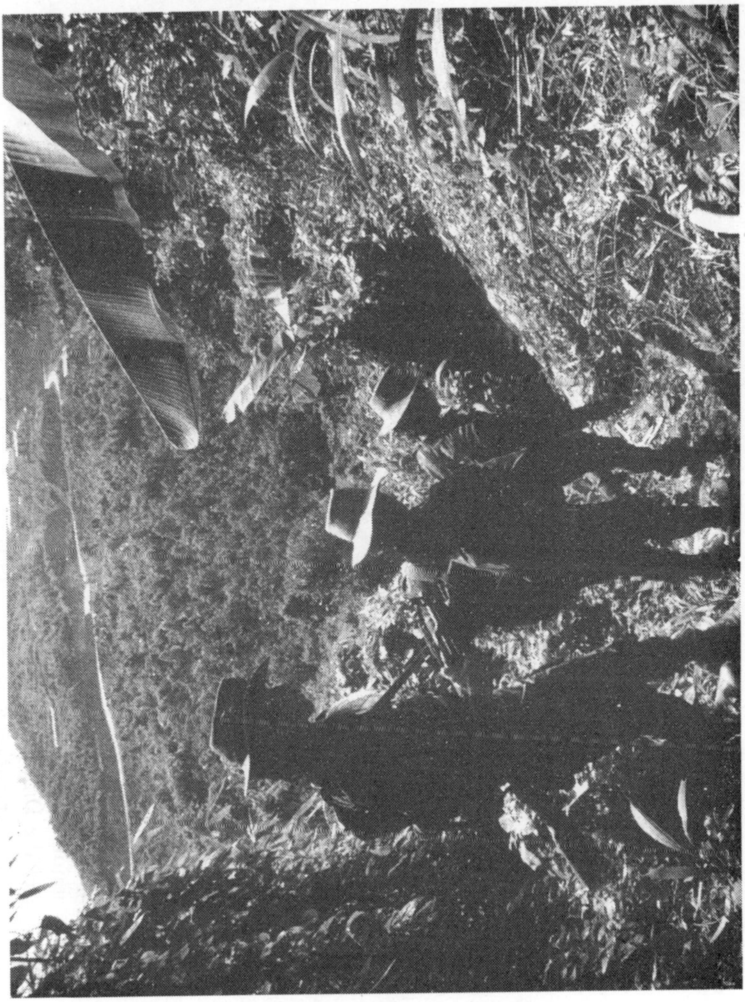

Plate 15.4: Journey of Jeopardy: Mizo insurgents in a hide-out near Aizawl. Commonly the hide-out treks involve several hours of uninterrupted strenuous climb up the acclivity, through dense forests with little food and water.

Plate 15.5: A *Hebron Naga insurgents' camp*: Football tournament on the eve of Xmas at their headquarter base. December 2008.

Plate 15.6: Not without passion: A Naga insurgent patrolling inside the camp with his pet dog. December 2008.

Plate 15.7: NSCN Cadre: The largest insurgent group in Nagaland. More recently they created a well-trained and well-equipped women's brigade. December 2008.

Plate 15.8: Shaving the head: An UNLF insurgent in a hideout in a local tribal settlement near the capital Imphal. In the 1980s, the area of operation of the insurgents, including their hideouts, covered the valley districts of Imphal, viz., Thoubal and Bishenpur. However, from early 1990s they started to expand their radius of operation into the relatively inaccessible hilly areas of the state of Manipur, including the Churachandpur and Chandel districts.

Plate 15.9: Under the shadows of gun: A young insurgent having a bath in a hideout in Manipur.

Plate 15.10: A group of UNLF insurgents in Manipur having lunch. August 1998.

Plate 15.11: Reconciling with the past, fighting with the present: A Chakma refugee settlement in Tripura. Apart from the Chittagong hill tracts, Mizoram and Kaptai Dam Reservoir, about 50,000 Chakma aborigines have recently crowded the state of Tripura since 1988, in order to flee the Bangladesh Army's operations against their villages in Chittagong hill tracts. A number of slum-like settlements sprung up eventually, which are being euphemistically termed as 'refugee camps' all over Tripura where they lead a dreary life.

Plate 15.12: Photogenic poverty: Surrendered MNF insurgents couple's at the rehab camp near Aizawl 1986.

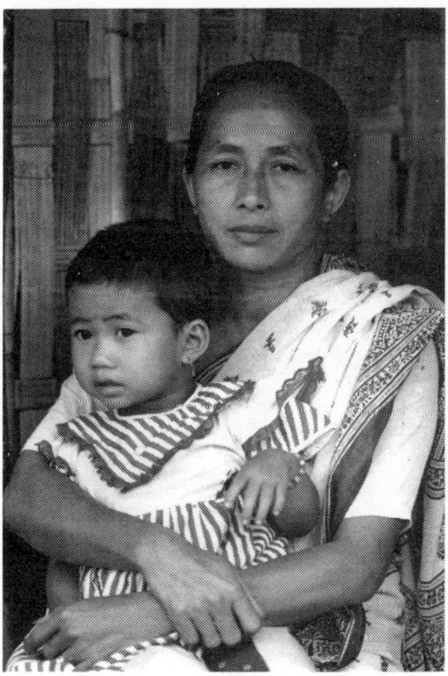

Plate 15.13: Human Security: A Chakma mother with her child waiting for ration at refugee camp in Tripura 1991.

Plate 15.14: Inhaling the venom of death: The popular bamboo-pipe for tobacco smoking. It is a popular custom in the states of Tripura, Manipur and Nagaland to combine tobacco with cannabis, marijuana, or other psychoactive herbs like the hops flowers and then smoke the concoction through a bamboo pipe, rather than smoking them in the form of joints. However, this form of smoking is highly carcinogenic and exposes the smoker to the highest risks of lungs cancer not only because the organic materials used are not 'cured' or filtered, but also because of the decreased gas exchange capacity and existence of particle residues in the smokers lung due to smoking from these pipes. Apart from the HIV/AIDS, lungs cancer thus accounts for the considerably low life expectancy of the people in the North-East due to high-scale addiction to this from of tobacco smoking.

Plate 15.15: The Green Gold: A Tripura Chakma refugee camp 1991.

Plate 15.16: Argus-eyed: An armed BSF guard on alert at a Mizoram-Burma border village. Commensurate with the separatist and ethnic turmoil in Mizoram, the sensitive international Indo-Burma border zone became highly porous. The infiltration of the insurgent groups from Burma and traffickers of small arms, light weapons and narcotics through this precarious border zone pushed it high on the radar of Indian government's security calculus, necessitating vigilant, armed patrolling of this area.

Plate 15.17: Mission accomplished: An ULFA camp in Upper Assam, captured by the Indian army in 1990. Apart from the deployment of 'hard' armed forces, the political manipulation of pitting one ULFA faction against the other has been a successful strategy for eviction of the ULFA from the Upper Assam. The ULFA had, by late 1980s, already split into two factions—The ULFA in Upper Assam and the ULFA based in Lower Assam, the latter being controlled by its top leadership in Bangladesh which includes its Commander-in-Chief Paresh Baruah and Chairman Arabinda Rajkhowa, who was recently held in Bangladesh in December 2009 and handed over to Indian custody. This has afforded the government a rare opportunity to launch a successful counter-insurgency policy in Assam.

Plate 15.18: Faces unknown: TNV insurgents in long queue during the arms surrender ceremony.

Plate 15.19: Operation Rhino: Assam Lakhipathar forest, after more than a week long encounter with UNLF and Army looks like a battlefield, 1993.

Plate 15.20: Smile of Hope: An election campaign in programme in frontier Assam, 1992.

Plate 15.21: New Generation and New Politics: An election campaign scene in Mizoram, 1987.

Contributors

ALI AHMED is a Research Fellow at the Institute for Defence Studies and Analyses, New Delhi.

DILIP BANERJEE is a photo journalist and Project Fellow at Maulana Abul Kalam Azad Institute of Asian Studies (MAKAIAS), Kolkata.

M.P. BEZBARUAH is a Professor of Economics at Gauhati University, Guwahati.

RAKHEE BHATTACHARYA is an economist and presently a Fellow at Maulana Abul Kalam Azad Institute of Asian Studies (MAKAIAS), Kolkata.

H.N. DAS is former Chief Secretary of Assam during 1990-5.

RANGAN DUTTA is a former Secretary to the Government of India and he is currently a Scientific Consultant in the office of the Principal Scientific Advisor to the Government of India, New Delhi.

JAYANTA MADHAB is an economist and was previously with the Asian Development Bank.

BINODA KUMAR MISHRA is a Fellow at Maulana Abul Kalam Azad Institute of Asian Studies (MAKAIAS), Kolkata.

PAPORI CHETIA PHUKON is pursuing her Ph.D. from Gauhati University on Tai ethnic community and is currently engaged in a project that seeks to explain insurgency in North-East India.

SANJAY PULIPAKA is presently a Fellow at the Maulana Abul Kalam Azad Institute of Asian Studies (MAKAIAS), Kolkata.

B. RAMAN is Additional Secretary (retd.), Cabinet Secretariat, Govt. of India, New Delhi, and is currently, Director, Institute for Topical Studies, Chennai. He is also associated with the Chennai Centre for China Studies.

M. AMARJEET SINGH is a researcher at the Institute for Defence Studies and Analyses (IDSA), New Delhi; and also the Assistant Editor of the *Journal of Defence Studies* (*JDS*).

LT. GEN. S.K. SINHA is a former Governor of Assam.

KRISHNAN SRINIVASAN is a former Indian foreign secretary and is currently a Senior Fellow at the Maulana Abul Kalam Azad Institute of Asian Studies (MAKAIAS), Kolkata.

Index